Introduction Digital Media

This book offers a clearly written and engaging introduction to the basics of interactive digital media.

As our reliance on and daily usage of websites, mobile apps, kiosks, games, VR/AR and devices that respond to our commands has increased, the need for practitioners who understand these technologies is growing. Author Julia Griffey provides a valuable guide to the fundamentals of this field, offering best practices and common pitfalls throughout. The book also notes opportunities within the field of interactive digital media for professionals with different types of skills, and interviews with experienced practitioners offer practical wisdom for readers.

Additional features of this book include:

- An overview of the history, evolution and impact of interactive media;
- A spotlight on the development process and contributing team members;
- Analysis of the components of interactive digital media and their design function (graphics, animation, audio, video, typography, color);
- An introduction to coding languages for interactive media; and
- A guide to usability in interactive media.

Introduction to Interactive Digital Media will help both students and professionals understand the varied creative, technical, and collaborative skills needed in this exciting and emerging field.

Julia Griffey, M.A., M.F.A., is a creative technologist, entrepreneur and associate professor of interactive digital media at Webster University in St. Louis, MO. At Webster, she teaches a variety of courses within the realm of interactive media design/development and its intersection with marketing, promotion and online business. When not teaching, Griffey builds apps and websites and runs her own creative online businesses.

Introduction to Interactive Digital Media

Concept and Practice

Julia Griffey

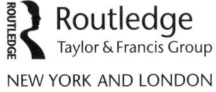

NEW YORK AND LONDON

First published 2020
by Routledge
52 Vanderbilt Avenue, New York, NY 10017

and by Routledge
2 Park Square, Milton Park, Abingdon, Oxon, OX14 4RN

Routledge is an imprint of the Taylor & Francis Group, an informa business

© 2020 Taylor & Francis

The right of Julia Griffey to be identified as author of this work has been asserted by her in accordance with sections 77 and 78 of the Copyright, Designs and Patents Act 1988.

All rights reserved. No part of this book may be reprinted or reproduced or utilised in any form or by any electronic, mechanical, or other means, now known or hereafter invented, including photocopying and recording, or in any information storage or retrieval system, without permission in writing from the publishers.

Trademark notice: Product or corporate names may be trademarks or registered trademarks, and are used only for identification and explanation without intent to infringe.

Library of Congress Cataloging-in-Publication Data
A catalog record for this title has been requested

ISBN: 978-0-367-14862-1 (hbk)
ISBN: 978-0-367-14863-8 (pbk)
ISBN: 978-0-429-05365-8 (ebk)

Typeset in Univers
by Integra Software Services Pvt. Ltd.

Printed and bound in India by Replika Press Pvt. Ltd.

To my husband who helped me edit, even when he didn't want to.

And to the wonderful people who allowed me to interview them for this book: Heidi McDonald, Elizabeth (Jake) Feinler, Tim Frick, Chris Cox, Ana Monte, Brian Lucid, Jans Carton, and Julie Gaieski. Thank you for sharing your time and knowledge.

Contents

	Introduction	**1**
	Why Learn About Interactive Digital Media?	1
	How This Book is Organized	1
	References	2
1	**What is Interactive Digital Media?**	**3**
	Introduction	3
	What Makes Interactive Digital Media Different from Other Forms of Media?	3
	Forms of Interactive Digital Media	6
	Developing Interactive Digital Media	10
	Essential Skills for the Interactive Digital Media Developer	13
	The Impact of Interactive Digital Media	14
	Career Opportunities in Interactive Digital Media	16
	Practitioner Interview—Heidi McDonald	18
	Discussion Questions	21
	References	21
2	**History of Interactive Digital Media**	**23**
	Introduction	23
	Origins of the Computer	23
	Evolution of the Computer	26
	The Computer Gets Personal	28
	The Graphical User Interface	30
	Video Games	33
	The Birth of the Internet	35
	Growth of the Internet	37
	The Birth of the World Wide Web	37
	Multimedia	40
	Web 2.0	40
	Interactive Digital Media in the 2010s and Beyond	42
	Practitioner Interview—Elizabeth (Jake) Feinler	44
	Discussion Questions	48
	References	49

■ Contents

3 The Interactive Digital Media Development Process and Team — 50

- Introduction — 50
- Team Members — 50
- Pitching the Project — 55
- The Development Process — 58
- Practitioner Interview—Tim Frick — 65
- Discussion Questions — 69

4 Fundamental Components of Interactive Digital Media — 70

- Introduction — 70
- Analog vs. Digital Media — 70
- Bits and Bytes — 70
- File Formats — 72
- Analog to Digital — 74
- The Pros of Digital Media — 77
- Compression — 78
- Description vs. Command-Based Encoding of Media — 79
- Color on the Screen — 80
- Practitioner Interview—Chris Cox — 84
- Discussion Questions — 89

5 Media Content — 90

- Introduction — 90
- Graphics — 90
- Pixel-based Images — 90
- Vector-based Images — 94
- 2D Animation — 96
- 3D Graphics and Animation — 99
- Audio — 102
- Video in Interactive Digital Media — 107
- Text — 112
- Practitioner Interview—Ana Monte — 116
- Discussion Questions — 119
- References — 120

6 Aesthetics in Interactive Digital Media — 121

- Introduction — 121
- Typography — 121
- Color — 127
- Layout Principles — 133
- Practitioner Interview—Brian Lucid — 145
- Discussion Questions — 148
- References — 148

7 Authoring Interactive Digital Media — 149

- Introduction — 149
- Multimedia Authoring — 149
- Making Video Games: Casual and Console — 151
- Building Apps — 153
- Building Interactive Media for Performance and Public Spaces — 155
- Building Websites — 156
- Practitioner Interview—Jans Carton — 165
- Discussion Questions — 168
- References — 169

8 Usability — 170

- Introduction — 170
- Why Good Usability is Important — 170
- Achieving Good Usability in Every Phase — 171
- Guidelines for Good Usability — 175
- Guidelines for Fun — 177
- Usability and Play Testing — 178
- Practitioner Interview—Julie Gaieski — 181
- Discussion Questions — 184
- References — 185

Index — *186*

Introduction

WHY LEARN ABOUT INTERACTIVE DIGITAL MEDIA?

Interactive digital media is becoming more and more pervasive in our everyday lives. As our world has grown increasingly digital, interactive and online, new job opportunities in this field emerge every day. This book provides an opportunity for students to learn about the burgeoning interactive industry and see where their existing skills align or where they might want to develop new ones.

I wrote this book to support my own Introduction to Interactive Digital Media class, (one I have taught for the past 10 years), because I could not find a suitable text to meet my needs. I wanted to demystify the field, expose students to new potential careers, and motivate them to build interactive digital media skills to support their own career or business objectives. I needed to provide a solid foundation for students majoring in the field while giving students from other disciplines a taste for what might be in it for them.

Initially, many of my students are mystified by interactive digital media and have no idea what is involved in the development process. For this reason, I partner the reading and discussions with hands-on projects (building a website as well as a prototypical app) that provide real, practical know-how. I believe that the production experience is beneficial for any student as it exercises skills deemed valuable by employers such as critical thinking, problem solving, paying attention to detail, communicating and writing (Ikaiddi, 2017). After completing these assignments, students tend to feel empowered and left wanting to learn more, which is always a joy to witness. I share these projects on my website: www.juliagriffey.com/idmbook.

HOW THIS BOOK IS ORGANIZED

Each chapter in this book focuses on one aspect of interactive digital media, specifically: what it is, where it came from, how it is conceived, what is in it, how should it look, how it is assembled and what makes it good.

Chapter 1 defines interactive digital media, its various forms and what impact it has had on our lives. Because interactive digital media is so pervasive, career opportunities are copious and diverse. This chapter also begins to address the

■ Introduction

question of how interactive media is made and what makes an interactive product more or less complex.

Chapter 2 dives into the history of interactive digital media, starting with the invention of the computer, the birth of video games, and the founding of the Internet. Throughout history, innovations in hardware and networking have inspired new forms of interactive media and methods of delivery, including the Web, multimedia, kiosks, apps, social media, casual games and augmented and virtual reality.

Chapter 3 outlines the process and the team involved with developing interactive media. While the types of projects under the umbrella of "interactive media" is broad, every project requires a process and a team. This chapter explains typical development processes and the various team members.

Chapter 4 addresses the nuts and bolts of digital media. How do we convert analog media into a digital form and what are the compromises that must be made? Once media is in a digital form, how does our software understand it?

Chapter 5 focuses on media content within an interactive experience: graphics, animation, audio, video and text. What are the formats used and the best practices when working with them?

Chapter 6 is about media aesthetics. Layout, color and typographic choices can have a dramatic effect on how an interactive application is experienced. This chapter provides guidance in how to make those choices.

Chapter 7 uncovers how interactivity is authored. There are a variety of coding languages and authoring environments used to build interactive applications. Developing for the Web involves an additional set of challenges such as acquiring a domain name, setting up hosting, a content management system and transferring files.

Chapter 8 looks at usability. What processes and techniques can help us build memorable, functional and lovable interactive experiences?

In addition to the main content, each chapter features an interview with a professional whose work relates to the topic. I am so grateful for their contributions and learned something from every conversation. Because I was only able to include brief excerpts from our conversations in the text, I have made the entire interviews available on my website: www.juliagriffey.com/idmbook.

REFERENCES

Ikaiddi, U. (2017) The Top 5 Skills Employers Say Recent Grads Lack and How to Learn Them. *Study Breaks*. Online. Available at: https://studybreaks.com/college/employable-skills.

1 What is Interactive Digital Media?

INTRODUCTION

When I tell people that I teach "interactive digital media," it is often followed by the question: "what's that?" Although I've become quite accustomed to explaining my field of study, I'm still surprised how many people don't know what, exactly, interactive digital media is. The definition I think best describes interactive digital media is *a computer-driven experience (most often screen based) that facilitates an interaction between the device and a user*. Or, as one of my students put it: "you do something to the device (computer, tablet, screen, etc.) and the device does something back," which I actually think is a good definition too.

An interactive digital media application could be a website, a traditional stand-alone kiosk, an app running on a mobile device, a video game, or a computer/sensor-driven, physical experience in a museum or public space. All are developed with different programming languages, run on different types of hardware and serve very different purposes. However, the common link is that they all facilitate a *two-way conversation between the user and the system*.

WHAT MAKES INTERACTIVE DIGITAL MEDIA DIFFERENT FROM OTHER FORMS OF MEDIA?

Two words: *user interaction*. When a user experiences other forms of media, for example, viewing an image, reading text, watching a video or listening to audio, the media does not respond to the user. These forms of media may trigger some sort of response from the user, but the user does not interact with it.

Interactive digital media is also different from other forms of media because it is a *non-linear experience*. It is unlike video, audio and text which usually have a distinct beginning, middle and end, and users experience the media in a sequential fashion. While some films have a non-linear narrative structure where the ending is shown at the beginning, viewers still experience the film in the same sequence. A classic example is the 2000 film, *Memento*, which has two plot lines that simultaneously develop in opposite directions, and then join in the final scene. In that sense, the film has a non-linear narrative, but the way the audience experiences the film is controlled by how the film editor put it together.

What is Interactive Digital Media?

Every user might have a different experience when using an interactive application. For example, I may open the AroundMe app and start looking for pharmacies, where someone else might pull up AroundMe and look for grocery stores. Even with a fairly straightforward app like AroundMe, the variations of paths users can take are almost infinite. For each user, the experience is dynamic and unique.

There are, however, some portions of interactive digital media applications that are intended to be experienced linearly. For example, in a training application, information is often presented in a linear way if the user needs to understand certain content before moving on to the next module. Another example of a linear experience within interactive digital media is the checkout portion of an e-commerce website. An online shopper must review the cart before entering an address, reviewing the order, adding credit card information, and finally checking out.

Designing interactive digital media experiences that are less prescribed can be quite challenging, because it's hard to predict user behavior. Oftentimes, people use applications in ways that the designers and developers never considered. Many interactive applications have failed because designers and developers didn't understand what the users wanted and how they would use the product.

An important step in the interactive application development process is to try to predict how users will use the application. Designers create scenarios such as the ones pictured below to figure out how their application will meet the needs of different types of users.

Sometimes, even despite careful planning, interactive applications fail because users don't like using them. For example, in 2009, Google launched a product called Google Wave which was intended to simplify group emails. It got a lot of hype and publicity. People were excited to use it, as group emails can often be hard to follow with all the threads and replies. Unfortunately, the application did not live up the hype. It had an overly complicated user interface resulting in a product that merged features of email, instant messages and wikis, but ultimately failed to do anything significantly better than the existing solutions. The developers did not expect the users to be overwhelmed and not use the app, and eventually it went away (Fitzpatrick, 2010).

How do interactive digital media developers avoid these pitfalls? One way interactive digital media developers learn how users are going to interact with an application is to do some usability testing during the development process. What that means is that once you have a prototype or a portion of your project done, you give it to representative users to see how they interact with it. This process is intended to point out the flaws and tell you what needs to be fixed. It's often very surprising to see how users interact with the application you build. It can be disappointing to watch, because what you might have thought was intuitive, may not be to the user. But understanding usability flaws early on in the development cycle is much better than later.

What is Interactive Digital Media?

1.1
User scenarios created by one of my students working on an app design project

User Scenario 1.

Cecilia is a 16 year old girl who wants to adopt a baby kitten. Her price range is anything less than $200. Also it has to be within 25 miles.

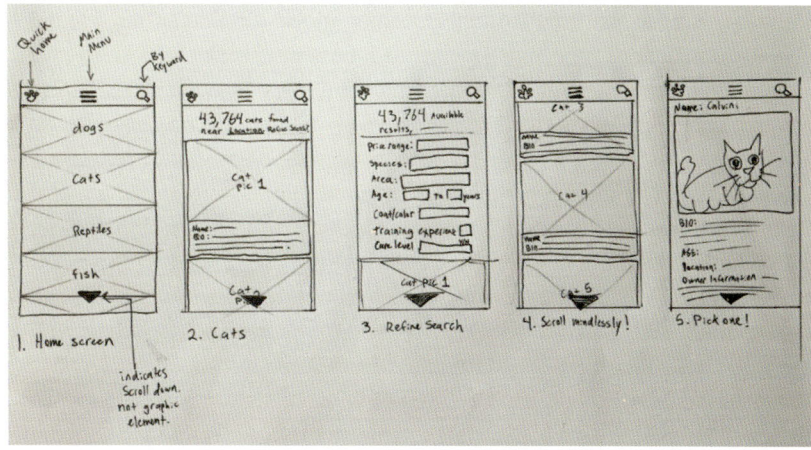

User Scenario 2.

Bobby is a 32 year old male who owns a Black King Snake. He is looking for rodentia to serve as his snakes natural dinner. He is specifically trying to find a feeder rat supplier that is cheaper than PetCo.

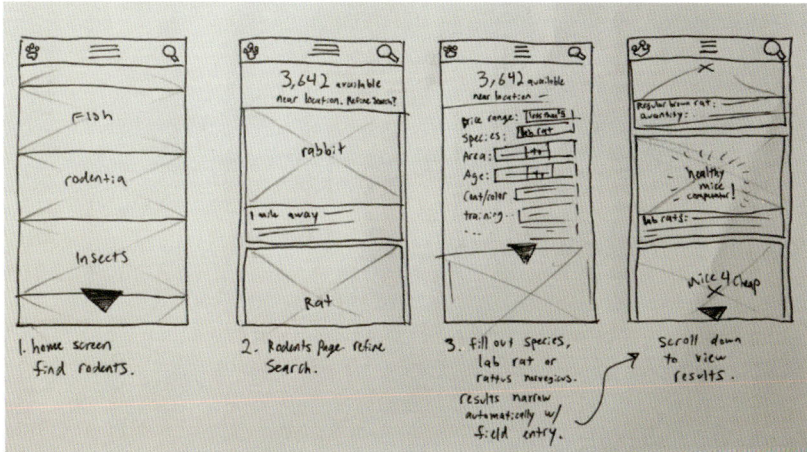

Fortunately, some usability issues can be solved with quick fixes. For example, inconsistent titling can confuse a user. If you call a page an "Order Form" in one location but "Product List" in another, a user will likely be confused. While you may understand that these are one and the same, a user may not.

I inadvertently created a usability issue when developing an e-commerce application by not being explicit in my labeling. This particular e-commerce site had a login area for designers to upload items to sell. Before we launched,

■ **What is Interactive Digital Media?**

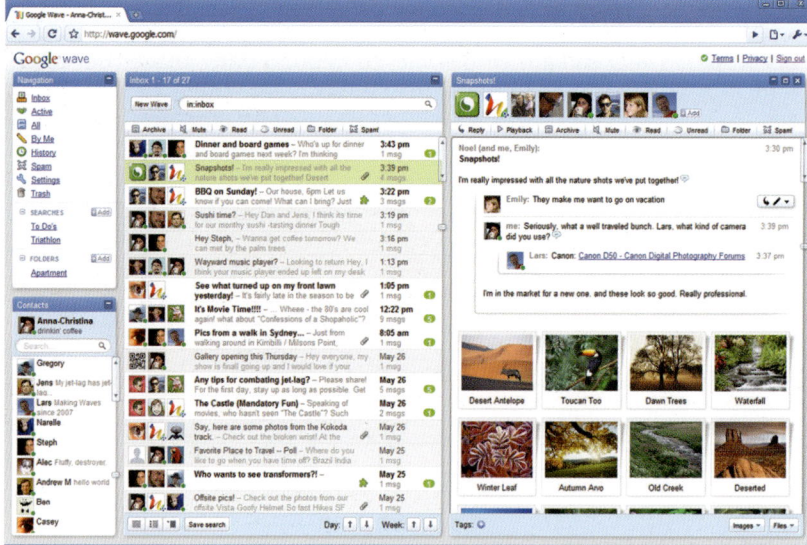

1.2
Google Wave interface

designers were logging in and editing their profiles and adding product data. Once I added a customer login, designers reported no longer being able to login. I couldn't figure out why the login suddenly no longer worked. Finally, I asked a designer for more information about what she was trying to do, and I discovered that she was trying to login via the customer login. Because I had not labeled the customer and the designer logins differently, the designers who had been using the application simply assumed that I created another place for them to login. Fortunately, in this case, it was a pretty easy fix to solve a major usability issue, and I was reminded of how unpredictable users can be.

FORMS OF INTERACTIVE DIGITAL MEDIA

Since interactive digital media has been in existence, hardware has evolved, triggering the emergence of new forms, uses and modes of interaction which impact the way we communicate, shop, learn and are entertained.

Traditional Stand-Alone Kiosks

A kiosk is a location-specific, interactive (typically touch) screen-based experience that is designed to provide instruction, improve productivity, facilitate communication, deliver entertainment or enable a transaction that is specific to its location. Interactive kiosks were some of the first forms of interactive media to exist, years before the world wide web was even invented. Self-checkout kiosks in grocery stores and pharmacies and airline check-in kiosks are becoming more commonplace as they have been shown to increase productivity (Sabatová et al., 2016). In a museum setting, kiosks are used to engage and inform visitors, adding another dimension of information or proving an experience that relates to

What is Interactive Digital Media?

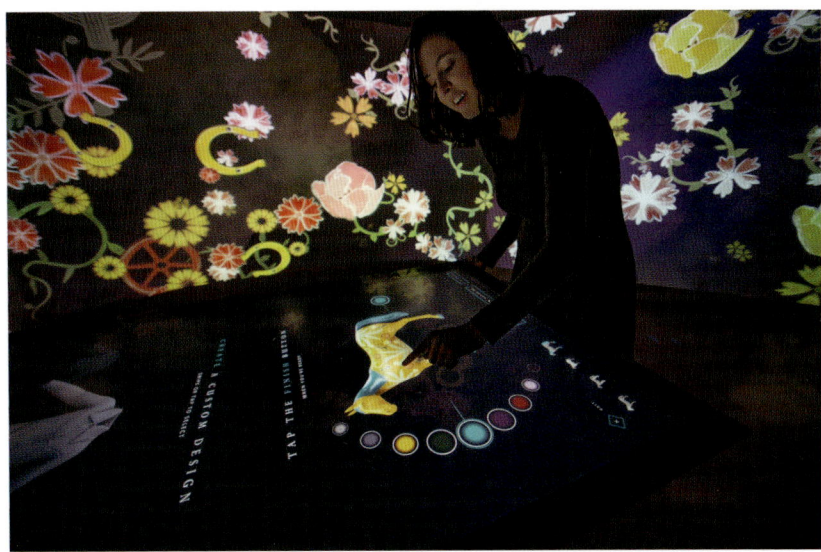

1.3
This unique interactive experience in the National Cowgirl Museum and Hall of Fame in Fort Worth, Texas uses a multitouch table to allow visitors to design cowgirl-themed objects and see their work on the walls in the space.
Source: © National Cowgirl Museum and Hall of Fame and Ideum

the content being presented. These modern touchscreen kiosks can now even facilitate collaborative interactive experiences.

Websites

A website is a combination of interlinked web pages, all under the same domain name that are displayed within a web browser and accessible from any computer with an Internet connection. Early websites were primarily "brochure-ware," comprised of a few static pages with some interlinking text, but they became more sophisticated as technology, bandwidth and protocols evolved. In the late 1990s e-commerce sites boomed. Then shortly thereafter, blogs and social media platforms popped up on the world wide web.

Modern websites have evolved significantly since their early counterparts. Because we now access websites from a variety of devices, most websites are designed to be responsive, meaning that their layout and content adapts based on the device that has requested it. This advanced requirement has presented a new challenge to both the web designer and web developer.

Mobile Applications

Mobile applications (or apps) are a distinct form of interactive digital media that emerged after the birth of the modern smartphone. They differ from desktop applications (programs like Microsoft Word that run on your computer) and web applications (specialized programs that run in a web browser), because they are designed to run on a tablet, smartphone or watch and are typically designed to perform a specific task. Some apps come installed on the device such as a web browser or an email program. Other apps must be purchased and downloaded through the app marketplace associated with the device, e.g. the Apple app store for iPhones and iPads.

What is Interactive Digital Media?

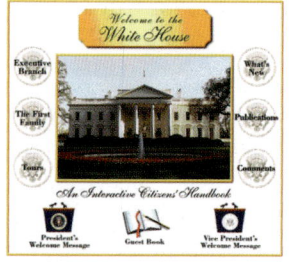

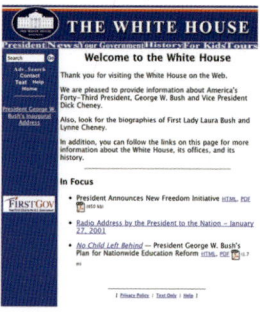

1.4
The website of the U.S. White House has evolved significantly over the past few decades reflecting changing web technology

1995

2001

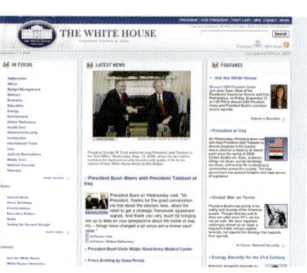

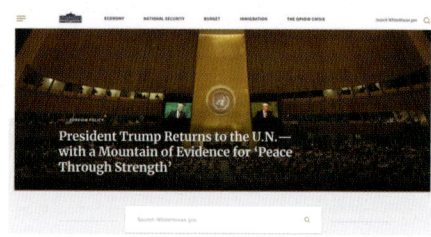

2008

2018

Apps have grown in popularity since they first became available because they are typically inexpensive, easy to download, update and remove, and provide fun and useful enhancements to a device. Apps can also be developed and sold by anyone with a clever idea and a bit of programming knowhow which ensures continual innovation and always something new and exciting in the app stores.

Apps are sometimes confused with mobile versions of websites, but websites are always viewed within the app browser. Companies often produce apps which have some of the same functionality of the website, but are designed to make certain tasks easier. Savvy companies know that if you download their app, the company can push you notifications such as coupons and reminders to the benefit of their business.

Video Games

A video game is a game that is run off of a computer, mobile device or specialized console where the user interacts with the system using some type of physical controller, sensor or directly touches the screen. The first video games accessible to the general public were housed in casings the size of phone booths and installed in arcades. *Pong*, released in 1972, is known as the first video game, where the objective was to bat a virtual ball back and forth on the screen. The graphics were simple—black and white—and the game was easy to understand and fun to play (Newman, 2017). Excitement about *Pong* and the other early video games released in the late 1970s and early 1980s helped to build the arcade culture: kids hanging out at the arcade dropping quarters into video games.

By the late 1970s, video games were available in the home, playable via specialized consoles, the first successful one being the 1977 Atari 2600 (Newman, 2017). Video game consoles have evolved significantly since this time. Over the past 40 years, we have seen several generations of gaming devices come and go, from handheld consoles to the latest, most sophisticated ones that facilitate collaborative game play across the Internet and ones without any controller at all, simply sensing the players' gestures as a form of interaction.

Video games have now made their way onto all of our devices. We can play a video game on our computers, or through a web browser, on tablets and smartphones and even on our watches. There is also tremendous variety in the types of games that are available. Some console games are super-involved with deep stories that can take hours and hours to explore and master. Augmented reality (AR) games blend real-world and digital spaces and virtual reality (VR) games immerse players in game worlds through embodied play. "Casual games" are simple enough to be played on an iPhone while waiting in a line. Games are no longer solely for entertainment; they are used to educate and train both students and professionals. Gaming is a growing industry with interesting niches and opportunities

Physical Installations, Exhibits and Performance

Museums have become a popular venue for unique interactive experiences where exhibit designers strive to create experiences with "technological novelty and open-endedness" to hold visitors' attention (Sandifer, 2003). This new generation of interactive exhibits encourages visitors to engage with the content in innovative ways, oftentimes fostering a collaboration among visitors. For example, at the Franklin Institute, visitors can "discover the hidden beauty of the deep sea, fly to the farthest reaches of outer space, [and] take a ride through the complex inner-workings of the human body" with the help of sophisticated sensors in an Oculus Rift (a headset incorporating goggles and headphones that immerses the wearer in a 3D virtual world) (The Franklin Institute, n.d.). At the Smithsonian's "Skin and Bones" exhibit, visitors can see skin and the movements that would have accompanied the bones when viewing the artifacts through an augmented reality app (Billock, 2017).

Unusual and elegant participatory interactive digital experiences are sometimes installed in public spaces. David Small's "Hall of Ideas" is a crowning example. Located in the Mary Baker Eddy Library for the Betterment of Humanity in Boston, the exhibit features animated letters that appear to bubble out of a fountain. From the fountain, they spill onto the floor, congregating in areas where people are standing. Then they slowly make their way up the wall where they form into quotations (Small Design Firm: Hall of Ideas, n.d.).

■ What is Interactive Digital Media?

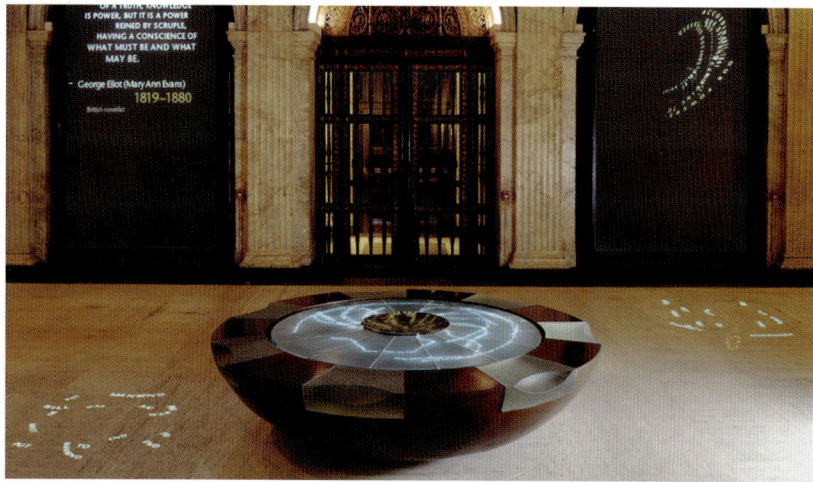

1.5
"Hall of Ideas" created by Small Design Group. Source: © Small Design Firm

Interactive media has added a new dimension to live theatrical performances. Choreographers at Portland, Oregan-based Trokia Ranch are fully exploiting its capabilities in their dance performances. For example, a recent piece is choreographed, in part, by audience movements. As the performance begins, cameras record audience member movements. These images are then interpreted by software which sends signals to the dancers telling them which sequence of movements to perform (Kaufman, 2013).

Non-screen based interactive experiences

A relatively recent innovation within the field of interactive digital media are non-screen based experiences which serve different purposes and are used in different contexts. While they still facilitate communication between a user and some type of computer-based device, they do not incorporate a traditional computer screen. An example of a very practical non-screen based interactive device is Amazon's Echo. The Echo can serve up different types of media based on the user's voice commands.

DEVELOPING INTERACTIVE DIGITAL MEDIA

Interactive digital media projects vary tremendously in form, medium, functionality and scale which undoubtedly affects its development team size and cost. For example, an experienced web developer can build a website in a few hours. But a large corporate website or custom web application can take months to build and have a large team of people working on it. A simple word game app might be made by an individual, whereas a AAA console game might require a team of hundreds. A project budget could be a thousand dollars or a million dollars. It just depends on what is needed.

Nevertheless, there is some common ground among these disparate types of projects with tremendously different scopes. The size of the team may vary, but the tasks and process remain the same. On a smaller project, team members must play multiple roles.

Several factors affect the complexity of an interactive budget, which in turn affects the team size and budget:

1) The Type of Interactivity that is Needed

Unconventional interactivity (e.g. an interactive application that responds to a user's facial expressions) will require specialized programming and therefore a larger budget and team.

2) The Required Functionality

If the application needs to be able to do a lot of different things, then it's going to be more complex and take a longer time to develop. For example, an app that allows you to set a timer for a given amount of time will be easier and quicker to develop than an app that allows you to set a timer with intervals and plays music while the timer is working.

3) The Level of Adaptability

An adaptable application is one that changes based on the user and her history of interaction. For example, the products displayed under the "you may like" heading are based on your shopping and browsing history that Amazon keeps track of. In other words, the application is adapting to the information you have given it in the past. To make an adaptable application, you will need to store customer behavior data and then dynamically display content to a user based on some algorithm and the data that has been stored in the database.

Many video games are adaptable, remembering the player's history within the game and offering new challenges and rewards based on their previous interactions. Clearly, this requires some skill to develop and will make the application more complex.

4) The Database Behind it

A database is a set of related tables of information. If you have ever worked with Microsoft Excel or Google Sheets then you have built a table, one of which is sometimes referred to as a "flat file." But, with respect to interactive digital media, we are most often working with relative databases, where a column of data in one table "relates" to a column of data in another table.

Almost every interesting application you use is connected to a database. For example, the AroundMe app must communicate with a database of different types of businesses (bar, pharmacy, grocery store, etc.) and their corresponding locations so that it can compare your location data against theirs. Based on these two locations, the app makes a calculation of the distance and then displays the

■ **What is Interactive Digital Media?**

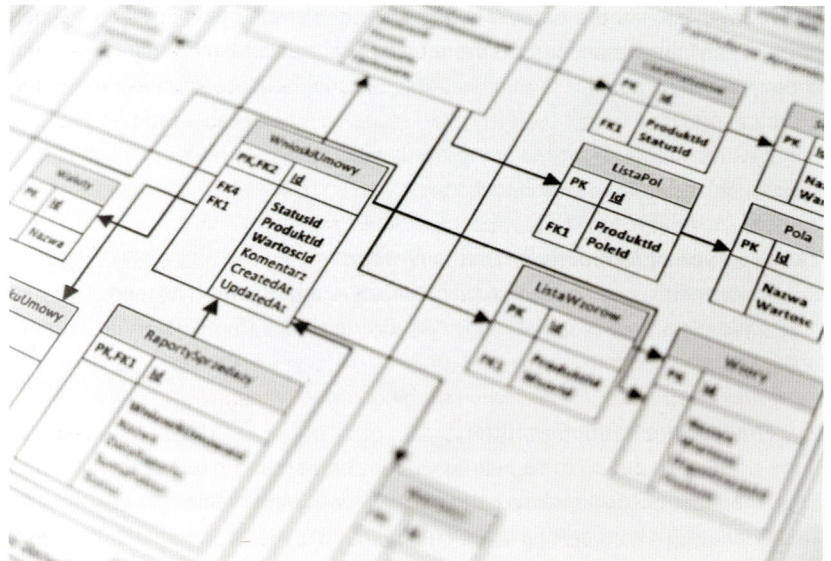

1.6
Database diagram. Source: © Krasnopolski; Shutterstock

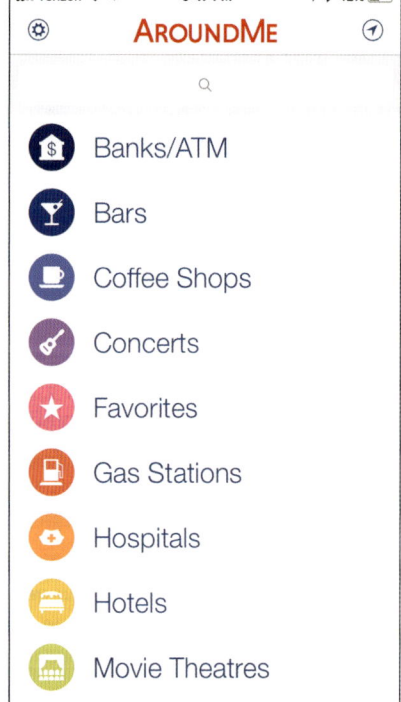
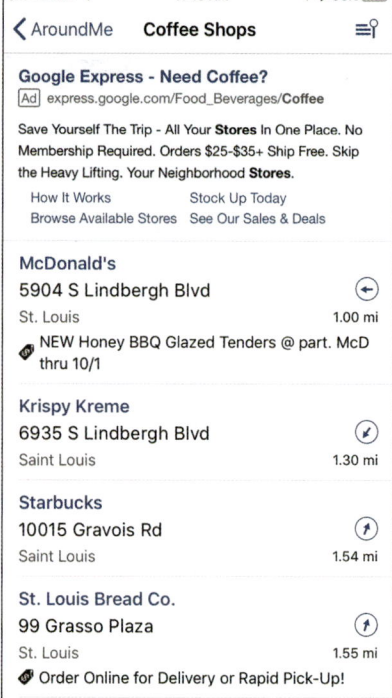

1.7
The AroundMe app compares the user's location to the locations of businesses which are stored in a database

results. An application like this could not work without having access to all that information in a database.

Clearly, databases are important and necessary, and, the more complex the database, the longer the application is going to take to develop, especially

12

if you have to build the database itself. But in the case of many applications (like AroundMe), the developers were able to take advantage of databases that already existed (businesses of different types and their locations) as well as the device's built-in GPS, and developed an application that presented that information creatively relative to the individual's location.

5) **The Amount and Type of Content Included**
If your application has a lot of content such as pictures, text, videos, illustrations, music etc., then it will take longer to develop. Think about the production involved in building an adventure video game; a story needs to be written, characters designed, worlds 3D modeled, and original music composed and recorded. The content requirements for this type of project are immense.

Oftentimes, the content you incorporate will not need to be created because it already exists. If this is the case, your development team will always need to obtain the appropriate permissions to use it. Securing these rights can be time consuming and costly, adding to the overall complexity and budget of the project.

Now, think about the websites, apps and games you use and play on a daily basis. Do you have a better understanding of how complex they were to develop and why?

ESSENTIAL SKILLS FOR THE INTERACTIVE DIGITAL MEDIA DEVELOPER

The skills required to develop interactive digital media depend on the role one plays in the development process. A game artist does not necessarily need to be a great writer. However, having some working knowledge of the various forms of media and how the interactivity is authored would be expected skills for someone to have who is entering the industry regardless of the job.

Knowing the Media
Video, audio, animation, text, graphics, illustrations, are the "meat" of an interactive experience and often referred to as the "content." Each form of media requires special consideration and is associated with a set of best practices when integrating them into an interactive experience.

Consider the job of a video game designer; familiarity with the media could increase the likelihood that his game will be produced. For example, knowing that 3D art can be very time consuming (and expensive) to create, he may not propose the most elaborate 3D environments and multiple characters in the story when there is a limited budget.

User Experience Design
Interactive media usually has a large visual component, therefore visual communication skills are needed to ensure users understand what the application is and how to use it. But design for interactive media applications is quite different from design for static forms of media (poster, flyers, brochures, etc.) Interactive

■ What is Interactive Digital Media?

media is more akin to product design because it is an experience, and not just a message. Therefore, the end users must guide every design decision through the development process.

Coding and/or Authoring the Application

Interactive products are either scripted by someone writing code or built within an authoring application (software that allows a developer to assemble media elements, synchronize content, design the user interface and script the interactivity), or by doing a combination of both. For example, Adobe Dreamweaver (a web editor) allows a developer to toggle between writing code and using tools and menu items in the software to build the interactivity.

The programming language and the authoring tool used to build the interactivity depends on the final format and context of the interactive application that is being made. For example, a web developer might code with HTML, CSS, JavaScript and PHP within Dreamweaver while an Apple app developer might code with Swift within Xcode, and a game developer might write C# code within the Unity editor.

THE IMPACT OF INTERACTIVE DIGITAL MEDIA

I'm actually quite surprised that so many people don't know what interactive digital media is because, frankly, it is everywhere! And, the pervasiveness of interactive media technology has made such a dramatic impact on our everyday lives.

Smartphones and tablets have only been in popular use for the past decade, yet, as of 2017, 3 billion people own and use a smartphone (Bajarin, 2017). While the smartphone was primarily designed for communication, it is now used as a research tool, entertainment device, documentation assistant, a fitness motivator, a GPS and a personal shopper (among many other things). Smartphones have become so useful that "smartphone addiction" has become a concern. Researchers surmise that extensive smartphone use leads to anxiety, depression and "ruminative thinking" (Chen et al., 2017).

Social media applications that emerged before the proliferation of smartphones took on a new life once they became accessible in the palm of our hands. Anytime, anywhere, via a few swipes in Facebook, we can access a myriad of banal content such as what our high school acquaintances ate for dinner. But social media is no longer just for being social. Nearly half of social media users receive news from the people they follow on social media (Hermida et al., 2012). Unfortunately, not all of this news is accurate, and with the ease in which content can be shared over these channels, news—both authentic and fake—is everywhere. Traditional news media outlets have struggled with readership and viewership due to changed consumer behaviors (Rieder, 2014). And misinformation disseminated through social media has been blamed for undermining the 2016 U.S. Presidential election (Lardner & Riechmann, 2017).

While new interactive digital media technologies have had some negative consequences for certain industries, they can also radically upend an entire industry in unexpected ways. For example, consider Uber and Airbnb. These companies built applications that completely changed the long-standing transportation and hospitality industries by taking advantage of the prevalence of smartphones and their new capabilities, and the availability of high speed data transmissions in most urban areas.

However, the impact they have made is not what we might have expected. For example, Uber has far from obliterated the U.S. taxicab industry. Instead, in U.S cities, employment has risen in self-employed drivers, as well as in traditional taxi services! This may be due the fact that Uber drivers are willing to work at off-peak hours when there is still a demand for rides while traditional taxi drivers are not willing to work. Uber drivers do tend to make more money than traditional taxi drivers because the Uber app allows the driver to "better optimize their time and services" (Gaskill, 2017).

Airbnb has impacted the hotel industry more directly. When there is a big event in a city and hotel rooms are scarce and expensive, residents can use the Airbnb app to determine what nightly rate they could fetch if they offer up their home to visitors, a phenomenon that has kept hotel rates in check during peak times. Latest research has shown that "in the 10 cities with the largest Airbnb market share in the US, the entry of Airbnb resulted in 1.3 percent fewer hotel nights booked and a 1.5 percent loss in hotel revenue" (Gerdeman, 2018). Uber and Airbnb are just two of the many companies and organizations who have proved that a well-designed interactive digital media application can create a revolution within an industry (Stone, 2017).

The explosive growth of the global video game industry has undoubtedly impacted many aspects of our lives. Once relegated to arcades and specialized home consoles, a video game is now accessible to anyone with a smartphone. Across the globe, we are gaming more now than ever before, and the growth of the video game industry is not expected to stop anytime soon (Sun, n.d.).

According to the American College of Pediatricians, 8–18 year olds spend approximately 1.13 hours per day playing video games (American College of Pediatricians, 2016). As a result, researchers are looking at the impact of video game play on players' levels of aggression, attention spans, obesity rates, etc., with a variety of conclusions. Some studies show gaming inspires violent behavior while others tout the benefits of gaming on perception and cognition (Bushman & Gibson, 2010; Boot et al., 2011). There is a push now in the industry for gaming companies to develop games with more positive outcomes, especially for teens.

People's interest in and addiction to games have inspired educators and even executives to use game constructs to motivate students or employees. This technique is called gamification, where game-design elements and principles are applied in non-game situations. The idea is that framing an objective within the context of the game will engage "players" who will be more likely to reach the desired outcome.

■ What is Interactive Digital Media?

CAREER OPPORTUNITIES IN INTERACTIVE DIGITAL MEDIA

The course of study for an interactive media professional would likely include design, programming and learning how to work with different forms of media. Eventually most practitioners specialize in one of these areas. However, it is not uncommon for independent producers of interactive digital media to do a little bit of everything. In either case, it's valuable to learn all aspects of the development process to either be able to do it yourself or to better communicate with the experts who do.

There is a wide variety of career opportunities in this industry. One of the most common career paths for my students is to become a designer or developer at a marketing, advertising or boutique interactive development shop. In this type of role and environment, you're doing client driven work. In a larger advertising/marketing company, the interactive projects might be a smaller part of a larger contract. But, if you were working for a smaller, boutique interactive development shop, your piece might be subcontracted out from a larger marketing firm, as a more specialized shop would be focused only on interactive work. In either case, these companies are service businesses with different areas of specialization. With demand for interactive media so high and the scope so wide, firms can specialize in one area, for example, some companies specialize in interactive museum exhibits, some may be experts in casual mobile games.

Career opportunities for interactive media specialists exist at almost any company or organization, as almost all have at least a website. Some even have internal web applications or an app that needs to be developed and maintained. Larger companies, especially those who conduct business on the web, usually have an internal team dedicated to it. School districts and universities offer career opportunities too, as they all have robust websites and social media channels that require constant maintenance.

Working for a video game company is another career path for an interactive digital media major. While triple A game programmers tend to come from computer science backgrounds, many games are now built with languages more commonly used within other forms of interactive media. In addition, skills in user experience design and media aesthetics are transferrable to the gaming industry.

Another career route might be working for a software company. Obviously, software companies hire programmers, but they also need expertise beyond writing code; design and usability are huge considerations. There are thousands of software companies besides the ones that may immediately come to mind like Microsoft and Adobe; different industries need specialized software or web-based applications to perform niche, industry-specific tasks.

Experts in interactive digital media are needed in fields where training must be developed. Consider all of the textbooks you have used in your life; most came with a companion CD or website to help teach the content in the book. Online classes have become more and more popular at universities, and most now have departments dedicated to online learning. Often within the development of these courses, interactive applications must be built to enhance the course content. Even in the corporate world, interactive training is common and vital to many organizations.

One of the great perks about having interactive digital media skills is that it's very easy to be self-employed or freelance. The tools required to produce many interactive applications are fairly inexpensive; a computer and some software. Compare that, for example, to an audio engineer who might need to book time in a studio and pay a hefty hourly rate to run his business. Another benefit is that you can work from anywhere (with a Wi-Fi connection). I've actually developed websites for clients that I've never met in person. So, if flexibility is what you like, then this may be the field for you.

Some companies rely heavily on freelancers because they may land a big project and need extra help but don't want to commit to hiring people full-time. Once you're known as a reliable freelancer, most companies will likely hire you back. One of the great ways to start freelancing is to work for a larger company for a while and then if you want to go out on your own you may have an opportunity at that company to come back and do freelance work for them from time to time because they know you and the quality of your work. Many freelancers do a combination of projects subcontracted out from larger companies along with projects in which they are working directly with the client. There are also many websites the help freelancers find gigs such as elance.com and upwork.com. Although freelancing does not offer the stability of a full-time job, you can typically charger a higher hourly rate since the company hiring you does not have to pay benefits or guarantee you a certain number of hours.

Even if you don't study interactive digital media as your primary discipline, there are still quite a few benefits in acquiring the skills, especially if you have entrepreneurial ambitions. Whether you want to start a bakery, open a recording studio, launch a PR agency, building a website will be one of your first steps, and if you can do it yourself, you will save a lot of money. But, even if you hire someone else to build your web site, you'll be able to speak their language and know how to enhance the site to better meet your needs. Once you get your site launched, you'll also better understand how to use social media strategically, optimize your site for search engine recognition and establish your credibility online. If you want to sell products and services online, you will have a better understanding of how to build an e-commerce site, including setting up the shopping cart, building product databases, creating imagery and finally marketing your store.

As you can see, there are many opportunities for a student of interactive digital media. While the acquisition of these skills requires ample hands-on practice, this book will provide an overview of the discipline. We'll cover many different aspects of interactive media, from where it came from to how it's made, the media content within it, to the design choices that make it fun and usable. Ready to dive in? Read on.

PRACTITIONER INTERVIEW

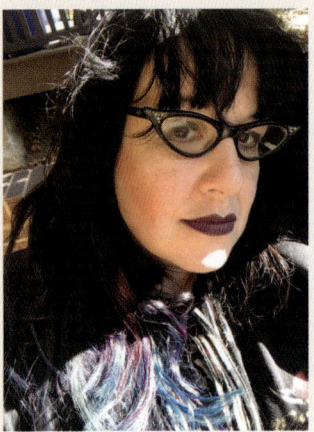

Heidi McDonald

iThrive Games—Pittsburgh, PA USA
Can video games have a positive impact on the player? Heidi McDonald thinks so and has the research to back it up. As the senior creative director for the Pittsburgh-based non-profit organization, iThrive Games, Heidi's mission is to "infuse meaningful, game-based growth opportunities into the virtual and physical settings where teens spend their time."

What does iThrive do?

iThrive works at the intersection of mental health and games for the benefit of teens, trying to find ways that games can be used for pro-social outcomes to make teens lives better. Its three divisions are mental health, education and industry outreach. The mental health division engages directly with mental health clinicians to learn how they can use games in the work that they're doing with kids. The education group helps educators use games as a medium to deliver important soft skills to their kids. And the industry outreach group tries to engage the game industry, providing resources about best practices for designing games that promote positive outcomes like empathy and optimism informed by the latest neuroscience and social psychology.

Has the industry responded positively to your mission?

Yes and no. We are very firmly supported in the university space, as well as in the indie space. It's a bit harder with Triple-A developers because they pretty much need a business reason to do anything. Therefore, our intention is to build a business case for creating more socially responsible games to try to get their buy-in.

What is your background and how did you land this job?

Although my fields of study at university were film and communications, I ended up taking a detour into video games courtesy of a game conference I snuck into. I'd been a gamer all my life but I never really considered it as a career. At that conference, I learned three life changing things: one, making video games is a job, two: women can do this job and three: a company in Pittsburgh, Schell Games, makes video games! I was hooked.

Eventually, through persistence and luck, I landed an internship at Schell Games, and since that internship, I have worked in various roles within the game industry, including client-side creative direction, business development, narrative design, systems, feature, level, and quest design and implementation.

How has the industry changed, since you have been involved with it?

I have only been in the industry a little over seven years and one thing that I've seen is that game writing is no longer enough. Writers at the Triple-A studios are also often expected to implement it. So, if I write a quest, I need to also know how to go into Unity and place the characters into the world and dictate the path that they walk.

I think the accessibility of state-of-the art tools like Unity and Unreal is amazing because now literally anybody who wants to make a game can download the same toolset the studios are using and make a game. It's amazing because now you've got all these voices who might not have been heard otherwise.

I've seen a lot of stuff happen with mobile games and monetization. Now it's pretty common for a free app to have in-app purchases. Back when I started in the industry, we had to do a lot of analysis of what was out there to figure out where the paywall should go, and I think it's a little bit more obvious now about what works and what doesn't.

I've also learned audiences are fickle and unpredictable. I've seen some games that are brilliant that like nobody noticed, and then you get a game like *Angry Birds* that goes bananas! You never know what's going to hit. *Goat Simulator* was probably historically the buggiest game to ever be released and it was a hit because it was buggy!

■ What is Interactive Digital Media?

How have video games changed?

AR (augmented reality) and VR (virtual reality) have definitely become a thing but I don't know how long it's going to take for AR and VR to be normalized in the consumer base because it's still very largely a rich white guy thing—ones who can afford the equipment. I've seen schools who apply for grants and get a VR headset and it just sits there and collects dust because they don't have the kind of game content their school needs or the computer wouldn't support it.

Escape room experiences are definitely a trend now. Big cities like Los Angeles and San Francisco have large communities of people who do these interactive theater experiences that are scripted that people pay to do together like a communal live/virtual game.

Fortunately, the gaming industry is starting to recognize the diversity of gamers in terms of age and gender and exploring different themes. The Entertainment Software Association has said that the fastest growing group of gamers is women over 35. So, a lot of companies will try to address that by saying "oh well those women all love match three games or hidden objects games so we'll make that" to try to reel in those women. But, that may not be the case. I think we need women in their thirties and forties to make games for women in their thirties and forties.

Have you witnessed a video game have a positive effect on a player?

We went to DigiPen Institute of Technology last September to host a game jam about empathy. There was a young, shy seventeen-year-old girl there who was very interested in going to DigiPen which is why she showed up at the game jam. Even though she had never made a game, the game she helped make won first prize!

We thought this was amazing, so we started filming and asked her why she wanted to be a game designer. None of us were prepared for the story that she told. She told us she was a big fan of the independent game *Brothers: A Tale of Two Sons*, which is about two siblings, one who runs away with a bad love interest and gets killed. This game helped her through losing her sister who ran away from home and was subsequently murdered by her boyfriend. She said that playing the game was the one thing that helped her feel close to her sister. The reason she wanted to be a game designer was because she wanted to make experiences for other people that helped them the way this game had helped her.

I was so moved by her story that I told the people at DigiPen. It turned out the guy in charge of scholarships happened to be in on the phone call and offered her a scholarship to the school. Now she's a freshman at DigiPen. And this year, at the game jam, she led a team of students who made another very thoughtful game. It was hard to believe this was the same girl.

It's great to witness firsthand when iThrive directly impacts the life of a teen. Those are the kinds of stories that are coming out of the work that we do.

DISCUSSION QUESTIONS

1) Have you ever downloaded an app on your phone and then deleted it because you found it too difficult to use? What was it? Why was it difficult to use? How might the designers and developers fix the problem?
2) What type of job might one be able to land after earning a degree or even taking courses in interactive media? Find a job listing and share it. Why do you think that this job would be suitable for an interactive media major? Do you find this job interesting/exciting?
3) Think about an interactive media application that you use. What new insight do you have about this application after reading this chapter? Do you think the application was complex to develop (explain using terms from this chapter)?
4) Can you think of an interactive digital media application that has changed your life? If so, what is it and how has it changed your life?
5) What are some of the positive and negative aspects of the pervasiveness of interactive media in our lives?

REFERENCES

American College of Pediatricians (2016). The Impact of Media Use and Screen Time on Children, Adolescents, and Families, (November). Online. Available at: https://www.acpeds.org/the-college-speaks/position-statements/parenting-issues/the-impact-of-media-use-and-screen-time-on-children-adolescents-and-families.

Bajarin, T. (2017). In a Mobile-first World, Don't Forget the PC. *PC Magazine*, 26–28.

Billock, J. (2017). *Five Augmented Reality Experiences that Bring Museum Exhibits to Life*. Smithsonian Magazine, June 29. Online. Available at: https://www.smithsonianmag.com/travel/expanding-exhibits-augmented-reality-180963810.

Bool, W., Blakely, D., & Simons, D. (2011). Do Action Video Games *Improve Perception and Cognition? Frontiers in Psychology*, 2 (226).Online. Available at: https://doi.org/10.3389/fpsyg.2011.00226>.

Bushman, B. J., & Gibson, B. (2010). Violent Video Games Cause an Increase in Aggression Long After the Game Has Been Turned Off. *Social Psychological and Personality Science*, 2(1), 29–32. Online. Available at: https://doi.org/10.1177/1948550610379506.

Chen, B., Liu, F., Ding, S., Ying, X., Wang, L., & Wen, Y. (2017). Gender Differences in Factors Associated with Smartphone Addiction: A Cross-sectional Study Among Medical College Students. *BMC Psychiatry*, *17*, 1–9. Online. Available at: 10.0.4.162/s12888-017-1503-z.

■ **What is Interactive Digital Media?**

David Small Design: Hall of Ideas (n.d.). Online. Available at: http://smalldesignfirm.com/project/mary-baker-eddy-library/#hall-of-ideas.

Fitzpatrick, S. F. (2010). Google Wave is all Washed Up. *American Libraries*, *41*(9),12. Online. Available at: www.jstor.org/stable/25734641.

The Franklin Institute (n.d.). Virtual Reality at the Museum. Online. Available at: https://www.fi.edu/exhibit/virtual-reality-museum.

Gaskill, A. (2017). Study Explores the Impact of Uber on the Taxi Industry. *Forbes Magazine*, January 26. Online. Available at: https://www.forbes.com/sites/adigaskell/2017/01/26/study-explores-the-impact-of-uber-on-the-taxi-industry.

Gerdeman, D. (2018). The Airbnb Effect: Cheaper Rooms For Travelers, Less Revenue For Hotels. *Working Knowledge, Harvard Business School*, 26 February. Online. Available at: https://hbswk.hbs.edu/item/the-airbnb-effect-cheaper-rooms-for-travelers-less-revenue-for-hotels.

Hermida, A., Fletcher, F., Korell, D., & Logan, D. (2012). SHARE, *LIKE, RECOMMEND. Journalism Studies, 13 (5–6),815–824. Online. Available at*: https://doi.org/10.1080/1461670X.2012.664430>.

Kaufman, S. (2013). Choreography and Computers. *Washington Post*. 15 March.

Lardner, R., & Riechmann, D. (2017). Russia "Used Fake News and Propaganda" to Undermine U.S. Election, FBI Says. *Time.com*. Online. Available at: https://time.com/4826603/russia-fake-news-us-election-meddling/#.

Newman, H. (2017). The History of Video Games, in One Infographic. *Forbes Magazine*, 29 March. Online. Available at: https://www.forbes.com/sites/hnewman/2017/11/29/the-history-of-video-games-in-one-infographic/#7ef630961a5c.

Rieder, R., (2014). Don't count newspapers out just yet. *USA Today*, October 2. Online. Available at: https://www.pressreader.com/usa/usa-today-us-edition/20141002/textview.

Sabatová, J., Galanda, J., Adam ík, F., Jezný, M., & Šulej, R. (2016). Modern Trends in Airport Self Check-in Kiosks. *MAD – Magazine of Aviation Development*, *4* (20)10–15. Online. Available at: https://doi.org/10.14311/MAD.2016.20.02.

Sandifer, C. (2003). Technological Novelty and Open-endedness: Two Characteristics of Interactive Exhibits that Contribute to the Holding of Visitor Attention in a Science Museum. *Journal of Research in Science Teaching*, *40*(2), 121–137. Online. Available at: https://doi.org/10.1002/tea.10068>.

Stone, B. (2017). *The Upstarts: How Uber, Airbnb, and the Killer Companies of the New Silicon Valley are Changing the World*. Boston, MA: Little, Brown and Company.

Sun, L. (2018). VR, Video games will Lead U.S. Entertainment Industry Growth. *USA Today*. 23 January. Online. Available at: https://eu.usatoday.com/story/money/markets/2018/01/23/a-foolish-take-vr-and-video-games-will-lead-us-entertainment-industry-growth/109097088/.

2 History of Interactive Digital Media

INTRODUCTION

Interactive media applications have become ubiquitous and impact many aspects of life today. We are so reliant on these technologies, it is hard to believe that they have only been around for a few decades. Within this time, ideas such as user-controlled interlinked media that once seemed far-fetched have become technically feasible. To make it all happen, however, took impressive creative thinking, collaboration and advances in computer hardware and networking.

ORIGINS OF THE COMPUTER

The computer is the most essential development and delivery tool for all forms of interactive media. While much of our interactive media is now consumed on handheld devices, these are still technically computers, albeit very small ones. The evolution of the computer was not driven by a desire to create and deliver interactive media. Instead, it was conceived as a timesaving device for making difficult mathematical calculations.

> The analytical machine weaves algebraic patterns just as the Jacquard loom weaves flowers and leaves.
>
> Ada Lovelace, 1843 (Evans, 2018, p. 20)

Countess Ada Lovelace was a well-educated, mathematically minded, Antebellum-era British woman who first learned of mathematician and inventor Charles Babbage and his amazing machines by visiting one of his weekly salons. Babbage routinely threw grand social events and showed off his latest inventions and acquisitions as entertainment. Babbage's most notable accomplishment was building a machine called the Difference Engine that could solve differential equations. It was inspired by Jacquard weaving machines that received instructions from punch cards and created woven designs as prescribed. Comprised of at least 8,000 individual components, the Difference Engine was "programmed" by setting initial values on the wheels and then turning a crank to get the results of the mathematical equation. The machine was far ahead of its time. Beyond its

■ History of Interactive Digital Media

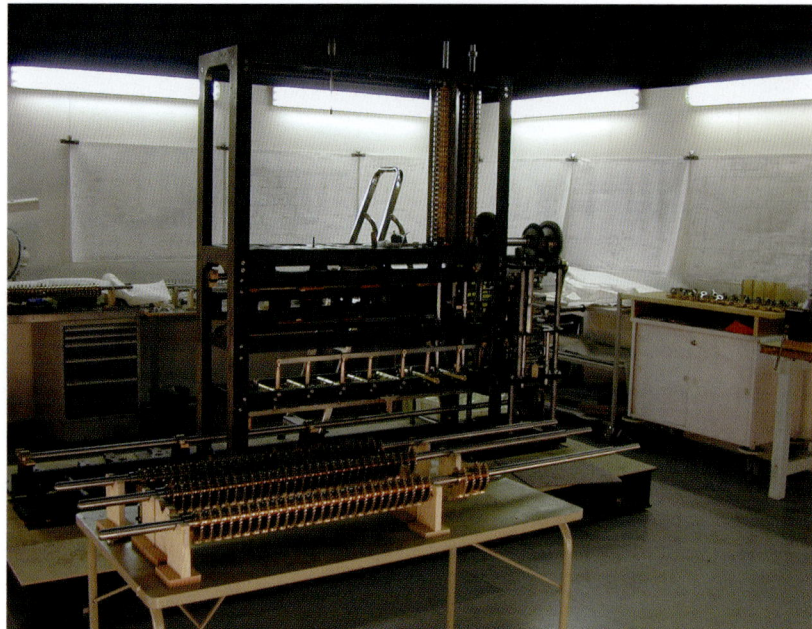

2.1
A recreation of Babbage's Difference Engine. Source: Wikimedia Commons. Online. Available HTTP: https://commons.wikimedia.org/wiki/File:Babbage_difference_engine.JPG

function as a great party trick, it sufficiently impressed the British government to offer Babbage funds to further develop the machine.

Lovelace became enraptured with Babbage and his machines, and the two began a correspondence. She started making notes for Babbage who had moved on from refining the far-from-perfect Difference Engine and had begun trying to build a bigger and better machine that he called the "Analytical Engine." In poetic fashion, Ada described what the Analytical Engine could do in addition to articulating its potential. Some believe that Ada understood the significance of Babbage's invention more than Babbage himself. In her writing, Ada described the Analytical Engine as a machine that could "be programmed and reprogrammed to do a limitless and changeable array of tasks" (Isaacon, 2014, p. 25). She explained that "anything that could be represented symbolically—numbers, logic, and even music—could pass through the machine and do wondrous things" (Evans, 2018, p. 20). Essentially, she described a modern computer in the year 1843.

Computer technology would stay at a standstill for almost another century until a visionary British mathematician named Alan Turing began writing about a device that could do so much more than making calculations. In fact, he portrayed a machine that looked and acted a whole lot like a modern-day computer using language even more precise than that of Lovelace. For example, Turing described a "read/write head" on a machine that would operate like a hard drive on a modern computer. And he did so somewhat unintentionally.

In 1937, while Turing was a graduate student, he published an article in the *Proceedings of the London Mathematical Society* titled: "On

Computable Numbers, with an Application to the Entscheidungsproblem." The Entscheidungsproblem (the decision problem) was a question posed by mathematical genius David Hilbert in 1928, which asked: "was there some procedure that could determine whether a particular statement was provable?" (Isaacon, 2014, p. 43). Turing argued that there was not. To make his argument, Turing described a machine that could solve any problem. If it came to a solution, the machine would halt, otherwise it would loop forever and never reach a solution. While Turing's proof was ingenious, the greater significance of his paper was that he "put into circulation the first really usable model of a computing machine" (Leavitt, 2006, p. 105). His visionary, theoretical machine became known as the "Turing Machine," and Alan Turing, "the father of the modern-day computer."

While Turing and Babbage never built their visionary machines, their work inspired the next generation of inventors. In 1937, a Harvard University physics doctoral student named Howard Aiken discovered a demonstration model of Babbage's Difference Engine in the attic of a building on campus and thought that it would be the perfect tool to help him make complex calculations required for his research. He successfully lobbied Harvard to further develop Babbage's Difference Engine in conjunction with IBM, resulting in a new machine that made its debut in 1941 called the "Mark 1." The Mark 1 was a functional, fully automatic "five-ton calculator" that could receive instructions from a paper tape (McCartney, 1999, p. 26), However, it was not electronic, only electro-magnetic.

In the early 1940s, a few other independent inventors around the world developed computing machines, each with different strengths, weaknesses and levels of functionality. The focus, primarily, for these machines was to make mathematical calculations which were of utmost importance to the Allies in the midst of World War II. At that time, it could take a week or more to calculate one missile trajectory. Computational power was lagging behind firepower. With so many American men overseas, mathematically-minded women were heavily recruited into "computing" positions to help make these calculations. These women were actually even referred to as "computers," which coined the term used today.

In 1943, the War was not going particularly well for the Allies; Hitler had taken over much of Europe and Japan was holding its ground. In desperate need for more computational power, representatives in the U.S. Army contracted with the Moore School of Engineering at the University of Pennsylvania for assistance in making these calculations. The University of Pennsylvania was sought after as a computational powerhouse due to its possession of a Differential Analyzer (another mechanical, analog computer designed to solve differential equations and invented by MIT electrical engineering faculty member, Vannevar Bush). The Moore School was also the employer of John Mauchly, a new professor with an idea to build an "electronic calculator that could take the place of all the [human] computers" (McCartney, 1999, p. 55). When the Army heard about his idea in 1943, they readily supplied the funding to bring Mauchly's idea to fruition.

At the Moore school, Mauchly partnered with Presper Eckert, a highly intelligent recent graduate of the electrical engineering program, and a team

■ History of Interactive Digital Media

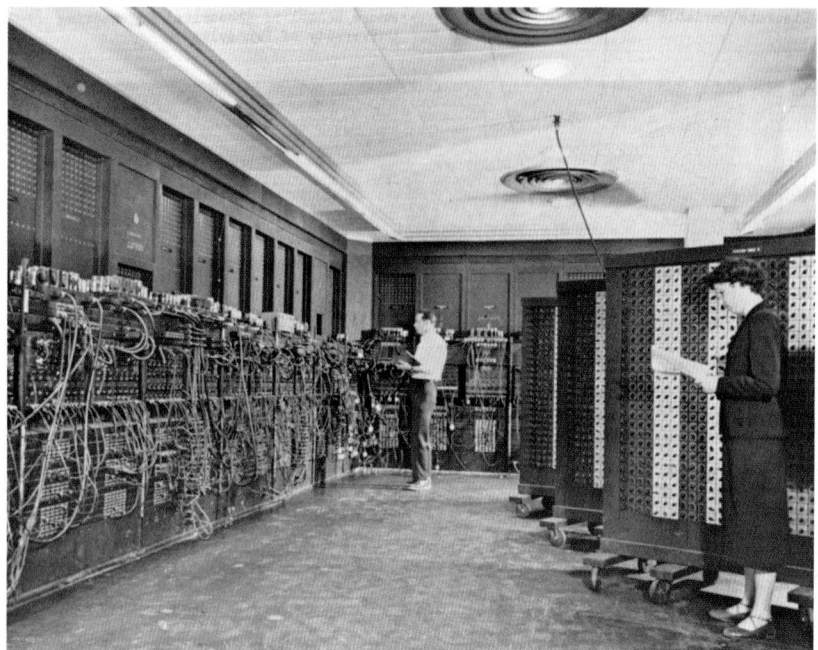

2.2
The ENIAC. Source: Wikimedia Commons. Online. Available HTTP: https://commons.wikimedia.org/wiki/ENIAC#/media/File:Eniac.jpg

of engineers to build the Electronic Numerical Integrator and Calculator which became known as the ENIAC. While aspects of their design borrowed ideas from other machines Mauchly had seen (which later resulted in legal disputes), it differed from them all in that it was completely electronic and general purpose, meaning that it could be programmed to do a variety of tasks. Ironically, the ENIAC was ready to go to work in 1945, just after the war had ended.

While the ENIAC could run different types of programs, loading a new program involved rewiring the machine by hand. ENIAC engineers needed to figure out how to make the computer perform a variety of tasks, so they recruited a team of the finest computers (six women: Frances Bilas Spence, Elizabeth Jennings, Ruth Lichterman, Kathleen McNulty, Elizabeth Snyder Holberton, and Marlyn Wescoff Meltzer) to figure out how to program the ENIAC (Isaacon, 2014, p. 87; McCartney, 1999, p. 95). These women essentially invented the field of computer programming, coining terms still in use today such as "subroutine" for a reusable block of code and "bug" for a glitch in a program. They even pulled off a major programming victory by getting the ENIAC to calculate a ballistic trajectory just in time for its public debut. The ENIAC is significant in that it was the world's first general-purpose, electronic computer.

EVOLUTION OF THE COMPUTER

Throughout the 1950s computers were enormous beasts that could fill an entire room. Their size was dictated by their contents: thousands of vacuum tubes (a glass tube without air that contains electrodes for controlling electron flow). The

ENIAC, for example, was the size of a 13' × 15' room, weighed 5 tons, and was comprised of 17,486 vacuum tubes (McCartney, 1999, pp. 101–102).

The 1947 invention of the transistor by William Shockley, John Bardeen and Walter Brattain at Bell Labs was the first step in allowing computers to get much smaller. A transistor is a solid-state electronic switch that can be used as an alternative to a vacuum tube. It was an exciting invention because it was physically much smaller and used a lot less power than the vacuum tube. It also generated less heat which kept it from failing as quickly (Watkins, n.d.).

The invention and integration of the microchip much further condensed the size of computers. A microchip is a set of electronic circuits on one small flat piece of semiconductor material, (normally silicon), replacing bulky individual electronic components such as transistors, resistors and capacitors. The microchip was actually conceived by two different people at two different locations: Jack Kilby at Texas Instruments and Ronald Noyce at Fairchild Semiconductor (and later Intel). Their competing claims to the invention led to legal disputes, however both were able to prosper from their invention (iProgrammer, 2010).

Intel became a leader in microchip (and later microprocessor) technologies, improving the speed and function of their technologies while making them smaller and less expensive. Gordon Moore, Intel co-founder, made a bold prediction in 1965 after noticing this trend. He surmised that computer power would double every year while the costs were halved. His idea became known as "Moore's Law" which proved to be remarkably accurate for many years to come.

The advancement of the computer was not just about improved performance in a smaller package, it was about an evolving mode of interaction. Like the Jacquard loom described by Ada Lovelace, early computers received instructions on punch cards which the computer would read, interpret and respond to. If there was an error in a program on a punch card, the card would need to be

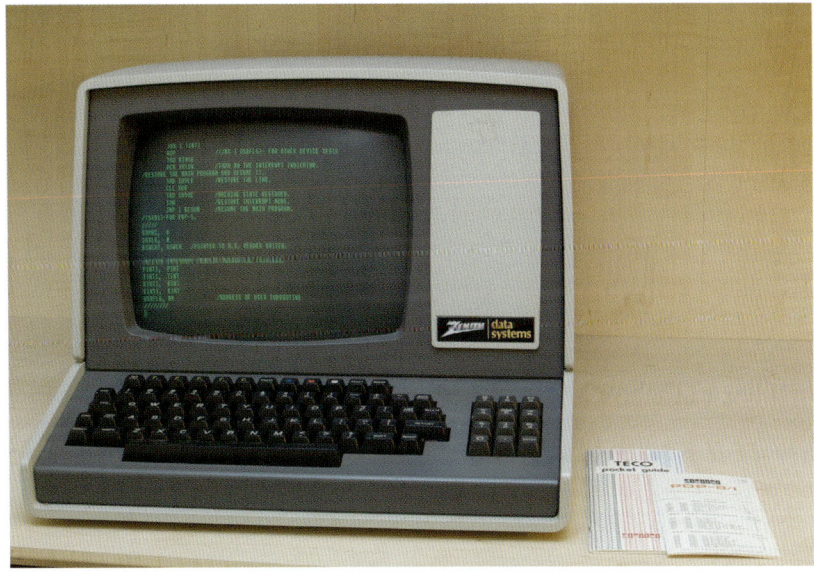

2.3
A dumb terminal from the late 1970s. Source: Wikimedia Commons. Online. Available HTTP: https://commons.wikimedia.org/wiki/File:Zenith_Z-19_Terminal.jpg

corrected and fed back into the computer. By the mid 1960s, dumb terminals (a computer station that relied on a mainframe for processing power) emerged which changed the way in which a user could interact with a computer. This new mode of human-computer interaction facilitated a real-time conversation between the computer and the user. However, because the mainframe computer was being accessed by many users simultaneously, computer time was limited and therefore precious and expensive. The lucky few who had access to computers got a leg up on the competition in the growing computing industry. In fact, access to computer time is one of the reasons why Bill Gates got so much coding experience. The forward-thinking mother's club at his high school raised money to pay for it.

Despite the fact that computers were still fairly inaccessible to the lay person in the 1960s and early 1970s, a few radicals dared to dream of having computing power in their own hands instead of having to share it among several users. The idea of individuals possessing their own computers went hand-in-hand with the prevailing "power to the people" philosophy of the 1960s. It is a not a coincidence that the California Bay Area was both the mecca for counterculture as well as computer technology. In the Bay Area, hippies intermixed with techies and formed groups such as the Palo Alto, California-based Homebrew computing club, frequented by Steve Jobs and Steve Wozniak. This mishmash of hippies and nerds were excited about getting computing technology into the hands of the people. And it would only be a few years for it to become a reality.

THE COMPUTER GETS PERSONAL

By the early 1970s, new technology companies such as Intel and Atari were establishing roots in the valley south of San Francisco thanks to an investment by Stanford University in a corporate park not far from the University. The area became known as "Silicon Valley," after reporter, Don Hoefler coined the term in a newspaper article about the local computer chip companies emerging in the area. However, despite the fact that so much high-tech energy was concentrated south of San Francisco, the first personal computer emerged 1,000 miles away in an Albuquerque, New Mexico strip mall (Bernard, 2017).

Ed Roberts was a serial entrepreneur who (out of a desperate need to rejuvenate his faltering calculator business) came up with the idea to build a computer that hobbyists could assemble themselves. Named after a star in the Star Trek series and the Intel microprocessor inside of it, Roberts introduced the first personal computer to the world: the Altair 8800. Expecting to sell a few hundred, Roberts' company (called MITS) sold hundreds each day and struggled to keep up with the demand. The Altair was featured on the January 1975 cover of the magazine, *Popular Electronics*, which drove up demand even further and became a rallying cry for computer geeks on the sidelines who dreamt of getting in on the personal computer revolution.

History of Interactive Digital Media

2.4
The Altair 8800.
Source: Wikimedia Commons. Online. Available HTTP: https://commons.wikimedia.org/wiki/File:Altair_8800_computer_at_CHM.jpg

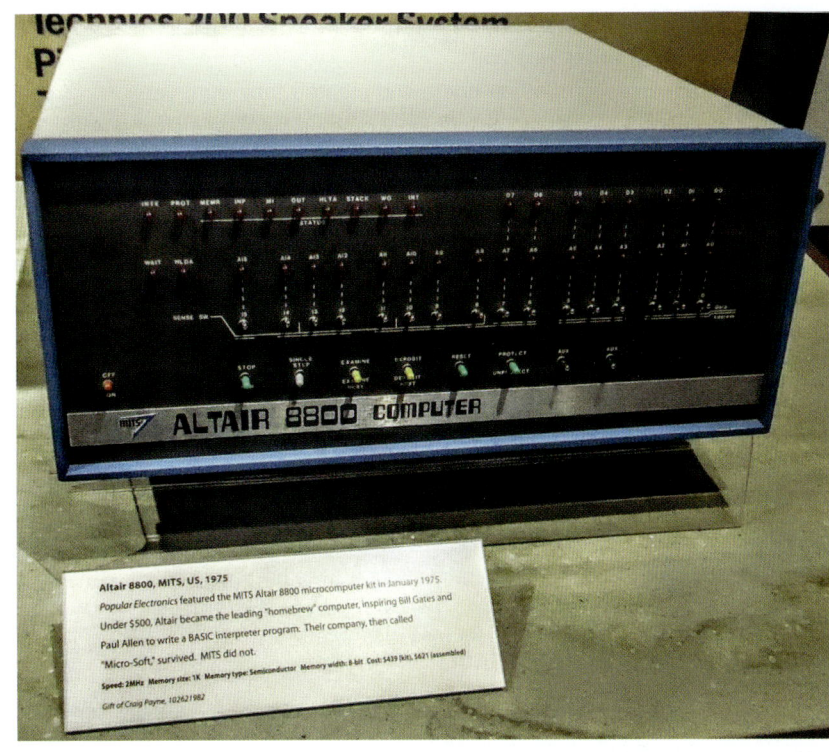

When the issue of *Popular Electronics* hit newsstands, Bill Gates was a junior at Harvard University. Already a proficient coder who took on projects with his older, more mature, business partner, Paul Allen, the duo realized that this was their moment to capitalize on the personal computer revolution. Calling their partnership "Micro-soft," they reached out to Ed Roberts at MITS and convinced him to license their version of the BASIC programming language interpreter for the Altair which would allow hobbyists to write and run programs on it. Roberts accepted, and this deal became a template for how Microsoft would grow their business going forward (Huddleston, 2018).

The Altair 8800 was not a computer everyone could use and love. Although it could be programmed to play music, games and do simple calculations and was embraced by geeky hobbyists like those of the Palo Alto Homebrew computing club, the Altair was not made for the average user. Homebrew member, Steve Wozniak was an electronics geek and recent Stanford graduate, living with his parents, and focusing his energy on building devices like a "dial-a-joke" machine. His friend and fellow computer enthusiast, Steve Jobs saw much more business potential in using Wozniak's engineering skills to develop a better, more accessible personal computer than the Altair. Jobs envisioned an all-in-one computer that could sit on a desk and be used by anyone and actually convinced a local hobby store owner that he and Wozniak could build

29

■ History of Interactive Digital Media

it. Remarkably, Wozniak and Jobs delivered the computers as promised, and in 1976 the Apple computer was born.

Other companies jumped on board and created their own versions of personal computers. IBM, which had primarily built hulking mainframes got in on the game and released their own personal computers. But as manufacturers introduced new computers to the marketplace, they realized that for consumers to be able to use them, they needed sell the computer with an operating system installed. Bill Gates and Paul Allen saw an opportunity and seized it.

Coming off of their success with their partnership with MITS and Altair, and having established their corporate headquarters in Seattle, Gates convinced IBM to license a personal computer operating system that he and Allen had written. They called their 1981 release MS-DOS, which stood for Microsoft Disk Operating System. Users could perform basic computing tasks such as run programs, write code, and manage files and folders on computers running MS-DOS. Because IBM was seen as a leader in personal computers, the new IBM clones that emerged followed suit and also licensed the MS-DOS operating system from Microsoft, and soon a software monopoly was born.

THE GRAPHICAL USER INTERFACE

In order for one to successfully interact with a computer running MS-DOS, the user had to learn a new language. MS-DOS was command-line driven, every task the user wished the computer to perform needed to be entered as text. For example, to change a directory, the user needed to type "cd" then enter the desired file path to navigate to the intended destination. At this time, personal computers also did not support a mouse or a graphical user interface. Ironically, however, several years before Microsoft's MS-DOS became the de-facto standard operating system on IBM PCs and their clones, a few innovators had built a much more user-friendly method of human-computer interaction.

Douglas Englebart was the director of a laboratory called the "Augmented Human Intellect Research Center" at Stanford Research Institute (SRI). His group was interested in inventing computer-related technologies (such as the computer mouse, bitmapped screens, and hypertext) that were designed to "augment" a user's intelligence. Englebart believed that as technology would make ,"the world increasingly complex, its power [needed to] be harnessed to help people collaborate and solve problems" (Douglas Englebart Institute, n.d.).

Englebart displayed his inventions at the 1968 Fall Joint Computer Conference in San Francisco's Civic Auditorium in a presentation titled "A Research Center for Augmenting Human Intellect," but it later became better known as "The Mother of All Demos." It was the "first public demonstration of the computer mouse, hypermedia and on-screen video teleconferencing," and it blew the audience away. Attendees saw a vision of computing 20–30 years ahead of its time. "It was the first time the world had ever seen a mouse, on-line processing,

History of Interactive Digital Media ■

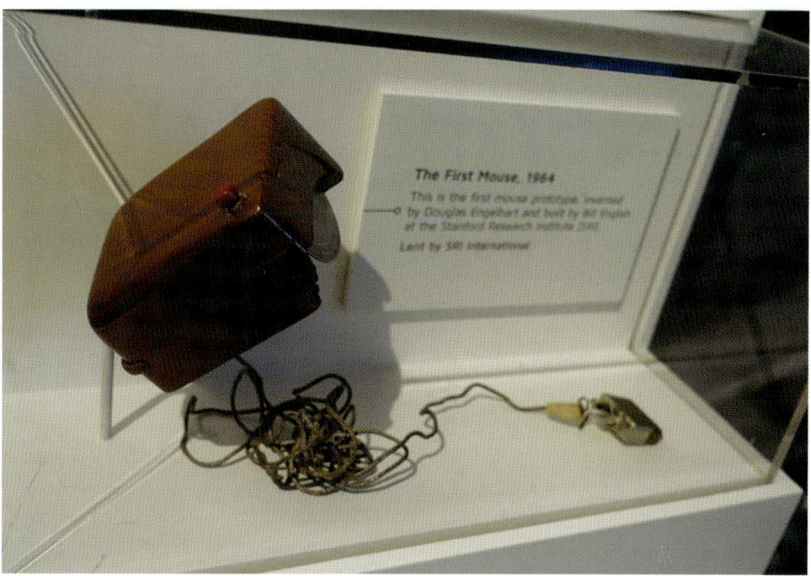

2.5
Douglas Englebart's first mouse. Source: Wikimedia Commons.

hypertext, mixed text and graphics and real-time video conferencing," explained Englebart (Fisher, 2018, p. 21).

SRI was not particularly interested in Englebart's work and failed to capitalize on any of his inventions, which was strangely similar to the attitude of Xerox at their West Coast research arm: Xerox PARC (Palo Alto Research Center), despite the fact that they were building on Englebart's breakthroughs. By 1973 Xerox PARC developed a computer, called the Alto, that supported an operating system with a graphical user interface (GUI) and a mouse. While they produced over 2,000 Altos, they didn't sell well because they were slow and underpowered. Also, executives at the Xerox corporate headquarters in Rochester, New York were more focused on their core business of selling copiers and did not see much potential in the Alto computer.

> The computer will never be as important to society as the copier.
> – Xerox Executive (Isaacon, 2014, p. 294)

In 1979, Steve Jobs, fresh off of his and Steve Wozniak's success in selling the first generation of Apple computers, paid a visit to Xerox PARC to get a better look at the Alto computer. Jobs was inspired by what he witnessed. Always the design innovator, he set off to build a more consumer-friendly version of the technology developed by Xerox. For example, to make the mouse cheaper and more durable, Jobs started disassembling deodorants to experiment with the track ball as the rolling mechanism inside the mouse.

Apple released its first computer with a GUI in 1983 called the Lisa, and it was a flop due to the fact that it was very expensive ($10,000), and it didn't

■ History of Interactive Digital Media

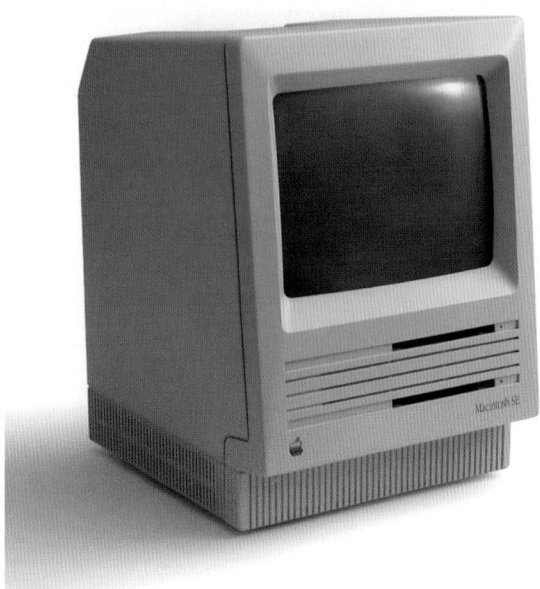

2.6
Early Macintosh computer. Source: Wikimedia Commons. Online. Available HTTP: https://commons.wikimedia.org/wiki/File:Macintosh_SE_b.jpg

perform all that well. The following year, Apple released a new computer called the Macintosh. Like the Lisa, it had a graphical user interface and a mouse. But unlike the Lisa, it was commercially successful because the cost was significantly lower (approximately $2,500), it performed well, and it came with some useful applications such as a word processor, a spreadsheet application, and a drawing program. Another reason why it was so popular is because Apple promoted it with a brilliant marketing campaign.

Apple's classic Macintosh ad was inspired by the 1984 summer Olympics in Los Angeles and the George Orwell book, *Nineteen Eighty Four*. The ad's message was that the year (1984) would not be like the dystopian 1984 described in the Orwell book because of the new Macintosh computer. The Cleo-winning commercial featured a beautiful, athletic female decathlete destroying (with her javelin) a projected Big Brother figure in the midst of lecturing to a group of zombie skinheads. The ad premiered during the Super Bowl halftime in January of 1984 and got even more exposure from the news stations who talked about the ad after the fact.

The Apple Macintosh was a huge commercial success, and it didn't take long for Microsoft to notice. They acknowledged that a computer with a mouse and a GUI made personal computers much easier to use. Therefore, in late 1985, Microsoft launched a GUI-based operating system called Windows which, from then on, came installed on all IBM PCs and their clones.

Mice and graphical user interfaces were becoming the standard method for interacting with a personal computer. Users no longer had to memorize and type cryptic commands to communicate with the computer. All they had to do was simply point and click on whatever application they wanted to run or the file they wanted to access. Now, all of a sudden, thanks to the mouse and the graphical user interface, the personal computer was able to be used by anyone.

VIDEO GAMES

Video games are a form of interactive digital media that emerged not long after the invention of the computer. Over the years, video games have taken many different forms, beginning as simple ping pong simulations and evolving into realistic virtual three-dimensional adventures. Video games were embraced by the public quickly and enthusiastically, and interest has not waned. The video game industry is "expanding at a double-digit rate, estimated to reach $180 billion by 2021" (Ballard, 2018).

In 1961, computers were hulking mainframes that primarily existed in businesses and universities, therefore only a privileged few had access to them. The Tech Model Railroad Club (TMRC) at Massachusetts Institute of Technology was one of these groups who had a computer at their disposal and was curious about what they could do with it, especially the PDP-1, a computer with a read-out display (a monitor). Junior TMRC member, Steve Russell, decided to write an interactive game for the PDP-1: a battle between rocket ships that he dubbed *Space Wars*. Players controlled the ships with toggle switches that were built into the computer. TMRC members spent hours playing the game and wrote code to add more features to it. They even built new controllers to play the game akin to primitive joysticks. While *Space Wars* was immensely popular among computer geeks, Russell and the TMRC never saw a profit from the game.

The next generation of video game developers did, however, turn a profit, and it was a very big one. In the late 1970s, Atari, one of the first video game companies to emerge, became one of the fastest growing and most profitable companies in the world. In 1981, Atari's gross profit was $3.2 billion, more than the entire movie industry in Hollywood (Fisher, 2018, p. 94).

Atari was founded by Nolan Bushnell, an engineering graduate from the University of Utah (a pioneering university in computer science) who funded his college education by working at an amusement park. Bushnell had witnessed countless visitors feeding quarters into mechanical games and decided to use computer components to build a standalone video arcade game. Although computer technology was somewhat primitive in the 1970s, Bushnell was able to create a video game by harnessing all the hardware power typically used in one computer for the purpose of running a single video game. Atari installed its first arcade game in a Palo Alto bar, Andy Capp's Tavern, in 1972, and it was an immediate success, setting Atari on its course to become a leader in the arcade industry.

Riding on the success of their arcade games, Atari decided to develop a console that would allow gamers to play video games in their homes. Their console, the Atari 2600, became the gold standard in home gaming systems; it

■ History of Interactive Digital Media

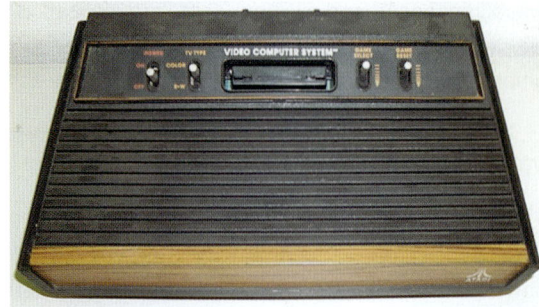

2.7
The Atari 2600.
Source: Wikimedia Commons. Online. Available HTTP: https://commons.wikimedia.org/wiki/Atari#/media/File:Atari2600wood4.jpg

allowed players to play a variety of games by plugging different cartridges into the console. Initially Atari designed all its own games. However, game developers at Atari felt slighted, as they were never given credit for their work, and they did not receive any extra compensation for successful games. Eventually a group of Atari game designers left and started their own company that made and sold video games for the Atari console. Their company, Activision, was the first third party game development company.

In the mid 1980s, arcade frenzy was waning, however, home game consoles were becoming big business. New players entered the market such as Nintendo, Sega, Sony and several other smaller companies, releasing a steady stream of home gaming consoles, each trying to one up each other with new improvements to their systems. These companies developed their own games internally as well as created licensing agreements with different third party game developers. In 1989, Nintendo had a surprise hit with their handheld gaming console, the Game Boy, proving that consumers loved being able to play video games on the go.

By the mid 1990s, home PCs were finally easy to use and powerful enough to run graphics intensive games. Some game developers focused their energy on making PC games, avoiding the restrictive licensing agreements inherent in making games for specific consoles. The release of Windows 95 provided a great opportunity for game developers, because unlike previous operating systems, it was able to run first person shooter games.

Despite the growing popularity of PC gaming, game consoles continued to evolve, and advertisers marketing them as the "hub of the living room," as they could be used to play CDs and DVDs (Kent, 2001, p. 521). Eventually consoles could even connect to the Internet, making networked game play possible.

In 2001, Microsoft decided to get into the video game business and released their console, the Xbox. While it might have seemed unlikely for a software company to get into the hardware business, Microsoft had a fleet of gamers on their staff who were passionate about the project and made it a reality, and the Xbox was a runaway success.

Microsoft continued to innovate in the video game hardware industry with the release of their Kinect motion sensing device in 2009 that worked with the

History of Interactive Digital Media

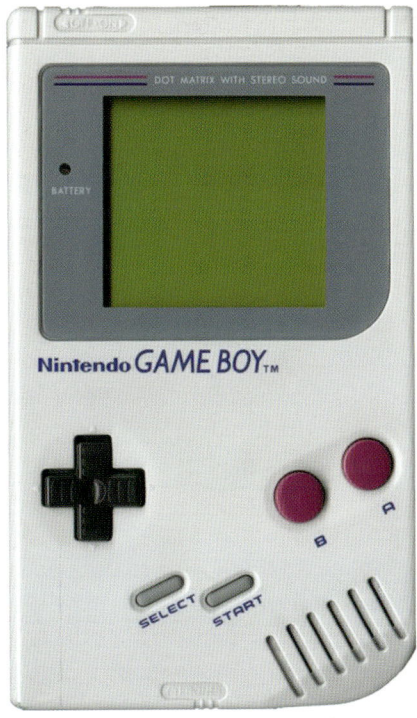

2.8
The first Nintendo Game Boy. Source: Wikimedia Commons. Online. Available HTTP: https://commons.wikimedia.org/wiki/Game_Boy_and_variants#/media/File:Gameboy.jpg

Xbox gaming system. The Kinect allowed the gamer to play video games using their entire body. The Kinect was marketed as being superior to other motion sensing devices such as Nintendo's Wii as it used a camera to track motion as opposed to Wii's handheld sensors that could only track arm movement. Virtual sports and dancing games were especially well suited for these platforms.

Smartphones have provided another platform for video game play as well as new opportunities for game developers. Smartphones lend themselves to "casual gaming," the types of games you can play while killing time. Games that have a simple objective like *Angry Birds* and *Candy Crush*, as well as simple networked games that allow players to challenge their friends, like *Words with Friends*, thrive on tablets and smartphones.

THE BIRTH OF THE INTERNET

> A network of such [computers], connected to one another by wide-band communication lines [would provide] the functions of present-day libraries [linked] together with anticipated advances in information storage and retrieval and [other] symbiotic functions.
>
> – J.C.R. Licklider, *Man-Computer Symbiosis*, 1960

Alongside of the computer and video game revolution, a different but related technology was evolving which would soon be known as the Internet. Unlike the

■ History of Interactive Digital Media

personal computer, the Internet was not developed in a garage in Silicon Valley. It was a government-funded project that involved research institutions from around the United States. Also, unlike the personal computer, which was seen as a tool for individual empowerment, the Internet was originally built to facilitate collaboration.

In the 1960s, when computers were large mainframe systems only used at research institutions and government agencies, access to them was quite limited. Getting time on the computer was precious and protected. J. C. R. Licklider (or "Lick") was a computer visionary as well as director of the Information Processing Techniques Office (IPTO) of the Advanced Research Project Agency (ARPA) of the United States Department of Defense. Lick believed that efficiency and collaboration could be improved if computers were networked together, and he articulated these ideas in a (now famous) 1960 paper called "Man-Computer Symbiosis." While Lick's ideas were considered pretty radical, they generated excitement in the emerging computing world, despite the fact that no one had any idea how to build such a network.

In 1965, Bob Taylor, a psychologist from Texas, who, like Licklider, studied psychoacoustics in college, became the director of IPTO. He was very much interested in Lick's ideas about computer networking and lobbied his superiors for the funds to build a network of computers at major research institutions throughout the United States. Without much effort, Taylor was given a million dollars from ARPA's budget to finance this network which eventually became known as "The Arpanet."

After securing the funds, Taylor's team put out a request for proposals to build the Arpanet. The winning bid was submitted by Boston-based, Bolt, Beraneck and Newman, otherwise known as BBN, which was also (not totally coincidentally) the former employer of J. C. R. Licklider. BBN had strong ties to Massachusetts Institute of Technology and were known for their technical prowess. They were excited to do the job, despite the fact that they didn't completely understand why they were being paid to build such a network.

The engineers at BBN started the project by connecting computers at two ARPA funded research centers: The University of California at Los Angeles (UCLA) and Stanford Research Institute (SRI) at Stanford University. They used telephone lines to get the computers to communicate with one another, but not in their usual mode of operation. Instead of tying up the lines with a continuous stream of communication, they sent the data in small packets through the phone lines.

Packets are small chunks of data that are numbered and addressed. Packets can travel any route to their destination, they are simply reassembled back together once they arrive at their final destination. Packet switching is the data transmission method that allowed the Arpanet to work and is still used today.

Connecting the first two computers (and the subsequent computers at other universities) on the Arpanet was a huge technological victory. However, despite the fact that these sites were now connected, the Arpanet got very little use because most users found it difficult to work on other people's systems. This all began to change, though, once the Arpanet found its unexpected niche: email.

Ray Tomlinson was a BBN engineer who came up with what he called a "little hack," a program that allowed you to send a message to someone at some computer on the Arpanet. He tested it out on himself. It seemed to work, so he asked others to give it a try. Once they did, email quickly took over Arpanet traffic. Years later, Bob Taylor stated that ARPA would have never agreed to fund the Arpanet had they known email would be its primary use. But there was no denying the fact that the Arpanet had tremendous potential as a communication medium.

GROWTH OF THE INTERNET

During the 1960s and 1970s other networks sprouted up independent of the Arpanet. But, in order for these networks to communicate, they needed to be speaking the same language. This conundrum prompted the development of Transfer Control Protocol/Internet Protocol (TCP/IP). TCP/IP specified how data should be packetized, addressed, transmitted, routed, and received which allowed other networks to connect to the burgeoning Arpanet. By 1975, the Arpanet became an international network with the addition of nodes in England and Norway. Shortly thereafter the Arpanet became known as the Internet.

In the 1980s, networking technologies made great strides, allowing the Internet to grow exponentially. Prior to the 1980s, the idea that computers in a room or in a building could be networked together and share resources like printers, etc., and connect to the Internet was a new concept. Bob Metcalfe, an engineer at Xerox PARC, took on the challenge of building a local area network by inventing the Ethernet protocol which is the standard used to network computers and connect them to the Internet. Since Xerox PARC was not interested in capitalizing on the invention, Metcalfe took the technology and launched a very successful networking company called 3COM.

Another networking challenge that needed to be solved was to network networks together. In the late 1980s, married Stanford University professors Len Bosack and Sandy Lerner worked in different areas of the Stanford Campus and wanted to be able to communicate with one another through their computers. They figured out how to do it by pulling wires through Stanford's campus and inventing the hardware that would allow their networks to talk to each other. Stanford wasn't impressed. So, Len and Sandy started their own company, Cisco Systems, which is still the largest networking company in the world.

THE BIRTH OF THE WORLD WIDE WEB

In the 1980s, while personal computers were becoming more commonplace, the Internet was growing by leaps and bounds. It was even possible for individuals to connect to the Internet from home using telephone dial up connections with primitive modems. The problem was that it wasn't easy to use. Once connected to the Internet, users would need to launch specific applications to perform

History of Interactive Digital Media

different tasks such as transferring files, chatting and posting messages on bulletin boards. The Internet was also entirely text-based and command-line driven, and was therefore seen primarily as a tool for techies.

The nature of the Internet completely changed once the world wide web was invented. The web put a graphical user interface on the Internet which made it much more accessible to a non-technical user. The web did for the Internet what the Macintosh did for the personal computer.

The world wide web was officially invented by Tim Berners-Lee, a research scientist at the particle physics lab, CERN, near Geneva, Switzerland. Berners-Lee was frustrated by having to navigate through networks to share documents with different departments. He wanted the scientists to be able to make their findings immediately and easily available to others. To solve this problem, he came up with the idea of a web page which could be seen by anyone with access to the Internet and a piece of software he invented, called a web browser. A web page could incorporate hyperlinks to other web pages and documents which allowed the author of the web page to connect his ideas to those of others.

While Tim Berners-Lee's invention of the world wide web changed the face of the Internet and made it much easier to use, it was not the first time interlinked media had been conceived. In the 1940s, M.I.T. professor Vannevar Bush, inventor of the Differential Analyzer, published a paper called "As We May Think," in which he described a machine that operated a lot like the modern day world wide web. Bush called the machine "The Memex," a tool that could record "trails of interest" and connect related documents via links. Because, at the time of his writing, computers had not yet been invented, Bush described the Memex as a stand-alone machine the size of a desk. While his description of the Memex seems clunky and naïve from a modern point of view, it was significant because Bush articulated the concept of interconnected media 50 years prior to the invention of the world wide web. For this reason, Vannevar Bush is often referred to as the "father of interactive media."

Another person who envisioned a web-like application long before the world wide web existed was a philosopher named Ted Nelson. In a 1974 paper, he articulated a system of interconnected documents called "Project Xanadu." Nelson didn't actually build Project Xanadu, but his ideas are worth noting because he described a system that operated very much like the world wide web years before its time. In addition, Nelson coined the term "hypertext," text that is clickable and leads to another location, just like a hyperlink we are accustomed to on the world wide web.

As word caught on about the world wide Web, Berners-Lee encouraged developers to improve upon his original freely available browser software. A 22-year-old University of Illinois student named Marc Andreesen did just that, and improved the original browser software so much that it became a hot commodity among early web users. Andreesen's browser, Mosaic, was probably "the most successful software product designed for and released on the Internet" (McCullough, 2018 p.16). His invention caught the attention of a Silicon

2.9
Netscape Navigator 1.0. Source: Wikimedia Commons. Online. Available HTTP: https://commons.wikimedia.org/wiki/File:Netscape_Navigator_1.22_Screenshot.png

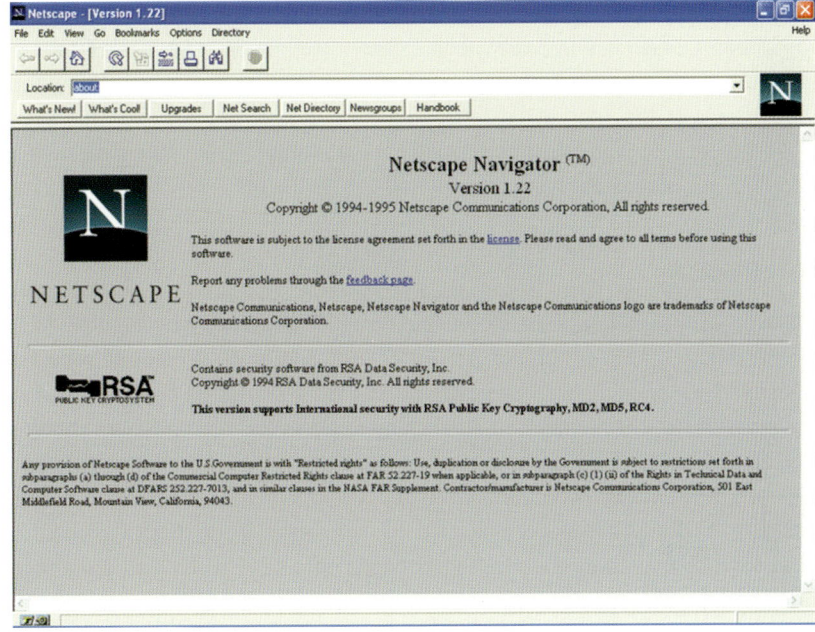

Valley venture capitalist, Jim Clark, (founder of Silicon Graphics) who invested in Andreesen's idea and rebranded the browser as Netscape Navigator. Netscape Navigator was freely available to individuals, but business users were charged a small fee.

In the mid 1990s, business was booming for Netscape. However, it wasn't long until Microsoft saw what they were doing and wanted in on the game. Their strategy to kill Netscape Navigator was to package their own browser, Internet Explorer, with the operating system Windows 95, that was being installed on every new PC. Bill Gates and company figured, if people were getting Internet Explorer for free with Windows 95, why would they pay for Netscape Navigator? Their strategy worked, Netscape sold out to AOL and Internet Explorer became the dominant browser by the late 1990s. It also created a legal battle between Netscape and Microsoft in which Microsoft was accused of anti-competitive practices.

As the world wide web attracted more and more attention from the general public, it didn't take long for enterprising-minded individuals to wonder how they could profit from it. Because the Internet was conceived as a government-funded network, commerce over the Internet was illegal. In 1991, however, this law was repealed in the United States, and it ignited the business world. Shortly thereafter, mainstays of the web shopping world such as Amazon (in 1994) and eBay (in 1995) emerged, as well as thousands of other e-commerce sites with varying amounts of success. The rush of excitement to do business online created the dot com boom of the late 1990s.

■ History of Interactive Digital Media

The world wide web has become the most commonly used application on the Internet which is why many people cannot distinguish it from the Internet. For many, their only experience with the Internet may have only been using the web. However, the Internet existed long before the birth of the world wide web. The difference between the Internet and the web is that the Internet is a network and the web is an application running on it.

MULTIMEDIA

Many other interactive applications existed prior to the invention of the web, they simply did not run over the Internet. In the 1980s interactive content, typically referred to as "multimedia," was distributed and consumed on floppy disks, and eventually CDs. CDs presented an exciting opportunity for interactive content distribution because the storage capacity was much higher than that of floppy disks and the newest computers were being shipped with CD drives. CDs also packaged well inside of a textbook, so publishers began using them to distribute bonus interactive content with their books. Music companies also embraced multimedia, including interactive content incorporating music video clips, images and interviews on the audio CDs as a bonus.

Multimedia kiosks were also around prior to the web. One early pioneer of the kiosk was Florsheim Shoes. In 1987, they introduced kiosks into their retail stores, allowing customers to order shoes that were not available in the store, which were then delivered to their homes a few days later (Key, 1987). This type of electronic retailing was pretty revolutionary for its time.

WEB 2.0

Most websites in the 1990s were really pretty simple. In fact, a lot of websites were referred to as "brochure-ware" because they were static pages of hyper-linked content with pictures. But, by the 2000s, that began to change. This was not due to any specific technological breakthrough. It had more to do with how websites were being used. Instead of one author creating the content for a website, new sites were evolving that were comprised of user-generated content. This shift became known as Web 2.0.

A classic example of a Web 2.0 site is Wikipedia—the world's largest encyclopedia built entirely of user-generated content. Ironically, the creators of Wikipedia started another web-based encyclopedia project at the same time as Wikipedia where the articles were all written by experts. That project didn't get very far because it took too long to create expert authored content. Wikipedia, on the other hand, grew like wildfire because users enjoyed contributing to the collective knowledge base and took ownership of the content.

Blogs are another type of web-based user-generated content that emerged in the Web 2.0 movement. In 1999, a website called Blogger.com emerged. On this site, anyone could set up an account and simply start creating content.

2.10
A hallmark of the Web 2.0 movement was an influx of user generated content

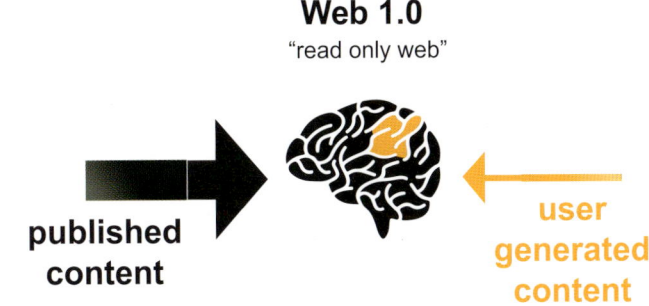

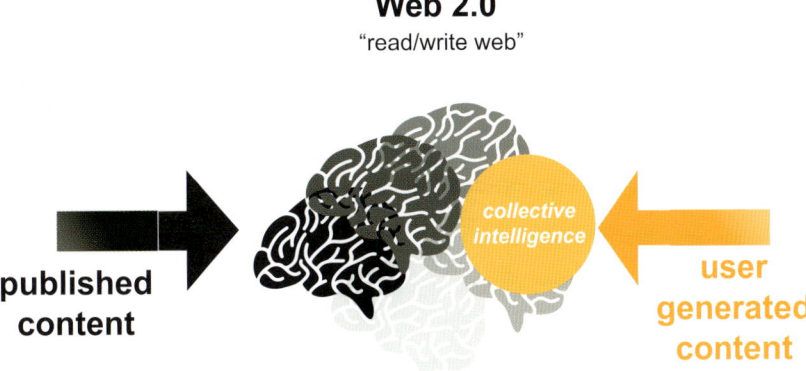

It allowed anyone to establish their own web presence in a space where any other user could add comments and start a discussion, which is a very Web 2.0 notion.

In the early 2000s, the solution to the problem of being able to easily update websites grew out of the blogging concept. If your company or organization had a website in the 1990s that needed updating, you would need to contact the developer to get these small changes made. It wasn't a great use of the company's money nor the web developer's time to make simple text edits. There was clearly a need to allow website owners a way to make simple edits to their content. Content management systems were created to address this issue.

A content management system, or a CMS, is a software application that allows a non-technical user to make changes to a website. CMS architectures are increasingly used to facilitate user website modifications without knowing any coding whatsoever. There are several CMS applications on the market that website owners can download and there are also CMS *architectures*, in which a website is built on a platform with an integrated CMS. WordPress (originally

■ History of Interactive Digital Media

founded as a blogging platform) is a very common CMS, but there are several others such as Joomla and Drupal.

The 2000s also saw the birth of social media, another Web 2.0 construct, as it allows people to publish on the web and have conversations. One of the first and most popular social media sites was Myspace. Founded in 2003, Myspace was a place for users to post content, create personal profiles, start blogs, join groups, and network with others. Myspace was overtaken in popularity in the mid 2000s by Facebook when it emerged in 2004. Facebook's speed in adding new features and helping people make connections made it more attractive to users. Twitter arrived in 2006 with a new concept: users were encouraged to make updates in short 120 character or less "tweets." New social media platforms continued to emerge throughout the late 2000s and 2010s, replacing each other in popularity, and further allowing anyone to be an online publisher.

INTERACTIVE DIGITAL MEDIA IN THE 2010S AND BEYOND

The biggest change that the web has seen in the 2010s is the prevalence of the smartphone. While there were several models of cell phones on the market in the 2000s that allowed users to surf the web, Apple's iPhone (released in 2007) took it to a new level. It was sleek, easy to use, and allowed users to surf the web, listen to music and even download applications. The iPhone quickly became the gold standard for smartphones, but also created challenges and opportunities for developers.

One challenge for web developers was the screen size of the smart phone. Many websites were difficult to view in their entirety on a smart phone screen. Since more and more people were accessing web content from their mobile devices, developers had to adapt. Fortunately, the core coding languages used to

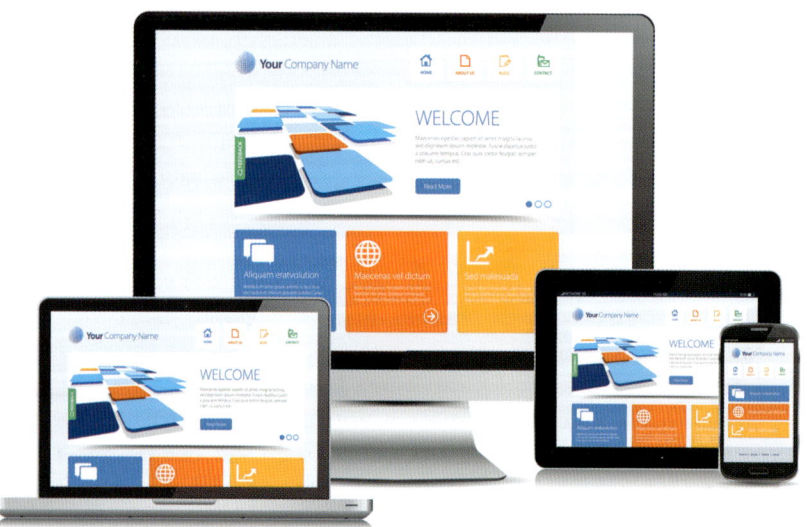

2.11
Responsive websites deliver content in different ways depending on the device that requested it. Source: © bagiuiani; 123rf.com

42

build websites evolved to the point of allowing developers to build websites that are responsive. A responsive website is one that changes its appearance based on the device that is accessing it. Responsive web design is now the standard for web development.

The iPhone and iPad (and subsequently Android and other smartphones) created new opportunities for interactive developers with the birth of the app market. Interactive designers and developers can invent an application and make it accessible to millions to purchase and download. Initially apps developed for the iPhone and iPad had to be created in the specific development environment created by Apple, but can now be developed in other environments.

As the general population has become increasingly reliant on their devices, websites have collected a lot of data on user behavior. These sites use the data to serve us content they think we might be interested in. We are now accustomed to seeing ads pop up in our Facebook feed, or on a side panel on a search engine, for some item or service we might have been shopping for on another website. We are not surprised by Amazon suggesting a product that we actually are interested in. This website behavior is called adaptability, as the application adapts to what it thinks we want, or what they can get us to buy.

Interactive media has evolved beyond a point and click experience. Interfaces are more gestural; we use a pinching motion to zoom in and out of screens on our iPhone. We play video games with our whole bodies. As we have become more aware of the detrimental effects of a sedentary lifestyle, interactive developers have devised interfaces that are more physical in nature.

The field of physical computing has grown beyond a niche area of research and been embraced by artists, hobbyists and inventors interested in building interactive systems that respond to the physical world. The popularity of physical computing has grown with the maker movement and as inexpensive circuit boards and sensors have become widely available.

Interactive applications that incorporate virtual reality are being used for a wide variety of purposes, from training to therapy to entertainment. Virtual reality employs the use of specialized headsets that put a user into a virtual 3D space by projecting 3D imagery and an audio feed inside the darkened goggles. The user can look around and explore this virtual world as well as interact with others. While the term "virtual reality" was coined in the 1980s when early hardware was just being developed, interest has grown recently as the technology has become more accessible and powerful. Most notably, the Oculus Rift, released in 2016, signified a remarkable advancement in virtual reality goggles. Virtual reality has many practical applications beyond entertainment; it is a powerful for training, education and even therapy.

Augmented reality is a form of interactive media in which a computer-generated image, text or sound is imposed on a live view of the real world. Many people got their first taste of this technology playing the popular mobile game, *Pokemon Go*, which took advantage of the mobile device's GPS capabilities and inserted characters into the players' real-world location. Augmented reality has

■ History of Interactive Digital Media

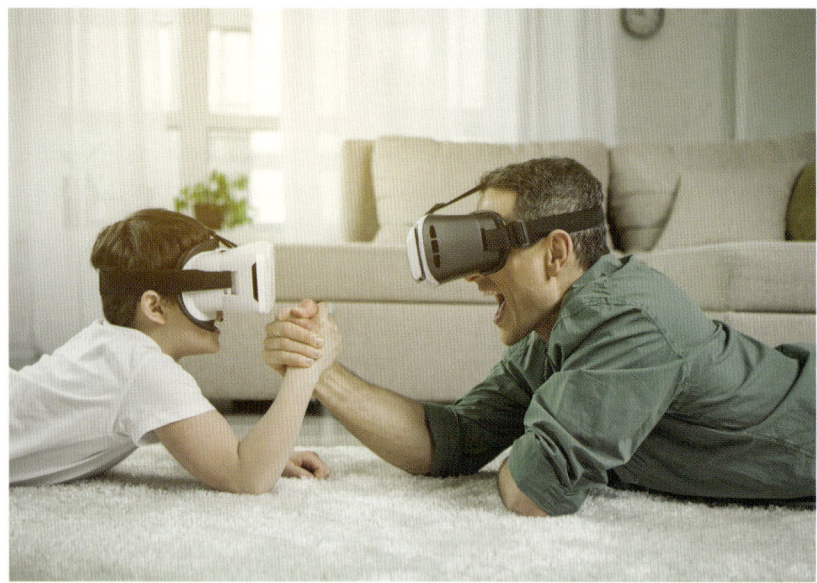

2.12
3D goggles facilitate virtual reality gaming. Source: © Olena Yakobchuk; 123rf.com

many other practical applications beyond finding and capturing virtual creatures. Imagine music students seeing actual notes appear while playing the music, or shopper customizing a car she was interested in buying while in the showroom (Paine, 2018). Its disparate uses will likely grow in the years to come.

PRACTITIONER INTERVIEW

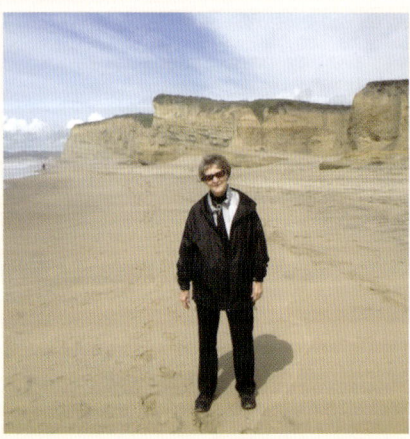

Elizabeth (Jake) Feinler

Former director of the Network Information Center, Palo Alto, CA USA
"Before Google and Godaddy, there was Elizabeth Feinler" (Metz, 2012). *Elizabeth (Jake) Feinler served as the director of the Network Information*

History of Interactive Digital Media

Center (the NIC) from its establishment in 1972 until 1989. She was hired by Douglas Englebart (inventor of the mouse and the graphical user interface) to create a directory for the newly established Arpanet and subsequently formed a group who developed the top-level domain name system and managed the first central domain name registry. Anyone who wanted to know where any resource was on the Arpanet, would first go to Jake.

How did you become the Director of the Network Information Center (NIC) at Stanford Research Institute (SRI)?

I went to West Liberty State College in West Virginia and decided to major in chemistry. Then I went on to graduate school at Purdue to study biochemistry. I finished my coursework for a PhD, but I got tired of living on minimal amounts of money, so I got a job at Chemical Abstracts in Ohio. I was fascinated by the amount of information they had to deal with and the fact that they were just barely getting computerized. The whole idea of handling information just intrigued me and so I never went back to chemistry.

In 1960, I took a job at Stanford Research Institute (SRI) [as a research specialist] where we were farmed out to various research groups to help them get the information they needed. I had never been to California before, but it sounded like fun. At SRI, I met a lot of people at the Institute including Doug Englebart.

Douglas Englebart ran the Augmentation Research Center Lab at SRI which created the computer mouse and the graphical user interface. Englebart believed that the best way to solve problems was to use the computer to augment humans' intelligence.

Doug did this thing called "The Big Demo" (the 1968 "The Mother of All Demos") which just blew everybody away because it had people interacting with computers and things that [they had] never [seen or] done before. Doug wanted computers [and information] to be at your fingertips. I was fascinated by what these people [Doug and his augmented human intelligence group] were doing.

[Doug] bid on a project coming out of ARPA to build an Information Center for the Arpanet. He came back down [to my office] and talked to me about it, and I said "why don't you hire me, Doug?" And he said, "I don't have a job at this time." But, when his project came in [in 1972], he came down and said, "I have a job now. Do you want to come work for me? We need a resource handbook." And I said, "what's a resource handbook?" And he said, "I'm not quite sure but we need it." So that's how I joined Doug's group and [became involved with] the Internet.

What was Doug Englebart like as a person?

Oh, Doug was a really, really nice guy. He was very soft-spoken, and he was driven. He had this vision that he wanted to see the world have any

■ History of Interactive Digital Media

information they needed at their fingertips. He was definitely a step ahead of everybody else.

SRI was an important center in the evolution of the Arpanet as SRI and UCLA were the locations of the first two Arparnet servers. After Jake joined Engelbart's group in 1972, she became Principal Investigator for the Network Information Center (NIC) project in 1974 and was later made Director when the work expanded substantially in 1985.

How large was the Arpanet when the NIC was established and what did your role involve?

I believe there were about 30 sites [on the Internet], and [my job was to] write up what resources were available at those sites. People contacted me to learn about the computer resources across the network.

What kind of resources would they be interested in?

There were two things happening; they were building the Net at the same time the users were using the Net. And that was rather confusing. Things were slightly broken all the time, so users were confused about where to go. It was very fundamental questions at the beginning, but we set up a network of technical liaisons at each site that knew all the details and protocols. So, if people were calling and saying "I'm having problems doing something because I can't get to that resource." Then we would call that liaison and let them know. So there was this very tight network of knowledgeable people that kept in touch with each other and we were just kind of the hub. We didn't try to answer everybody's question so much as we would send them to the right person that could answer the question.

I've heard that the Arpanet wasn't initially used all that heavily until email was invented.

Well, I would say [email] was the killer app mainly because it changed the whole way people communicated. It just opened up the doors of communication between different types of people. [In places, such as in the military], you had to go up three channels to the top and then across to another agency and down those channels [to communicate with different people.] [With email] that just went out the door because everybody started talking to everybody. It really did change the way the whole world communicated.

When did the Arpanet grow so large that the directory became difficult to maintain?

We started out [publishing the Internet directory] with lots and lots of paper and sending all this stuff out by snail mail and then in the mid 80s, we made it available via FTP. But we still published the Arpanet directory [on paper] like the phonebook, until, maybe 1986, when WHOIS [was standardized.]

I read somewhere that you are credited with coming up with the top-level domain naming scheme, e.g. .gov for government sites, .com for commercial sites, etc.

Well, I'm not going to take credit. We were a team, so we all worked on this together. But there were finally so many computers on the network that the address space [on each packet traveling through the Internet] was no longer large enough [to hold address information], and we had to come up with a different naming system.

Feinler's group decided to designate generic top-level domains to describe the type of host that was on the Internet. GOV was used for government sites, EDU for education, and COM as an afterthought for anything that didn't quite fit, since the Internet was not commercial at the time.

We came up with a naming scheme that was hierarchical. You came to the top and then went down a tree. That required that you have top-level naming domains. We wanted to have [the top-level domains] based on networks. We picked these very generic [top-level domains] for two reasons: they were generic and those were the communities that were developing [on the Internet]. Plus, there was a standards body under every one of those top-level domains that would determine what the rest of the structure [of the domain name] was going to be.

Did SRI manage the database that matched IP addresses to domain names that was the precursor to the DNS system?

Yes. The Network Information Center managed the host tables until the network went commercial. Places like GoDaddy [and other domain registrants took it over.] What we gave away is now a multi-million-dollar industry.

Prior to the DNS system, could anyone register whatever domain name they wanted?

Well, no, it was managed [by the person] that was in charge of the top-level domain. Each domain managed itself in a sense. They each had a structure that they wanted to follow. [For example,] the military was very different from the universities.

When you were at SRI, did you have an appreciation for the historical significance of what you were doing?

Very! I mean I think everybody that was on the Net in the early days was very dedicated to making this thing work and seeing where it could go and

■ History of Interactive Digital Media

how far it could go. Computers were just exciting in those days and the whole network was exciting because look at all the people you could talk to and the things you could do!

One of the things that never seems to get emphasized is that although we were kind of the hub, it really worked because we had all these contacts at every site on the network (technical liaisons). The network of people working back and forth with us was what I think was very significant in getting the Internet built and then [establishing] the rules people played by.

You had this privileged position of seeing computers with mice and early graphical user interfaces. When personal computers first came out, were you disappointed or surprised?

No. Doug [Englebart's] concept of [a computer that could accomplish many different tasks via a graphical user interface] was well known, but it was too big for computers at the time.

In 1984, Apple computer released the Macintosh, a personal computer that had a mouse and a graphical user interface. The Macintosh was able to accomplish many of the tasks that Englebart had demonstrated at "The Mother of All Demos" 15 years prior.

Did Doug feel like Steve Jobs and Apple ripped him off?

Oh no, no—he wanted this stuff to get out, but he didn't like the way it went. Doug envisioned a computer as an assistant to augment a human, and that its services should essentially be at the knowledge worker's fingertips. It bothered him that things deteriorated so that one had to keep learning new interfaces, new passwords, etc., i.e., nothing was consistent for the user.

I saw that you were in the first group of inductees to the Internet Hall of Fame in 2012. That must have been a pretty unique and terrific honor.

It was! I [was] so surprised because you know most of the people that [were the first inductees to] the Internet Hall of Fame were people who built the network. Although we did not build the Internet, we told the world it was there! To be there with Vint Cerf or Bob Kahn or some of those people was just a true honor.

DISCUSSION QUESTIONS

1) Why do you think the history of interactive media is a worthwhile history to study?
2) It is often said that "those who cannot learn from history are doomed to repeat it." How does this apply to the history of interactive media?

3) What was your first encounter with interactive media? How has your use of it changed over time?
4) Do you think interactive media is a tool for empowerment or repression?
5) What do you think is the future of interactive digital media?

REFERENCES

Ballard, J. (2018). 5 Trends Explain the Growth of the Video-Game Industry. *The Motley Fool*, November 9. Online. Available at: https://www.fool.com/investing/2018/11/09/5-trends-explain-the-growth-of-the-video-game-indu.aspx.

Bernard, Z. (2017). Here's the Story Behind how Silicon Valley Got its Name. *Business Insider*, December 9. Online. Available at: https://www.businessinsider.com/how-silicon-valley-got-its-name-2017-12?r=US&IR=T.

Douglas Englebart Institute. (n.d.). Online. Available at: http://www.dougengelbart.org/content/view/183/153.

Evans, C. (2018). *Broadband: The Women Who Made the Internet*. New York: Portfolio/Penguin.

Fisher, A. (2018). *Valley of Genius: The Uncensored History of Silicon Valley, as Told by the Hackers, Founders, and Freaks who made it Boom*. New York: Twelve.

Huddleston, T. (2018). What Microsoft Billionaire Bill Gates was Doing at 20 Years Old. Online. Available at: https://www.cnbc.com/2018/03/29/what-microsoft-billionaire-bill-gates-was-doing-at-20-years-old.html.

iProgrammer (2010) Invention of the Microchip. *iProgrammer*. Online. Available at: https://www.i-programmer.info/history/machines/736-kilby-a-noyce.html.

Isaacon, W. (2014). *The Innovators*. New York: Simon and Schuster.

Kent, S. (2001). *The Ultimate History of Video Games: From Pong To Pokemon and Beyond—The Story Behind the Craze that Touched Our Lives and Changed the World*. Roseville, CA: Prima Publishers.

Key, J. (1987). Florsheim Shoe Stepping Into Future with Electronic Shoe Catalog. *Chicago Tribune*, 13 July. Online. Available at: http://www.chicagotribune.com/news/ct-xpm-1987-07-13-8702210287-story.html.

Leavitt, D. (2006). *The Man Who Knew Too Much*. New York: Atlas Books.

Licklider, J. C. R. (1960). Man-Computer Symbiosis. *IRE Transactions on Human Factors in Electronics*, HFE-1, 4–11.

McCartney, S. (1999). *Eniac: The Triumphs and Tragedies of the World's First Computer*. London: Walker Publishing Company.

McCullough, B. (2018). *How the Internet Happened: From Netscape to the iPhone*. New York: Liveright Publishing.

Metz, C. (2012). Before Google and Godaddy, there was Elizabeth Feinler. *Wired*, June. Online. Available at: https://www.wired.com/2012/06/elizabeth-jake-feinler.

Paine, J. (2018). 10 Real Use Cases for Augmented Reality. *Inc.com*, May 30. Online. Available at: https://www.inc.com/james-paine/10-real-use-cases-for-augmented-reality.html.

Watkins, T. (n.d.). History of the Transistor. Online. Available at: http://www.sjsu.edu/faculty/watkins/transist.htm.

3 The Interactive Digital Media Development Process and Team

INTRODUCTION

The development of any interactive project requires a team of experts with specialized skills who follow a prescribed development plan so that the project runs smoothly, and time and money are not wasted. With most projects, there are usually limited funds, so it is important to be as efficient as possible to prevent expending the entire budget before the project is done.

The interactive digital media development process tends to be collaborative and iterative. Team members frequently communicate with each other and the client or publisher to better understand what needs to be done. The process is also highly iterative, meaning that revisions result from development feedback. At regular intervals, the team meets to reflect on the completed work and revisions are made based on these reviews. Then the group returns to work. This cyclical process typically happens regularly throughout the development process.

The type of professionals on a team are dictated by the interactive product being produced. For example, if the project is an iPhone app, an Objective-C programmer will be needed on the team. If there is a virtual reality component to the project, there will be a 3D artist involved. Video game development teams include level and narrative designers. It just depends on what exactly is being built.

The size of the interactive digital media development team can vary tremendously depending on the scope of the project. If the project is small, members may play more than one role at a time. For example, if you are an independent website or app developer, you may be the project manager, information architect, designer, illustrator, and audio specialist simultaneously. Conversely, on larger projects, there may be multiple people working on the project with the same title.

TEAM MEMBERS

Team members working on interactive projects come from a variety of disciplines with a wide array of skills. You may be surprised to learn that you are well-suited to be a member of an interactive digital media production team even if you are not studying or have studied interactive digital media.

Project Manager/Producer

The project manager is responsible for delivering the product with promised features, on time, and on budget. She oversees all the business aspects of the development process and is oftentimes the point of contact with the client. A project manager must always be aware of how much time each team member is spending on the project. For example, there may be 20 hours of animation budgeted for a project. If the animators have already put in 18 hours of work and are not close to being done, the project manager would have to figure out how to get the animation portion done within budget or take some budget from other parts of the project and use it to cover the rest of the animation work. The best project manager is someone who is organized, focused, task oriented and not afraid to nag everybody else.

A producer role is similar to that of a project manager, but it is a term more typically used within the video game industry. Producers are ultimately responsible for a game's production.

User Experience Designers

The discipline of user experience design is focused on enriching user satisfaction with an interactive application. Typically, user experience design applies more to functional interactive applications as opposed to video games. Several roles fall under the umbrella of user experience design.

Information Architect

An information architect synthesizes the functionality and content required for a project and creates an overall structure for the piece. He researches how users classify information, develops labeling systems accordingly, and organizes content so that it can easily be found by a user. He then creates diagrams (called flowcharts) that explain the structure of the interactive application.

Visual Designer

The visual designer (or the graphic or interface designer) is responsible for the look and feel of the product. On a larger project, designers may develop a style guide which would articulate all design related choices such as what fonts are used for all text elements and what the images should look like and how are they placed within the application.

Interaction Designer

The interaction designer defines the methods in which the user interacts with the application for optimal satisfaction and usability. She answers questions such as: will the user need to click and drag or double click to access an option in a dropdown menu? The interaction designer defines the dialog that occurs between the user and the interactive application.

Video Game Designers

In the video game industry, the design roles are typically defined a bit differently.

■ The Development Process and Team

Narrative Designer
The narrative designer is responsible for the game's story and characters. He does a great deal of pre-production design work, writing game, level and quest design documents as well as cinematic scripts. Once the production work commences, the narrative designer helps with scripting, getting characters, dialogue and events into the game.

Level Designer
The level designer acts like the architect of the game, creating the various worlds and the physical layout of the game.

Game Artist
The game artist creates the structures, props, and characters in a game as well as the interface elements.

Systems/Gameplay Designer
The systems designer defines how the game will actually work, often using math and physics to make the game mechanics and interactions operate properly.

Sound Designer
Sound designers create the soundscape the player experiences in the game, adding sound effects, ambient sounds, and music to the game.
    On larger game projects, there are often designers that have more specialized roles, such as lighting designer and combat designer.

Programmer
The programmer writes the code to make the interactive application function, and there are several different ones that may be used, such as: HTML, CSS, JavaScript, JQuery, PHP, Objective-C, C#, etc. Each language has specific uses and are often used in combination.

Media Specialists
Media specialists are experts in creating, capturing and editing different types of media.

Illustrators
Illustrators create original artwork and illustrations such as original characters in a 2D game, or diagrams and charts, such as in an educational application.

Photographers/Photo Editors
Photographers would be part of the production team anytime original photos are required. In addition, photo editors would be needed to enhance and composite existing images.

Audio Engineers/Composers

Composers create original scores and soundscapes. And, if sound effects are required, an audio engineer would have to create and record the sound effects.

Animators/3D Artists

2D or 3D animators would be part of the production team if animated content is part of the application. If the application (especially a game) was based in a virtual, three-dimensional world, a 3D artist would be required to build that virtual world as well as the characters in it. 2D animation is often part of a casual game, and abstract 2D animated graphics are often used within a website or an app.

Filmmakers/Editors

Video content within interactive experiences has become increasingly common due to improved bandwidth on the Internet. When original video is part of the project, experts who can direct, shoot and edit the video are part of the production team.

Legal Specialists

Individuals familiar with the law are frequently needed on an interactive digital media production team.

Acquisition Specialist

The acquisition specialist secures the rights to use media integrated within the final product. Imagine you are building an interactive exhibit about the Civil War. Some of the images and text may come from copyrighted sources. An acquisition specialist would help secure the rights to use the material. He also would be involved in establishing agreements to protect the creative work of those involved with the project.

Contract Specialist

When a project is proposed and accepted, usually a contract is signed, and an individual with legal expertise is needed to create this document. Contracts are also needed when a portion of the project is subcontracted out.

Writers

Writing in different forms and styles is a crucial component throughout the development process of an interactive application.

Proposal Writer

Most projects start with a written proposal. The proposal writer plays an important role on the team because the proposal can determine whether or not the project is landed. The writing in the proposal should be persuasive, yet clear and concise to improve the likelihood that it is read.

■ The Development Process and Team

Game Design Document Writer
In the gaming industry, video games are often pitched internally or to a game publisher. Therefore, its objective is similar to that of a proposal in that it should be compelling, clear and concise, especially in the high concept and game treatment portions as they are used to "sell" the game. More detailed design documents are updated throughout the production process to keep a record of design decisions and to communicate with the entire development team.

Content Writer or Content Strategist
The content writer creates the text within the application. He must understand the audience and strike an appropriate tone and reading level. For example, the writing style within an app geared towards teenage girls would differ from the writing style in an app geared towards older men. When content is provided by a client, the content strategist's job is to shape the content so that it best supports the client's goals.

Technical Writer
A technical writer composes help screens, rules or other types of technical documentation. A good technical writer writes clearly and logically using consistent language and using terms that might be searched by a user needing help.

Content Expert
The topic of an interactive digital media project can range tremendously in subject matter. For example, you could be building an interactive 3D virtual heart or a game that teaches kids how to read. In order to build these specialized applications, you need input from the people that know most about these subjects. Content experts help the designers and developers understand the material which often informs the design and the function of the project.

Oftentimes clients serve as the content experts. If, for example, you were making a website for a group of dentists, the dentists would likely be the content experts. However, if a museum wanted to build an interactive piece about prehistoric animals and no-one on the staff knows much about them, a content expert may be consulted.

User/QA Tester
Large gaming companies typically have entire quality assurance (QA) departments dedicated to finding glitches within a game throughout the development process and before it is released. These testers try to identify any bugs by meticulously playing the game repetitively and systematically changing one variable, i.e. different character, different weapon, etc.

User testing is frequently performed on client-driven interactive projects like websites and apps where representative users are recruited to test the application as opposed to members of the development team.

Social Media Specialist

Social media channels often play a starring role in the marketing, promotion and customer services aspect of an interactive application. Can you imagine a game studio releasing a new title without it being all over Facebook, Twitter and Instagram? Any company or organization's website typically has corresponding social media channels. A savvy social media strategist offers a huge boon to an interactive project development team.

PITCHING THE PROJECT

Before you can get started producing an interactive application, you normally have to convince someone to hire your team or allow you to move forward with your idea. If the project is client-driven, the pitch is in the form of a proposal. However, if the project is being developed internally (e.g. a game company planning the release of a new title), the pitch would be in the form of a game design document. In either case, the following questions should be addressed in the project pitch.

Objective

What is the purpose of this product?
The objective statement should address the goals of the project. That is, what should the application accomplish? It is the most important question to ask a client, because the goal can completely change the whole focus of the project. For example, if the client's goal is to project a cool image online vs. to obtain online sales, the resulting website would be very different. When you identify the goal and reiterate it back to the client, you demonstrate an understanding of what the client is trying to accomplish.

Because a video game is created for entertainment and not to solve a problem as other interactive experiences often do, an objective statement would not necessarily be part of a game proposal. Instead, the document should begin with a clear description of the game.

Target Audience

Who is this product for?
The target audience is the population for whom the application is intended. Understanding the target audience is important because different users have different preferences and abilities.

Do not make assumptions about your target audience. One game company assumed that women over 40 preferred romance stories, but after polling their target audience, they learned that they actually preferred solving mysteries and puzzles. Knowing the preferences of their target audience greatly impacted the games they chose to develop.

■ The Development Process and Team

Sometimes the target audience will be segmented. Consider a university website. The target audience includes very distinct and different groups: prospective students, current students, employers, potential employers, faculty, prospective faculty, staff, and prospective staff. The website needs to address the interests of all of these different types of audience members.

Context

Where and how will this product be used?
Context answers the questions where, when and in what conditions the interactive application will be used and can dramatically affect design and development decisions. For example, if you are building an app for a worker on a factory floor where it is quite noisy, audio would be ineffective. Or maybe the user is wearing bulky protective apparel, how will he interact with the device? Think about the difference between a game developed for an iPhone vs. one intended to be played on an Xbox. A different type of game will be suited for each context.

Content

What text, images, audio, video, animation will be included and what form are they in?
Content is the meat of any interactive application. It is important to understand what types of content will be incorporated in the project and what form it is in. Will the project require your team to digitize video and scan thousands of images? Or will you need original art and music? Articulating what the content will be, how much already exists and what form it is in will help better define the scope of the project.

Interactivity

What type of functionality is involved?
Interactivity describes how the system must behave in order to accomplish its goal. For example, will the application need to anticipate what the user needs prior to her typing in a search field? Will the application need to recall the user's last interactions and behave differently based on previous behaviors? Answering these question in the project definition phase will help in generating a list of features that will need to be included.

Projected Outcomes

What is the expectation after making this product?
The projected outcomes build on the initial stated objective; if you meet this goal, what would you expect to happen? For example, let's say you are developing an interactive decision-making application for a kiosk in a sporting goods store that will help a woman pick out running shoes. The stated objective might be "to help

women choose the perfect running shoe." But the projected outcome might be that sales of women's running shoes will increase once the kiosk is in place.

Competitive Analysis

What competing products are on the market and what are their strengths and weaknesses?
Demonstrating a need in the marketplace for the product might encourage decision makers to move forward. In game pitches, a "unique selling points" section is commonly included that discusses competing games on the market and why the proposed one would be better.

Writing Style and Presentation
Since proposals are a determining factor as to whether a project is executed or not, it is important to write persuasively. A proposal is an opportunity to let a potential client or funder know that your team is best suited to develop this project and that it's worth doing. It's also in your best interest to write succinctly and clearly so that the reader gets to the point quickly and does not stop reading before you've made your case. You also should write with precision because the proposal is the basis of a cost estimate, and if you leave anything open to interpretation, your client or publisher may assume you are providing more than you anticipate delivering which could mean a lot of extra time on your part.

    The style, tone and look of a proposal matter. Avoid writing a personal narrative. The proposal should be written in the third person, with the project as the subject. The client wants to know how you will solve their problem, not about your hopes and dreams. The tone in your proposal should be positive. If your writing sounds negative and overly critical, you will not endear yourself to a client. Always keep in mind: presentation matters. The look and feel of your proposal is a preview of the work that you're going to deliver. Take the time to make your proposal look professional to make a good impression.

Budget and Timeline
While clients generally like to see that the person submitting the proposal understands their goals, they are most often interested in how much the project will

Table 3.1

Task	Hours	Rate	Total
Planning	10	$125	$1250
Product Photography & Editing of 100 products	50	$100	$5000
Interface Design	30	$125	$3750
Front End Programming (HTML, CSS)	40	$125	$5000
Back End Programming (PHP)	20	$150	$3000
		TOTAL	**$18,000**

■ The Development Process and Team

Project Development Schedule

Project Steps:	Qtr 1			Qtr 2			Qtr 3			Qtr 4		
	Jan	Feb	Mar	Apr	May	Jun	Jul	Aug	Sep	Oct	Nov	Dec
Explore Market Need												
Develop Concept for Product												
Begin Development Cycle												
Develop GUI												
User Interface Text Evaluation												
Alpha Version Release												
Quality Assurance Testing Phase 1												
Fix Outstanding Problems from Alpha												
Beta Version Release												
Quality Assurance Testing Phase 2												
Fix Outstanding Problems from Beta												
Design Box and CD Labels												
Begin Advance Advertising Campaign												
FCS Preparation												
Final Quality Assurance Testing												
FCS Release												
Production and Packaging												

Development   Marketing   Milestones
QA Testing   Box Art

cost and how long it will take. Because the development of digital products usually does not have any cost of materials (unless there are licensing or acquisition fees), the budget is most often structured in terms of task and hourly rate. A simple budget for a new e-commerce site might look like this.

Along with the budget, the proposal should include a projected timeline. Depending on the complexity of the project, the timeline can be presented in different formats. For simple projects, a simple bulleted list of expected completion dates for each phase in the project might suffice. For larger projects, such as in a proposal for a major video game, a Gantt chart might be used to communicate each project phase and the associated amount of time it is expected to take.

3.1
A Gantt chart helps a development team plan as well as communicate the project timeline with a client

THE DEVELOPMENT PROCESS

The client or publisher has accepted the proposal, a team is assembled, and it's time to start the project. How does a project commence, and what is the process? The terminology that each company uses may differ, but can generally be described in three phases: the definition, design and production phases. The objective of the definition phase is to articulate exactly what the team will be making. The design phase involves figuring out how all the parts will fit together and defining the look and feel. And, in the production phase, the team is actually building the piece as outlined in the previous phases.

Although we have just defined three distinct phases of development in a linear fashion, the reality is that the development process tends to be very iterative. As the project progresses, work is evaluated at regular intervals, and the result of this assessment may require recalibration and changes which should then be implemented before moving forward.

Each phase in the development process usually has some type of progress marker and associated deliverables that are identified at each stage. Deliverables are portions of the project that are developed as the project takes shape such as sets of wireframes or a preliminary prototype. Oftentimes payment schedules are tied to the deliverables.

Let's take a closer look at each of these development phases.

Phase 1—Definition

The purpose of the project definition phase is for all involved parties to have a clear understanding of what they are making, why they are making it and who they are making it for. Some of the project definition occurs through the proposal writing process, however, once the project is greenlighted, a greater level of research is conducted so that the development team is best suited to deliver a product that meets their goals.

Market Research

Market research involves learning more about the client, their identity, preferences and challenges. What data can you review to gain a better understanding of your client and their needs? For example, if you are building a website, it would be enlightening to see their web analytics to determine where traffic is coming from and how people behave on their site. Looking at competitive products and assessing what works and what doesn't can help guide the design process.

User Research

User research asks you to get in the head of the users. What are the preferences and habits of the people who will be using the application? What will they want to do, and how will they go about doing it? Tools such as focus groups and surveys help development teams learn more about the intended users. Sometimes user personas are created to help the design team think deeply about the users' needs.

Visual Research

Visual research is about collecting visual elements to hone in on a design direction. Web-based tools like Pinterest are perfect for storing bits of visual inspiration in one place and can be shared within the design team. Some designers create moodboards, a collage of images, text and visuals in a composition to begin to form a visual direction.

Once the research is done, the team should have a better sense of the interactive product's capabilities and contents which are then articulated in the form of a functional specification which provides a basis from which the design work can commence.

■ The Development Process and Team

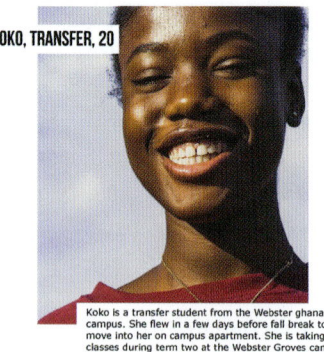

3.2
User personas help designers get into the heads of their users.
Source: © Adanma Ojukwu

Phase 2—Project Design

The objective of the design phase is to create visuals that communicate how the interactive application should look, feel and work. Like the architect who makes blueprints for a building that are handed off to a builder, the interactive designer builds design documents that serve as a set of instructions for the programmers. Designers use several different types of documents to communicate their ideas to the rest of the team, including flowcharts, wireframes, user scenarios, interface designs and prototypes.

Flowchart

A flowchart is a visual representation of the interactive application's structure. It is comprised of boxes (and other shapes) representing different pages or sections or levels of a game with lines between the boxes indicating links or pathways. Flowcharts can be quite simple and small for a project like an app that does only a few things. Or they can be quite large and complex for a large-scale website with thousands of pages.

A flowchart can be made in specialized software like Microsoft Visio. However, many designers prefer to use the graphic applications they are most familiar with (like Adobe Illustrator or Adobe InDesign) to build their flowcharts.

For content-rich applications, a process of organizing, categorizing and labeling the content must occur before a flowchart can be created. This is the job of an information architect who uses techniques to consider how users categorize and label content to build a structure for the application.

Wireframes

A wireframe is a blueprint indicating where all the interactive and content elements will reside on the screen. Wireframes should only be black, white and shades of grey, as omitting color forces the client and the team to focus on the

3.3
A flowchart describes the structure of an interactive application. Source: © Rosalie Kollefrat

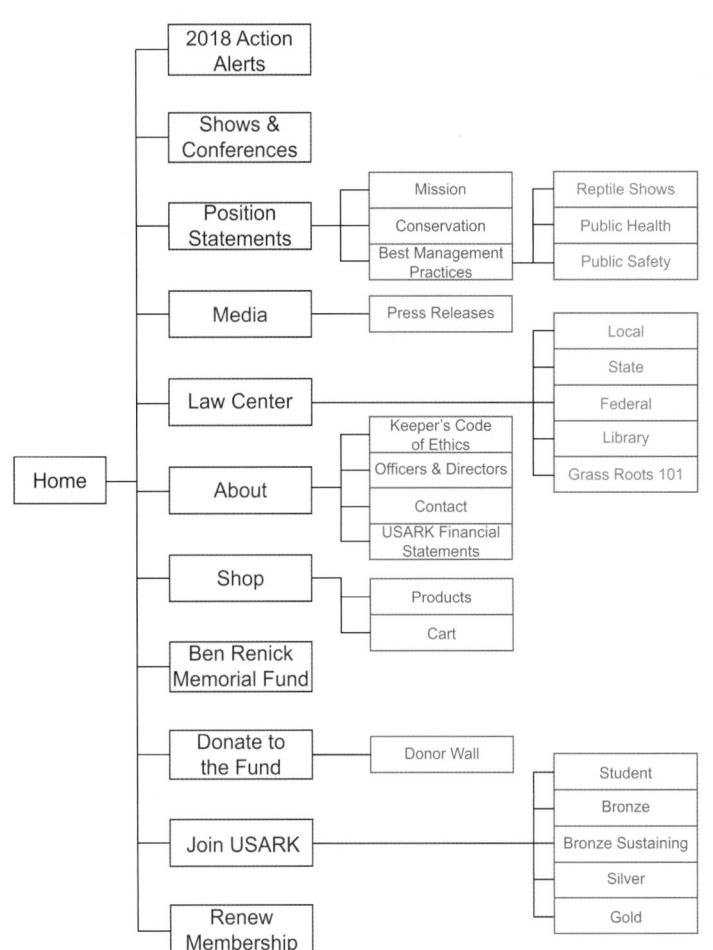

use of the space without being distracted by color, font and imagery. Wireframes are *not* made for every screen in the interactive application—just representative ones. If two screens have the same basic layout (but different content), only one wireframe is needed. The number of wireframes a designer makes depends on the complexity of the application.

The wireframe needs to match the proportion of the screen on which the final application will run. For example, you would not make a wireframe for a smartphone app that is in the proportion of a square because a smartphone screen is rectangular.

User Scenarios

A user scenario is intended to show how a user would travel through an interactive application. For each user scenario, you should describe who the

■ The Development Process and Team

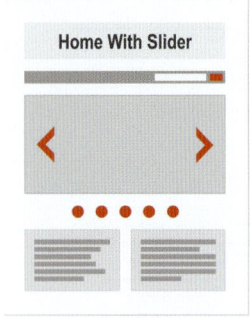 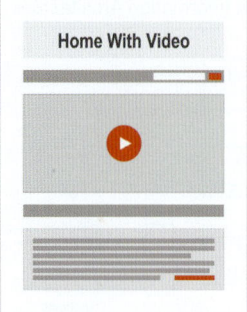 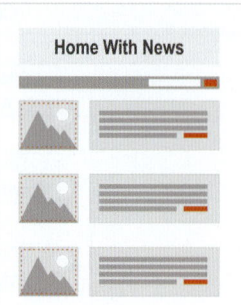
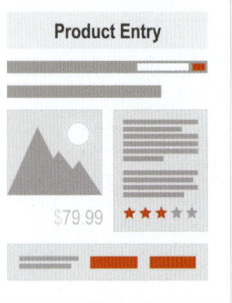 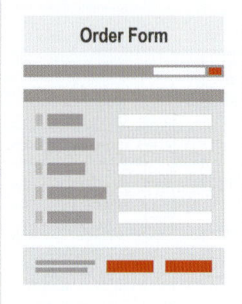 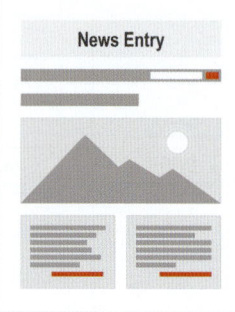
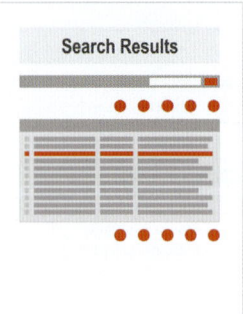 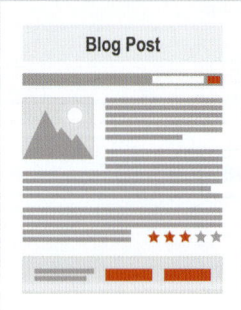 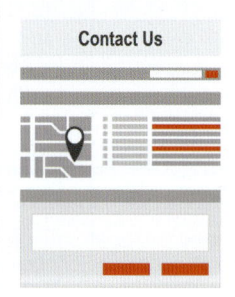

3.4
Wireframes describe the layout of elements on a screen. A wireframe should be made for each unique page layout. Source: © Viktor Gmyria; 123RF.com

user is and what she is trying to accomplish. Then, you would show how she would travel through the application to accomplish the task by visually connecting wireframes indicating what the user did on one screen to arrive at the next one.

Let's say you were developing an app that allows a user to locate Funko vinyl figures. Your user scenario might be:

Ollie, the family dog, has damaged a limited edition Pokemon Funko pop doll while Tammy is away at college. Tammy's mom wants to replace it before she's home for the holidays, but she only knows the color of the doll and nothing else. She's willing to pay any price for it.

The Development Process and Team ■

3.5
This user scenario shows one route a user may take through an interative application.
Source: © Adanma Ojukwu

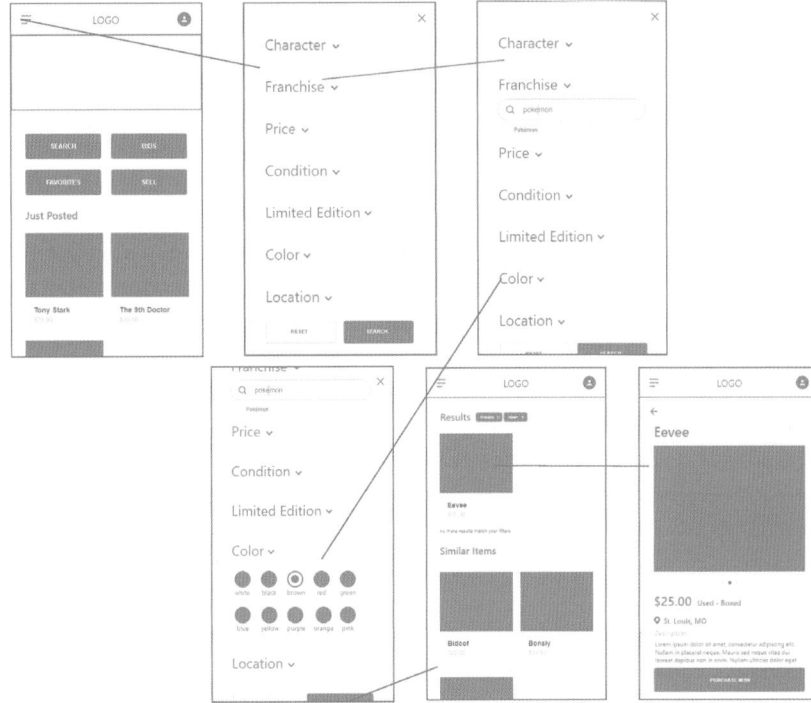

The following scenario shows how Tammy's mom would travel through the app to execute this task.

The process of creating user scenarios based on different user types with different needs helps designers identify repetitive behaviors and adjust the design to accommodate a wide array of user needs.

Interface Designs
Interface designs are essentially mockups of key screens of the interactive application. With the wireframes serving as a guide for screen layout, the interface design process involves choosing colors, type and designing icons to give the application a suitable look and feel while keeping in mind goal, audience, content and context.

Prototype
At the end of the interface design process, the team should have built a prototype—an incomplete working model of the product which provides an opportunity for the team to see how the product will work and possibly identify any problems. A prototype might also be shown to a client or publisher to elicit their opinion and make sure the development team is going down the right path.

63

■ The Development Process and Team

A simple prototype for an app might be a couple of screens mocked up in Photoshop that are linked together as an interactive PDF. Oftentimes, a prototype will be built using the language or within the platform where the product will ultimately be created. For example, a working prototype for a website project might be a couple of pages in HTML with some working links. A prototype of a game might be a small, working portion of the actual game built within the game engine.

Like an architect, the designer does not walk away from the project after the specs and prototypes are done; he often consults with the programmers throughout the development process and designs any additional graphics or mockups as needed.

Phase 3—Project Production Phase

The production phase commences when the design is approved and a prototype is made. At this point, primarily coding or authoring is needed. The product end use and deployment environment and the team's area of expertise will dictate what type of programming language and environment is used to develop the project.

Throughout the production phase, user testing should occur, with the goal of identifying problems with the application before rolling it out. User testing often leads to a lot of unexpected results.

Software and gaming companies always carry out user testing on their products as their budgets tend to be much larger than those for mobile apps or websites. Adobe, for example, releases beta versions of products to representative users to get feedback and identify bugs. Gaming companies will do quality assurance testing throughout the development process.

When larger interactive projects like games or apps are nearing completion, they are often rolled out in stages, and termed the "alpha version," the "beta version," and the "gold master." The alpha version includes most media elements but also many bugs. Those bugs are identified and fixed, then the beta version is released, which may still have a few bugs, but includes all media. And finally, the gold master is released which is the complete, (theoretically) bug-free application. The reason why it is rolled out in phases is because, when people start using the application, a lot of these bugs are identified along the way. Bugs become quickly identified when you have 1,000 users using an application as opposed to 10 testers. Therefore, while it may be annoying to early adopters, there is a lot of value for development teams to release an imperfect application.

After the product released, there is still work to be done. Depending on the product, there may be release notes, manuals, and packaging that need to be developed before it is truly complete. Also, it's important to archive materials. Archived files can save you a lot of time and pain down the road as clients may come back years later to request further work.

PRACTITIONER INTERVIEW

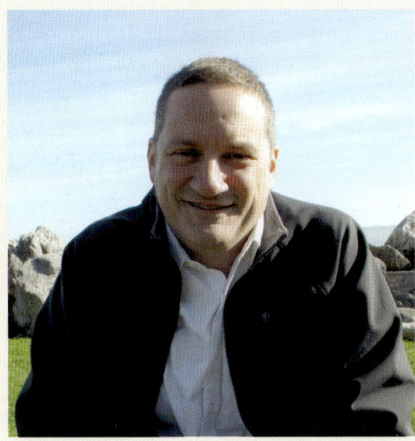

Tim Frick

Mightybytes, Inc. Chicago, IL USA
Tim Frick is the founder and CEO of Mightybytes, a Chicago-based digital agency and certified B Corporation that works primarily with mission-driven organizations such as non-profits and educational institutions. Tim started Mightybytes in 1998, after studying filmmaking in college and uses his background in filmmaking to help organizations tell their stories. Tim is also a seasoned conference presenter as well as book author on topics related to interactive digital media.

How did you make the leap from film to interactive media?

I was on this track to be a filmmaker when the Internet happened. I was excited by the promise of what it could do and how it could change the way we communicate. As a storyteller at heart, I was really interested in using this new medium as a way to push new ideas forward. So, it was a natural migration. But it was also a really exciting time to be doing this kind of stuff because there was a lot of opportunity everywhere.

What type of interactive projects does Mightybytes work on?

The majority of our projects are website redesigns for mission-driven organizations. We do a lot of work with publishers and universities. Those organizations, alone, have very different needs; a publisher may be trying to sell products while a university might be trying to increase enrollment. Our goal is always to get to the heart of what the business's goal is and ensure user needs and business goals are aligned.

What kind of questions do you like to have answered before you get started?

You know, the basics: timeline, budget, goals. It's important to have that first conversation about what they want to accomplish, why they want to accomplish it and in what timeline and with what budget. That just helps us very quickly find out if we are aligned. We do a little research ahead of time on the organization to see if it's a good fit. For example, as a Certified B Corp, we are very green, but have had fracking companies [ask us to do work for them,] and we politely decline. So, it's important to have that qualifying conversation so we're not wasting our time charging our fees and writing proposals for companies that aren't a good fit.

What makes a great proposal?

I think that it's important to make sure you're really clear about what is being asked of you. You shouldn't just memorize and reiterate what someone says they're looking for, but instead, interpret that in a way that you think is going to be most useful for the client, and showing them step by step how you will do it. I think a lot of companies get caught up in talking about their process and the proposal tends to be all about them instead of how they're going to address the challenges of the client. A good proposal is as specific as possible but also as flexible as possible. We want proposals to be succinct, clear, easy to understand and engaging. But we want clients to understand that we are flexible enough to roll with changes that inevitably come along.

How do you create a budget for a project?

Agencies have all kinds of different ways that they charge for their time. Mightybytes typically uses the fixed bid-managed scope approach on website projects, though we have a lot of retainer clients as well. We don't break our budgets down in that much detail, but instead find a mutually agreed upon budget range that we can work within. We provide regular budget reports, typically bi-weekly, and have ongoing conversations about how best to maximize remaining funds as a project progresses.

We are lucky, now that we are going into our 22nd year, as we have a lot of past project data that we can go back and [use as a reference]. Even if an old project is not an apples-to-apples comparison, we can at least make some assumptions that help us and our potential client get in the same ballpark in terms of cost.

On the client side, they have two things going on: a project with a bunch of goals and a company budget. We help them get clarity around how to manage that and get the most out of their project budget. We are also big fans of prioritization, and start working on the highest value deliverables first so that we provide the most value to the organization and help them get much closer to solving their problems as quickly as possible. If we nail that, then we can have some conversations about reprioritizing what's left based on what we've learned so far.

How many people and what types of people are usually on your project teams?

At the very least we would have a designer, a developer and a project manager. It depends on the nature of the project. If it isn't super content heavy, that might be enough for a team. But many of our clients have websites that are tens of thousands of pages, so one of the big challenges with those websites is doing the information architecture with lots of taxonomy and cross-references. If it's large project then we would have multiple designers and developers involved. But the flow of information typically goes through one project manager who works with one person on their end as it streamlines the communication.

Once the project gets going, what kind of design documents do you use in your process?

It depends on the project. Let's just compare two example projects: a large content strategy project website with lots of content to a beach cleanup app on your phone that may not be super content heavy but is dependent on users doing tasks. For a project like that [the beach cleanup app], we are doing user research and testing out our assumptions as much as possible by making user flows and journey maps, then wireframes. Much of that is done in a workshop setting with our client. We find that it helps us build consensus faster.

On a heavy content project, we do a lot of card sorting exercises where we work out taxonomy issues to make sure users can find what they are looking for. We [conduct tests where we ask] 20 people to find a piece of content. Then we track their path. Optimal Workshop's Treejack is a great tool to figure out user paths through websites with a large amount of content.

What happens after the design phase is complete?

So, I wouldn't say design phase necessarily. For us, design and development are as iterative as they can be. We tend to work in cyclical, collaborative sprints to build consensus more quickly. The sprint may be an internal sprint or a design sprint with a client where they co-create with us. We find that the process of getting approvals and moving forward goes more quickly when we work this way. We don't do the design, lob it over a wall, then do the development.

What is your project roll out process?

Sometimes it makes sense to just launch a big fat grand site, but for some projects, it makes sense to either make some tweaks to what is there, or do a soft launch so that you can actually pull user data. The nice thing about a launched product is that you can collect real data about how users are interacting with it and make some educated decisions about how to improve that moving forward. Depending on the client's needs and what they are looking for, we will advise them on one of those two approaches.

Either way, I still recommend to our clients that once they launch something, they consider long-term optimization processes. Some of that might be search engine optimization where we are just trying to drive more qualified traffic to the site. Or [we might discover ways to improve efficiencies, for example,] we might learn that there are three extra steps in a form we don't need and if we remove those steps, we're not going to have as much drop off in the funnel. It's doing that kind of ongoing optimization and testing that improves conversions and helps you meet your goals.

Does Mightybytes provide hosting for your clients or do you put them somewhere else?

We have taken both approaches. We do encourage our clients to use managed hosting, preferably powered by renewable energy. We offer a package, but some clients have their preferred vendors.

Do you primarily develop websites using WordPress as the content management system?

Yes. We were a WordPress and Drupal shop for years. In fact, we sponsored Drupal camp here in Chicago and we were big proponents of that. But it got to a point, as a small agency, [it was hard to offer both], because the development skill sets were so different. So, in 2011, we dropped Drupal and focused primarily on WordPress.

Do you do any usability testing after a product has launched?

Yes. We do three kinds of user testing: quantitative, qualitative and behavioral. On the qualitative side, it's doing interviews and getting personal feedback. On the quantitative side, we'll use Google Analytics. For behavioral, it's studying the behavior of users interacting with the application. Depending on what it is you're trying to accomplish, we use a specific kind of tool to track what a large number of users are doing on a specific page. It's really about tracking conversions and figuring out where in the process you can make changes and tweaks to optimize the process and reach better goals.

Is there any specific field of study or experience that you look for when hiring people?

I definitely look for great problem-solving skills. One of my favorite interview questions is "what was the hairiest situation you've been in and what was the solution you used to get out of that situation?" I can't imagine you could be a good designer [or developer] in 2019 without good problem-solving skills. You can train certain skills, but it's hard to train someone on creativity and innovation and creative problem solving. So, I definitely look for that.

I'm a writer myself, so I definitely appreciate someone who can write, because that means they can communicate well. [And if they communicate well,] I know that the projects that they work on are going to go much smoother.

What do you like about working in this industry?

I like the variety. I always have new challenges and new problems to solve. Because we work with non-profits who tend to be 5 years behind the business sector in just about everything, it's exciting to help those organizations get on-boarded regarding what good design is. Their eyes light up when they see the result of paying attention to good design practices, putting a good product out there that actually does what it's supposed to do, and seeing how it directly impacts them.

DISCUSSION QUESTIONS

1) What role on the interactive media development team is most appealing to you? Why?
2) What role on the interactive media development team is the least appealing? Why?
3) Have you worked on any projects in the past that were iterative? How so?
4) What is the most important part of a proposal? Why?
5) Why does a company like Mightybytes follow a prescribed interactive digital media development process?

4 Fundamental Components of Interactive Digital Media

INTRODUCTION

When we create any form of interactive digital media, all of our content: audio, video, text, graphics, etc., must be in a digital form. If the media is not digital, then we cannot store it on a computer, our main tool for authoring interactive applications. But what does it mean to be digital? How do we convert media into a digital form? And what guidelines should we follow when doing so?

ANALOG VS. DIGITAL MEDIA

Analog and digital media are two different ways of encoding information. Like words and numbers, they are two disparate methods of representation. Until the advent of the computer age, all media was analog: 8 track tapes, VHS, records, film, photographs, etc., where media is represented in a continuous form. Digital media is the opposite of analog media because it is represented in discreet sampled values.

BITS AND BYTES

A computer stores particles of information in the form of "bits". A bit is the tiniest piece of digital data and can either be a one ("on") or a zero ("off"). Therefore, all digital files are ultimately made up of a lot of zeros and ones. The larger the file is, the more zeros and ones contained inside of it.

Since all digital files are comprised of zeros and ones, you may wonder how complex media, such as video files, can be represented with only two digits. The answer is that by stringing together several zeros and ones, you can describe more complex information. If you have only one bit to describe some form of media, you cannot be very descriptive because there are only two possibilities: 0 or 1. However, if you put two bits together, you can now express four possibilities: 00, 01, 10, and 11. The number of possibilities you can express doubles with each additional bit you string together.

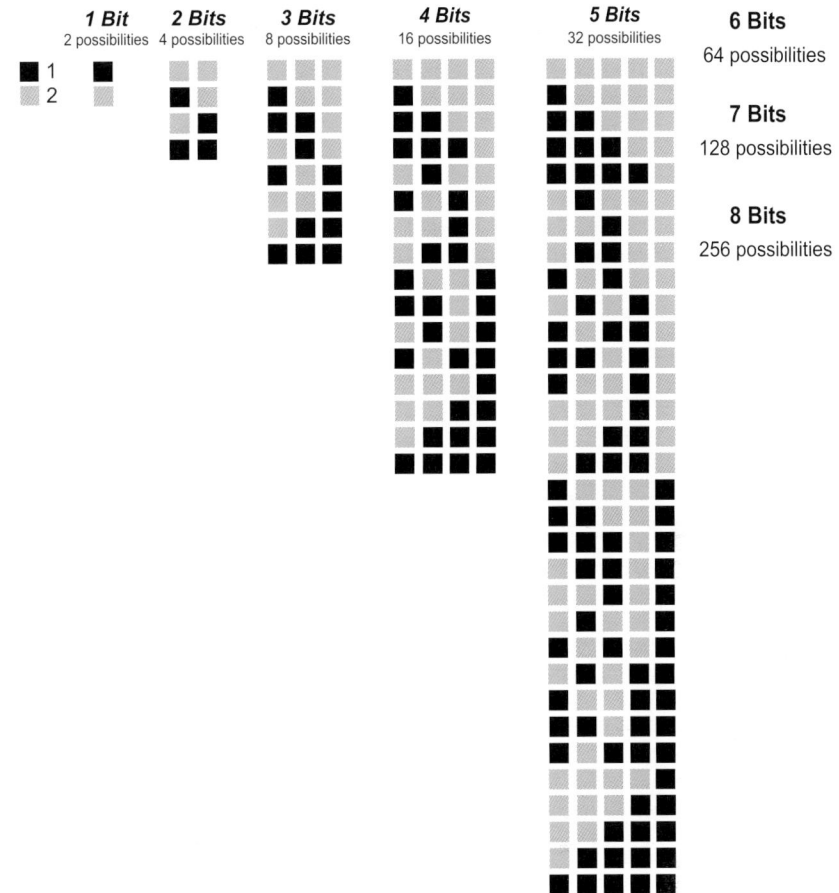

4.1 The number of items that can be represented doubles with each additional bit, a phenomenon known as "the power of two." For example, with eight bits we can represent 256 possible variations, but with 16 bits, we can represent up to 65,536 possible variations

In computer architecture, eight bits are a common quantity to represent different types of information. For example, the ASCII text system is an 8-bit system, where 8-bit codes are used to represent all 256 characters in the English language. So, for example, the letter A is represented by 0 1 0 0 0 0 0 1, whereas the number 5 is represented by 0 0 1 1 0 1 0 1.

In the early 1990s, 8-bit monitors were quite common which meant that the monitor could display up to 256 possible colors (and that's it!). Most modern monitors are now 24-bit color, where 8 bits are used to express each of the levels of the red, green, and blue light (24 bits total) for every pixel. Using the logic of the power of two, we can determine that a 24-bit monitor can generate over 16 million different colors (2^{24} = 16 million).

Because stringing together eight bits to represent information is quite common in the digital world, it has a special name: a byte. You're probably familiar with the term "byte" because we represent the size of our files in bytes. Most files are at least a kilobyte (1000 bytes) or a megabyte (1,000,000 bytes) or even a gigabyte (1,000,000,000 bytes). That's a lot of 0s and 1s inside the files we use!

■ **Fundamental Components of Interactive Digital Media**

Consider how many bits are in a 40 kilobyte file (e.g. a small Microsoft Word file).

- 40 kilobytes = 40,000 bytes
- 8 bits = 1 byte
- Number of bits = 40,000 × 8 = 320,000 bits

Therefore, the small Microsoft Word file is made up of 320,000 zeros and ones. Now imagine how many zeros and ones are in a video file!

FILE FORMATS

If every file is just made of 1s and 0s, how does your computer know what to do with it? This is job of the file format. The file format is dictated by the series of letters after the period in the file name. These characters are called the file extension, and are important because they tell the operating system what to do with the file when the user double-clicks on it. For example, the .DOCX extension added to a file name tells the operating system that the data inside the file should be interpreted by the Microsoft Word application. Sometimes, however, multiple applications can handle the same type of file. Perhaps you have experienced double-clicking on a file and an application that you didn't want to use launches? Either the operating system will pick an application by default or it will ask you what application you would like to use to open the file.

As operating systems have evolved over the last few decades, cross-platform file compatibility has become much better. It used to be that certain file formats were PC specific and couldn't be opened on a Mac, and vice versa. The web paved the way for better cross-platform compatibility as it is not platform specific and allows people to share files so easily.

While data files (ones that you can create and modify: images, sounds, text, animations, videos, etc.) are commonly cross-platform compatible, application files usually are not. Application files are files that contain executable instructions such as Firefox or Microsoft Word. When you download a new application onto your computer, you must be sure that you are downloading the appropriate version for your operating system, that is, if the application will reside on your hard drive. Now that the Internet is so pervasive and connection speeds have improved, many applications are web-based, running entirely through the web browser.

Most of the programs used for interactive digital media development have native file formats that contain the full, uncompressed version of the file from which you can make further edits. It's always a good idea to maintain the native files so that you can make future edits even if the derivative file is the one used within the final piece. For example, the Photoshop native file format is a PSD file (a file that has the extension .PSD). PSD files are intended to only be opened in Photoshop. They maintain all the layer information as well as any filters and adjustments you made to the image. If you have access to the PSD file, you can go back into the image and manipulate the layers or turn on or off the effects that you added and export a new version for use in your project. Because the PSD file retains all of this extra information, the file size tends to be larger than the image file you export from Photoshop.

When you work in some media applications, the native file format acts more like a container and pointer to different types of media. For example, Adobe InDesign, a page layout program that allows you to build multiple page and interactive documents, acts in this manner. The native (.INDD) file is quite small because it just contains instructions regarding how all of the media referenced within the document should be displayed. In InDesign, the native file would not be the one you would share for general consumption. Instead, you would export it into a more universally understood file format, typically PDF, which can be opened on most computers and within a web browser. Video editing programs like Final Cut and Adobe Premiere, video compositing applications like Adobe After Effects, and audio editing applications like Adobe Audition work much the same way. Because these applications act more like containers pointing to other files, you should organize the files referenced in the main project file into one folder and save them all together.

The following table outlines common applications an interactive digital media producer would likely use and their associated native file types.

While it's important to preserve both the original and the derivative files that are part of an interactive digital media project, it's also imperative to have a maintenance system for organizing and backing up all files associated with a project. One issue that can make accessing old files more complicated is deprecated

Table 4.1

Application	Description	Native File Format	Common Derivative Files
Adobe Photoshop	image editing	.PSD	.JPG, .PNG, .GIF
Adobe Illustrator	vector-based drawing	.AI	.PDF, .EPS
Adobe InDesign	page layout	.INDD	.PDF
Adobe Premiere	video editing	.PPJ or .PRPROJ	.MOV, .MP4, .AVI
Final Cut Pro	video editing	.FCPX	.MOV, .MP4, .AVI
Adobe Audition	audio editing	.AAC	.MP3, .AIFF, .WAV
Avid Pro Tools	audio editing	.PTX	.MP3, .AIFF, .WAV
Adobe AfterEffects	video compositing	.AEP	.MOV, .MP4, .AVI
Maya	3D graphics and animation	.MB	.OBJ, .STL, .MOV, .MP4
Adobe Dreamweaver	coding	.HTML, .JS, .PHP .CSS	n/a
Unity Technologies – Unity Game Engine	Game authoring	.UNITY	.EXE (PC game) App bundle (MAC) Xcode (iOS)

■ Fundamental Components of Interactive Digital Media

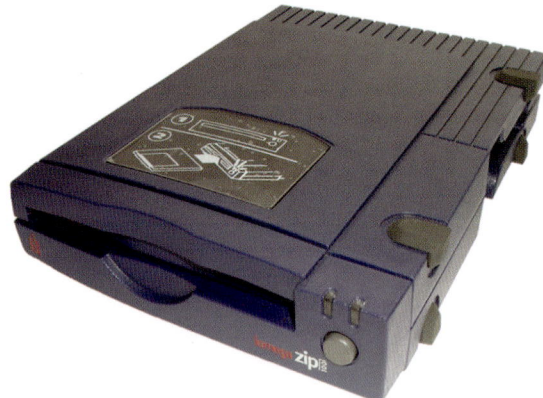

4.2
An external zip drive, circa 2000. Source: Wikimedia Commons. Online. Available HTTP: <https://commons.wikimedia.org/wiki/Category:Zip_drive#/media/File:Iomega-100-Zip-Drive.jpg>

storage media. For example, in the late 1990s and early 2000s, a popular storage media were zip disks. A zip drive, which was either built into the computer or added as a peripheral, read or wrote to a zip disk. Zip disks typically stored 100 or 250 Megabytes of data. If you had archived old files on a zip disk, it would be difficult to access those files, because you would have to find a zip drive and an appropriate driver so that the computer could use it. Therefore, when digital storage technology starts to become obsolete, it is a good idea to move files over to a more contemporary medium.

Storing files "in the cloud" has become increasingly common, offering the benefit of data loss prevention in the event of hardware failure. Dropbox is a common cloud-based file storage system. However, some file types don't lend themselves to being stored in the cloud, such as large video files. In this case, it's best to store them on a portable hard drive, and two different ones, if possible. Keeping large files off of your hard drive improves your computer's performance, and storing a backup on a secondary hard drive, helps prevent file loss if one were to fail.

ANALOG TO DIGITAL

Oftentimes, interactive digital media projects must integrate media that currently exists only in an analog form. In this case, the production team must convert the analog files into a digital format. For example, the audio might only exist on cassette tape, or, perhaps the video content is only available on film or, maybe, the visuals are original drawings on paper. In each of these cases, when converting the analog information into a digital format, you must make some choices that involve a bit of a compromise.

The process of converting analog to digital information is sometimes referred to as sampling because the digital representation of the original source file is just a series of samples of it. One example of sampling is when you use a simple photo scanner. When you do the scanning, you must decide how intensely you want to sample the information which is the "resolution:" the number of

Fundamental Components of Interactive Digital Media

samples that are taken of the analog source material in a given amount of space. If you need a lot of detail, you would sample at a very high resolution.

To better understand how resolution affects the quality of a scanned image, consider the following example. If we were to take 100 samples of a 1 by 1 inch square image, we can achieve a more realistic description of the analog image than if we take only 16 samples in that same 1 by 1 inch square. The more samples we take in a given area, the higher the resolution and the better the representation we are going to get of the analog source material.

Although we are talking about the area of an image, resolution is measured in dots (or pixels) per linear inch (dpi). A one-inch-square image comprised of 100 pixels is 10 dpi and a one-inch-square image comprised of 16 pixels is 4 dpi.

In the example below, you can see how a higher image resolution produces a much higher quality.

Images designed to be seen on a computer screen or mobile device do not need to be super high resolution. Typically monitor resolution is only 72 or 96 dpi, therefore better detail and clarity than that will not be evident when viewing the image on a screen. Images designed for print, on the other hand, are typically 300 dpi. Since screen-based images are often transferred via the Internet, it is fortunate that they are lower resolution because their file sizes are small and they download quickly.

Converting analog sound to digital involves taking samples of the original analog source. However, in this case, a high sampling rate means taking more samples in a given amount of time.

The image below demonstrates how a higher sampling rate yields a digital file that has a more accurate representation of the analog sound. The first illustration is a representation of the actual sound wave. The next illustration shows

4.3
More pixels in a given area offers greater potential for shape definition

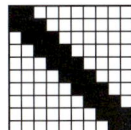

4.4
The picture on the right has a resolution of 300 dpi and it is significantly more crisp and clear that the 50 dpi lower resolution image on the left.
Source: Edited image based on original © Mariusz Blach; 123RF. com. Online. Available HTTP: <https:// www.123rf.com/ stock-photo/hot_air_ balloons.html?&sti=ms rqvkhk8dsfyam6p0|&m ediapopup=22831430>

1 inch x 1 inch
4 dpi

1 inch x 1 inch
10 dpi

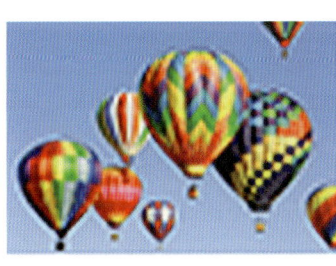

50 dpi

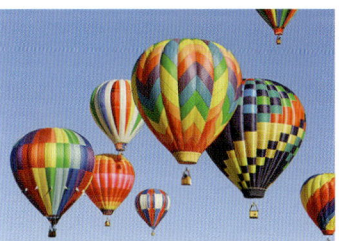

300 dpi

■ **Fundamental Components of Interactive Digital Media**

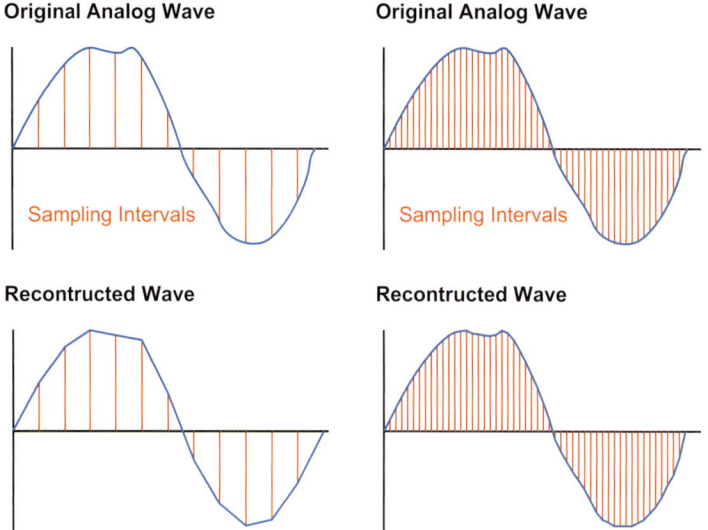

4.5
More samples in a given amount of time yields a better approximation of the original source

a low sampling rate (with the blue lines indicating the sampling points) and the resulting reconstructed sound wave. The second set of illustrations depict a high sampling rate and the resulting sound wave. You can see that in the first set of illustrations, the reconstructed wave doesn't look much like the original analog wave. But, if more samples are taken in a given amount of time (as in the second illustration) the digital file is a much more accurate representation of the original sound. The trade-off, however, is that a lot more data is collected when sampling at a high sample rate.

Sampling audio at the highest possible frequency is not always necessary or appropriate because the more information we capture, the larger the file size will be, and it's possible to capture information that is not even audible to the human ear. It doesn't make sense to capture sounds we can't hear (unless you are building an app for dolphins!). Therefore, it's important to keep end-use in mind. A good rule of thumb is to sample media at a sampling rate a bit higher than what is needed for your final end use. Then, discard any excess information.

Nyquist Theory states that the rate at which sound should be sampled is double the maximum possible frequency, as it ensures all the peaks and troughs of the original wave form will be captured. Therefore, if a digital recording is sampled at 44.1 kHz, then 22.05 kHz is the highest frequency sound that can be captured.

Bit depth (or the number of bits used to represent the digital sample) is the other factor that influences the quality of a digital file. If more bits are used to describe the media, the better the representation of the analog source.

For example, imagine you're trying to depict a landscape. If you have only 8 crayons to work with, you're not going to get a very accurate representation of it. On the other hand, if you have a box of 500 crayons, you will get a much

4.6
Images saved with a limited bit depth (256 colors) tend to have flat areas of color

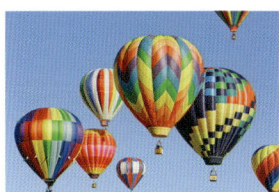
millions of colors

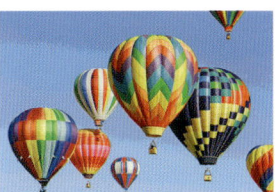
256 colors

more accurate representation. Old 8-bit monitors were a lot like the box of crayons because they had only 8 bits to represent all the colors on the screen. This presented a challenge for web designers at the time because they had to choose colors and design graphics that wouldn't look horrible on monitors with limited bit depth.

The example below illustrates how bit depth influences the quality of an image. In the photograph on the right, only 8 bits are being used to describe all of the different colors in the original image. The result is that it looks really splotchy and flat because with 8 bits we can only use 256 unique colors to describe the image, and 256 colors are not enough to capture the broad range of colors that were in the original image.

A low bit depth has a similar, detrimental effect when applied to sound. With a limited number of bits, you cannot precisely describe the level of the sound that you are sampling. The resulting digital sound sampled at a low bit depth would be a really distorted version of the original sound.

A best practice is to capture and keep digital files in the highest possible resolution, bit depth, sample rate, etc., until outputting the final product. Then, if further manipulation is required, or the finished product needs to be higher quality, the original files will allow for it.

THE PROS OF DIGITAL MEDIA

Although converting media to digital formats involves making compromises, there are several advantages to having media in a digital form. One major advantage is that it can be reproduced without generation decay. Generation decay would occur when duplicating analog media, such as when recording from one cassette tape to another. The copy would not be as good quality as the original.

Another significant advantage of working with media in a digital form is being able to make edits in a nonlinear fashion. Before film editing was done on the computer, editors literally had to cut and tape pieces of film together. If they cut off too much, it was a difficult mistake to fix. Analog sound editing worked in a similar fashion. Digital audio and video editing can now be done nonsequentially and without destroying the original source material.

Ease of distribution is another advantage of digital media, but has led to many copyright violations. Entire businesses, such as Napster, a peer-to-peer music sharing platform that emerged in the mid 1990s, were shut down due to

■ Fundamental Components of Interactive Digital Media

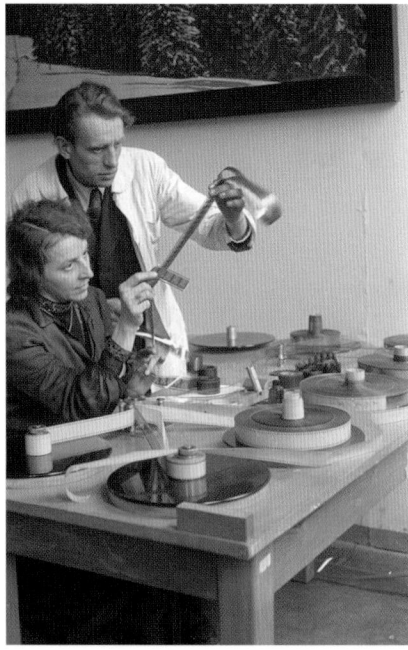

4.7
Film editing was a physical, destructive process. Source: © Deutsche Fotothek; Wikimedia Commons. Online. Available HTTP: <https://commons.wikimedia.org/wiki/Category:Film_editing#/media/File:Fotothek_df_pk_0000165_017.jpg>

unlawful sharing of digital media files over the Internet. The disappearance of Napster and improved Internet bandwidth paved the way for music and video streaming services like Spotify and Netflix, allowing users to consume digital content legally. In the early days of the web, though, streaming audio and video would not have been possible.

COMPRESSION

Compression is the process of reorganizing (and sometimes removing) digital data to reduce the file size. The method in which the compression is achieved is called a "codec." Advancements in compression codecs have made the delivery of digital content (especially audio and video) over the Internet possible.

While there are many specific types of compression codecs, they can be categorized into two broad groups: lossy and lossless compression. An easy way to remember the difference is to just look at the words themselves: loss less = nothing is lost when compression is done. TIFF images are an example of a file format that uses a lossless compression method to achieve a reduction in file size; the compression algorithm reduces the file size without disposing of any of the original data. Another example of lossless compression is a zip file. When you zip files together, you reduce the file size without losing any data.

Lossy compression, on the other hand, involves destroying some of the data to achieve a reduction in file size, and, as a result, a great amount of compression is achieved. Lossy compression strategies are used in MP3 and JPEG files which explains how they can have such a small file size while maintaining a decent quality.

When you compress media in a format that involves lossy methods, the software must decide what information to keep and what information is redundant or not noticeable in order to achieve high amounts of compression. The results are not always good on the first try. Sometimes you might over compress a file and achieve unsatisfying results which is why it is important to keep original uncompressed files so that you can open them up and export another compressed version of the file.

The most common type of compressed audio file is the MP3 file format due to its ability to maintain most of the integrity of the original sound while significantly reducing the file size. The amount of compression that can be achieved by converting a WAV file to an MP3 file is approximately 10 to 1. For example, a 30 MB WAV file can be saved as a 3 MB MP3 file. The invention of the MP3 format in the early 1990s ushered in the era of music downloads, ripping CDs and storing thousands of songs on your iPod. The MP3 format was revolutionary at the time because transfer speeds over the Internet were still quite slow, but with its extreme compression, MP3 files could be downloaded in a few minutes.

Digital video is even more complex than images or audio which explains why there are so many video compression codecs available and new ones being introduced all the time. Depending on the type of video you are compressing, one may achieve better results than others. A video editor should be familiar with many common codecs and recognize which ones are best suited for compressing different types of footage.

DESCRIPTION VS. COMMAND-BASED ENCODING OF MEDIA

The types of files that are most often compressed are stored in the computer as a description of the media it represents. A description-based file is a detailed representation of the discrete elements that comprise the media. For example, a JPEG image is encoded as a description because the computer stores the file information pixel by pixel. Audio files such as WAV, MP3, and AIFF files are all stored as descriptions. Compression can be achieved by summarizing and eliminating parts of the description.

Not all digital media files are stored as descriptions, though; some digital files are stored as commands. Command-based files are simply a set of instructions that the computer follows to produce it. An example of a digital media file that is stored as a set of commands is a vector-based image. When a program opens the file, it reads and interprets the instructions and recreates the image. For this reason, a vector-based image looks crisp and clear at any size. The only audio format that's encoded as a set of commands are MIDI files. The MIDI format is like a musical score instead of a description of the sounds themselves. To play a MIDI file, the MIDI software must interpret the MIDI commands and reproduce the sounds on the fly.

■ Fundamental Components of Interactive Digital Media

There are pros and cons to description versus command-based media. Graphics that are stored as descriptions can most closely represent natural scenes and sounds, and support very detailed editing. Graphics stored as a set of commands will never have an organic look or feel because they are mathematically generated, but the file sizes are typically smaller and they can be scaled without any kind of distortion or loss of quality. Similar pros and cons pertain to audio files as well. If you want to record natural sounds, it will have to be stored as a description. But, if you are composing a score and you want to edit the notes or apply a different musical instrument to those notes, the information must be stored as a set of commands.

In the example below, on the left is a pixel-based green circle (description-based media) and on the right, a vector version (command-based). The pixels on the edge of the left circle are evident, making it look blurry, but the edges of the right circle look crisp and clear. This is because the circle on the right is regenerated at any size based on the set of instructions. We can zoom in all we want and it will always look crisp and clear. A simple shape like a green circle is ideal to make in a vector-based drawing tool like Adobe Illustrator because it is a non-realistic looking graphic and can easily be stored as a mathematical formula. Logos are most often made in vector-based drawing programs because they can be reproduced at any size and maintain pristine quality.

COLOR ON THE SCREEN

Mixing Pigments vs. Mixing Light

In kindergarten, we learn the three primary colors: red, yellow and blue as well as the colors we can make by mixing them: purple, green and orange. The method in which a printer produces color is somewhat similar. However, printers produce colors from four printing pigments: cyan, magenta, yellow and black.

When a printer puts ink onto a paper, it is adding pigments to a page. These pigments absorb the light reflecting off the paper. For example, cyan ink absorbs red, leaving the green and blue light to reflect. If all pigments are mixed together in equal amounts, all light will be absorbed and you are left with black. But since the inks are not perfect and the result of combining cyan, magenta and yellow comes out more brown than black, a

4.8
Green circle created in Photoshop and rasterized. When it is enlarged, the edges look pixelated and blurry

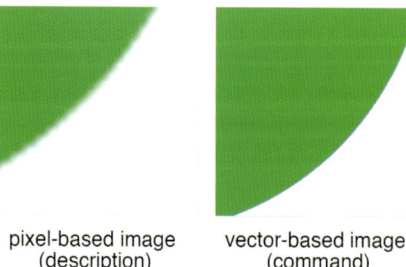

pixel-based image (description)   vector-based image (command)

Fundamental Components of Interactive Digital Media

4.9
Additive vs. subtractive color mixing

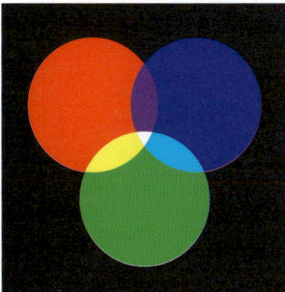

Color on the computer

Mixing light: red, green, blue
Additive color

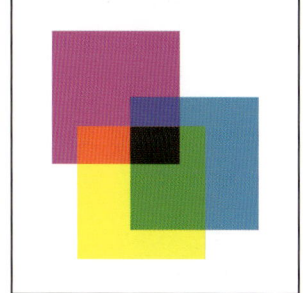

Color in print

Mixing pigment: cyan, magenta, yellow
Subtractive color

4.10
The complete color spectrum vs. CMYK vs. RGB color

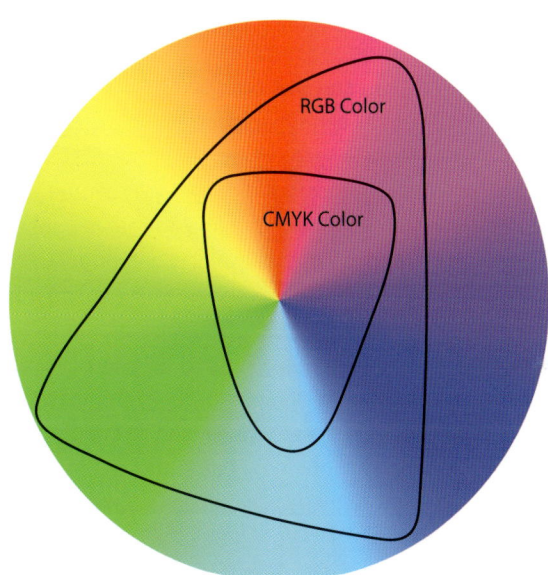

black pigment is used to achieve a pure black color. The process of mixing pigments to produce color is called a "subtractive" process.

Your computer screen generates color in a completely different manner. Color on a computer screen is made by the combination of different colored lights (red, green and blue). Computers are able to generate a very large spectrum of color by varying the amount of red, green and blue light for each pixel on the screen. If you mix maximum amounts of red light, green light and blue light, you get white. Producing color by mixing light is called an "additive" process.

The illustration below shows the visual spectrum of color (every color our eyes can see) and the subset that our printers (CMYK color) and computer

■ Fundamental Components of Interactive Digital Media

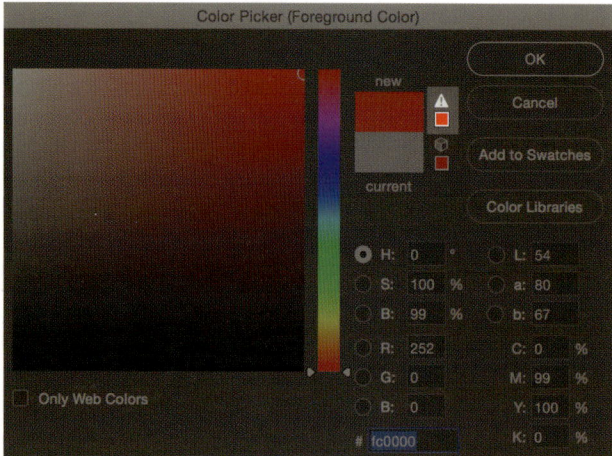

4.11
Photoshop provides a gamut warning when you select an "out of gamut" color

screens (RGB color) can recreate. You can see that both color mixing systems can produce a lot of different colors, but still can't make every single color in the visible spectrum.

Because printers and monitors produce colors differently, it can be challenging to design on the computer when your intended final format is print. As a designer, you must be careful not to choose (typically highly saturated) colors that are visible on the screen but not reproducible with the four printing inks. These non-printable colors are called "out of gamut." Software programs like Adobe Photoshop and Illustrator provide gamut warnings to let you know that the color you're mixing on the screen will not be able to be reproduced with printing inks. If you ignore the gamut warnings and include a lot of out of gamut colors in your design, the printed piece will look very flat in the out of gamut areas as the printer has to simply substitute the nearest in-gamut alternative.

The warning in the Photoshop color picker below the gamut warning is the web safe color warning. Clicking this button will jump to the closest web safe color. While this is still a feature in Photoshop, it's no longer relevant to interactive designers. In the 1990s, when most people had 8-bit color monitors, standard color palettes were established across web browsers to help web designers pick colors that would look most consistent across different platforms and browsers. This set of 216 "web safe" colors were chosen because it was less than the 256 colors the 8-bit monitors could reproduce, and left a few extra colors for the computer's own use while dividing the levels of red, green and blue light into 6 equal intervals ($6 \times 6 \times 6 = 216$). Needless to say, monitors have gotten much, much better and web safe colors are a distant memory.

RGB Color

Because interactive digital media is screen-based, RGB color is the standard method of specifying colors when creating graphics or specifying color in code.

Fundamental Components of Interactive Digital Media

In Photoshop, for images designed for screen-based media, you will always choose RGB color mode. And when you code web pages, you will specify the RGB value of the colors you want to use.

The way in which you specify RGB color is via hexadecimal code: a six-character string that specifies the level of red, green and blue light needed to comprise the desired color. Each character in the hexadecimal code is a base-16 number.

To understand what base 16 means, consider our regular base 10 number system. Base 10 numbers are comprised of 10 different digits: 0, 1, 2, 3, 4, 5, 6, 7, 8 and 9. A base 16 number uses those same 10 digits, but requires 6 more unique characters to encode 16 possibilities: 0 through 9 and then A, B, C, D, E and F. Since each character represents one of 16 possibilities, a pair of base 16 numbers can represent 256 possibilities. In a hexadecimal (or hex) code, each pair of base 16 numbers represents each of the levels of light (right, green and blue) with 00 being the absence of light and FF meaning full strength. Because each pair can be 256 possibilities, when 3 pairs are combined, over 16 million different colors can be described.

To get a sense for how the hex code corresponds to color, see some of the examples below. Notice the hex code for black is all zeros which is somewhat counterintuitive. But, if you recall that RGB color is additive and pertains to light, it makes sense because black is the absence of light. Conversely, if you turn on maximum red light, maximum blue light, and maximum green light, you will produce white which is why the hex code is the maximum hex value: FFFFFF.

Graphics applications like Photoshop and Illustrator will tell you any color's corresponding hexadecimal code. In the example below, you can see how this code is entered in CSS code to specify the color of the background of a web-based application. Notice that the syntax for describing the color is the pound character (#), then the hex code.

4.12
Examples of a few colors and their corresponding hexadecimal codes and RGB values

Color	Hexidecimal Value	RGB Values
	#000000	rgb (0,0,0)
	#FFFFFF	rgb (255,255,255)
	#2d3d96	rgb (44,63,149)
	#cc1515	rgb (203,32,39)
	#338841	rgb (51,136,65)
	#efe919	rgb (239,233,25)
	#a94d9d	rgb (169,77,157)
	#f39220	rgb (243,146,42)

■ Fundamental Components of Interactive Digital Media

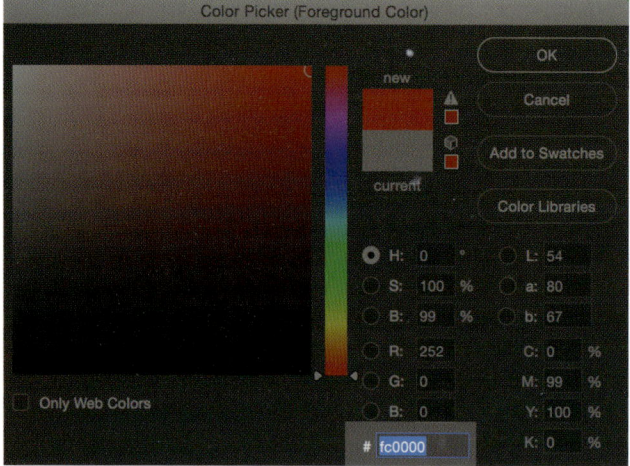

4.13
Adobe Photoshop displays the hexadecimal code for every color

4.14
An example of background color specified in hexadecimal format within a CSS document

PRACTITIONER INTERVIEW

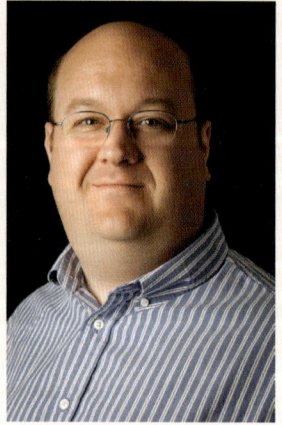

Chris Cox

Former senior computer scientist for Photoshop—Adobe Systems, Inc., CA, USA
Chris Cox worked as a senior computer scientist on the Adobe Photoshop team from 1996 to 2016 and was instrumental in developing the program

over this 20-year span. He holds several patents related to this work on Photoshop, and, he is 2010 inductee of the Adobe Photoshop Hall of Fame.

How did you end up getting your job at Adobe, and how did your career evolve there?

During college, Photoshop came out and I wrote a lot of plug-ins for it using the developers kit available through America Online. When I left college, I had been studying physics, but basically nobody was hiring in physics, so I looked at graphics programming and ended up working with a company that developed a Photoshop accelerator card. I did a lot of work there with the Photoshop team for about a year and a half. When that company started downsizing, I contacted Adobe. They said, "how soon can you be here?"

[When I started at Adobe], Photoshop had a lot of bugs and a lot of problems, so the first couple of years, I was mostly focused on performance problems. As time went on, I started writing more features. When new processors came out, I had to adapt the program to make it as fast as possible.

Why did working on Photoshop appeal to you?

I had some background in photography, working for the yearbook and the newspaper [in school] and also a little bit of an art background, so the idea of Photoshop appealed to me, not only painting stuff, but taking images in and manipulating them. A lot of the plugins I wrote were for taking an image off a supercomputer, bringing it onto a desktop system, and converting it into something the desktop could use. Everyone had proprietary image formats then; there were no standards.

So, what year did you join Adobe, and what was it like then?

I joined the Photoshop team in 1996. At that time, Photoshop was more of a professionals' tool. It wasn't an everyday person's thing, because there was no easy way to get photos into a digital form. At that time, it was an expensive process. Also, the desktop printers were horrible and digital cameras existed if you had a hundred thousand dollars to spend.

Then digital cameras and scanners and printers became cheaper and the world wide web took off and made it more accessible for people to share their images. So, it was an interesting time to start with [Adobe Photoshop] and watch it grow and eventually snowball into this popular culture thing. I heard somebody the other day say: "Photoshop, you mean what people do to their photos?" I'm like, "no the program." It's become a verb.

■ Fundamental Components of Interactive Digital Media

When the web came around, were you feeling pressure to adapt Photoshop to make it more useful for web developers?

Yes. We started with a side program that was designed for web imaging (Adobe ImageReady), but, as the web became more popular, we got pressure to put its features into Photoshop and not just have it as a separate program. So, we improved the quality of the plugins writing and reading web format images and added a few web specific features to Photoshop, some of which were liked, and some of which were kind of technological dead ends.

What do you mean by a technological dead end? Slices?

Right. You know, it's still there and it still has some uses and some people do use it. It was a big thing for web designers at one time that was superseded by a lot better stuff afterward and left in the dust. CSS changed things a lot. The evolution of HTML changed things a lot. But we had no way of knowing. Some of it we got right, some of it—not so much.

The slice tool in Photoshop allows you to divide an image into smaller pieces that fit back together like a puzzle. It was useful before Google Fonts were widely used and navigation bars were comprised of images containing the text. You would lay your navigation bar out as one big image than slice it up to get the individual images representing each menu element. Slicing was also useful when tables were used for web page layout and images could be used to force areas to be a certain width.

What were some of the big performance challenges that you had? Everyone used to say that Photoshop ran so much better on a Mac vs. a PC, but how much truth was there to that?

Yeah, there was some truth to it. Apple was shipping fairly optimized hardware. But in the Windows world, you had a mix. Some [systems] were good; some were bad. Some [PC makers] cut corners to keep the cost down and they made it slower. The compilers on the Mac were a little bit ahead of the Windows compilers. And, for the Mac you're targeting a few models, but for Windows, you're targeting hundreds of different motherboards and configurations. We had to try to keep [Photoshop] fast for everybody, but there were limits and there were things beyond our control.

What were some of the biggest challenges during your time developing and working on Photoshop?

It was always Windows or Apple changing their APIs, and we would have to adapt to that. There were a lot of crashing bugs that we should have caught before we shipped and just missed somehow. But then we would try to jump on these crash reports and get on the biggest stuff as quickly as possible.

Were there any features that you worked on a lot that weren't used as much or how you expected?

There are some features where some people understand it and a lot of people shake their head. [A great example] is the channel mixer. If you think like mixing [chemicals] in a dark room, it's obvious how it works. But to a lot of people, it's totally not obvious. Originally, I wrote that for the guys who were in the darkroom doing serious work, and they got it. But then I started reading books and other tutorials [about the channel mixer], and [discovered] a lot of people just did not get it.

With some of this stuff, even though you think nobody is using it, somebody is. A great example of that was when we took the shortcut off of the brightness and contrast command. It had been assigned randomly and all the teachers said "don't use this command, it's horrible, it's destructive." So, we took the shortcut away and reassigned it to something else that made a little more sense. [Shortly thereafter,] the entire comic book industry complained. They had workflows built around the brightness and contrast command. They would paint something in a solid color, make a selection within that, and use the brightness and contrast command to make it a little lighter or darker fairly quickly. Without that shortcut key, their work got a whole lot slower. Fortunately, we'd already been thinking about how to make keyboard shortcuts customizable and so we sped that up a little bit and made it so that they could assign shortcuts as needed. But up until that point, we didn't know people were using Photoshop for comic books.

Were there any other weird industries that are using Photoshop that took you guys by surprise?

Yes. A lot. [One was] the defense industry. Before they go try to sell weapons to Congress, they [use Photoshop to enhance their photos.] They have a picture of a plane and a picture of a tank bursting into flames but the laser is infra-red, and there's nothing visible. So, they paint in [a laser] to show to the congressmen, because otherwise they don't understand.

Also, the weaving industry people have some rather odd steps to prepare an image to be woven into a pattern on a jacquard loom, because you've got to occasionally have an overlap of the threads for the fabric to remain solid. So, they created a process of preparing the images for the loom to create different mixtures of different thread colors to keep it solid as they weave.

■ Fundamental Components of Interactive Digital Media

[The 3D artists who make] Pixar movies have to paint texture maps that go on all these models. It's not done in 3D software. They paint in Photoshop but then they have to work with the 3D software to render the [resulting image of the 2D texture on the 3D object.] [We had to figure out] how we could help them speed up this workflow.

It's interesting to learn these different industries, workflows and techniques and try to make it all work great.

From your time at Adobe working on Photoshop, do you have any one highlight moment?

When Photoshop was written, it was written for 16-bit image coordinates, and an image could not be bigger than 30,000 pixels in height or width. At the time, that seemed huge. Then, years later, people started making these scanning back cameras that could capture up to 120,000 pixels wide and they wanted to [work with them] in Photoshop. Well, it took six months or so of hard code and lots of work where my branch of the app didn't even compile most of the time to make that transition [while I was trying] to get all the math right to deal with larger coordinates. But it finally came together and now nobody even thinks about it. It just works. They make huge images, and occasionally if they want to exceed the 300,000 pixel limit, the code is there to do it.

It must be satisfying to see people use Photoshop in that way knowing that you worked on it.

Yeah, especially to see the comic book industry grow and use more modern techniques. By giving them a little more control, they were able to work faster and keep the same level of quality. When Photoshop started, the daily comic strips were almost all hand drawn and hand inked. Now almost all have switched to just drawing and inking and coloring straight in Photoshop. It's an interesting change. Unfortunately, it means a lot of them no longer have original copies of the strips to sell.

I ran into a well-known airbrush artist several years ago and he was no longer using [a real] airbrush at all. He was doing everything in Photoshop and he said it was so much faster, so much more productive, and so much healthier for him. He never wanted to go back. No fumes. No blowing his nose and getting a multicolor result. This was a guy I had admired when I was growing up. I saw his illustrations in magazines and aspired to do as great as he did. And [I see now that] we just totally changed that industry.

Isn't that an ironic twist?

Somewhat, yeah.

DISCUSSION QUESTIONS

1) Why do you think some people collect and even prefer forms of analog media?
2) Do you have experience converting analog media into a digital form? If so, how did you do it and what compromises did you make? Would you do anything differently?
3) Have you created media in a format or stored it on an obsolete medium that is now inaccessible or unusable? What would you do differently to prevent this from happening?
4) How would your life be different if media was not available in a digital form?
5) What are some of the advantages of the hexadecimal color system?

5 Media Content

INTRODUCTION

Content is the "meat" within an interactive experience and comes in many different forms: graphics, animation, audio, video and text. It's helpful to know best practices when working with each form as you may need to produce the content yourself, or interface with a specialist in the discipline.

GRAPHICS

Graphics of different types: buttons, charts, diagrams, photographs and illustrations are expected components within any interactive experience. Graphics also play a large role in the planning process, as wireframes and flowcharts must be created to explain how the application will look and work. Having facility with graphics applications, knowing the appropriate file formats and being able to apply good design principles to the creation of these graphics are all useful skills.

The two different types of computer graphics are pixel-based (often called raster or bitmap images) and vector-based images. Pixel-based images are comprised of small squares of color (called pixels) and are created and edited in photo editing applications like Adobe Photoshop. Vector-based images are stored as mathematical equations and are created and edited in drawing programs like Adobe Illustrator.

PIXEL-BASED IMAGES

What They Are

Pixel is short for "picture element": a square dot that can only be one color. If you zoom into a pixel-based image, you can eventually see the individual pixels that make up the image. However, from afar, you can't see each one; the color appears continuous.

There are pros and cons associated with bitmap images. One major advantage is that the tiny pixels allow you to create photorealistic representations. Pixel based images can also easily be displayed within a web browser when saved in an appropriate format (JPEG, GIF or PNG).

Media Content

5.1
Every bitmap image is comprised of pixels.
Source: Edited image based on original © Mariusz Blach; 123RF.com

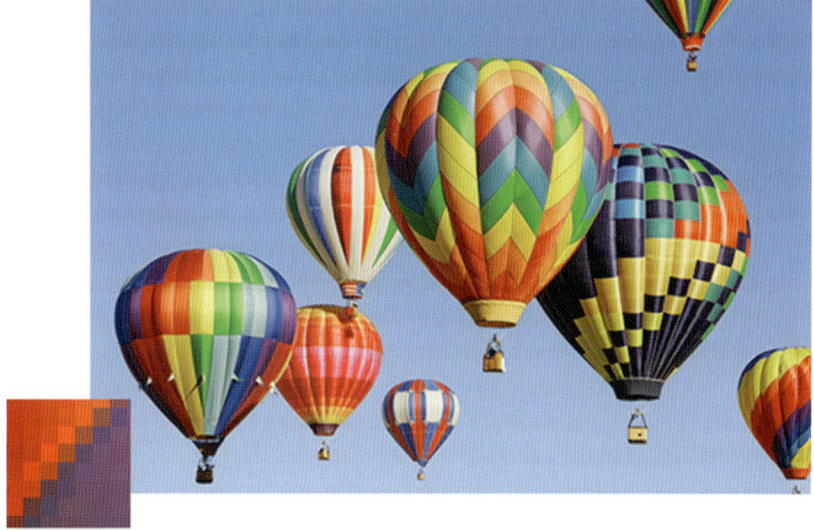

5.2
Every bitmap image has a finite number of pixels, which is shown in image editing programs.
Source: Edited image based on original © Mariusz Blach; 123RF.com

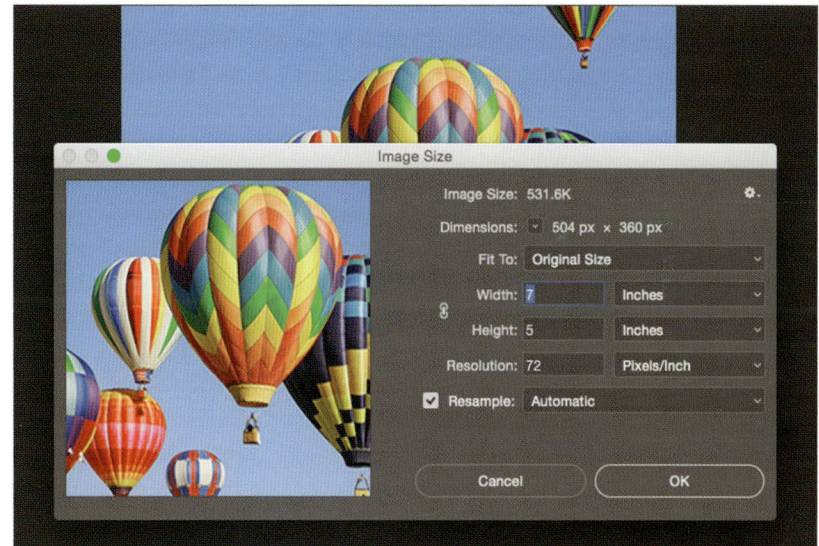

One downside of pixel-based images is that the file sizes can get quite large. And, every bitmap image has a finite number of pixels, so if you enlarge a bitmap image too much, you will lose the photorealism because the individual pixels become apparent.

Resolution and Bit Depth
When working with pixel-based graphics, it's important to be cognizant of resolution and whether it is appropriate for the intended end use. Graphics programs (like Photoshop) will tell you the resolution of the image you are editing.

■ Media Content

In the following Photoshop screenshot, you can see that this image is comprised of 504 pixels horizontally and 360 pixels vertically because it is 7 by 5 inches with a resolution of 72 pixels per inch.

- 7 × 72 = 504 pixels (width)
- 5 × 72 = 360 pixels (height)
- 504 × 360 = 181,440 (total number of pixels)

In the previous chapter, you learned that images used within interactive media applications are typically 72 dpi or 96 dpi to correspond with screen resolutions. Printers, on the other hand, are capable of generating images at a much higher resolution, therefore images designed for print should be captured and saved at a higher resolution (typically 300 dpi). Integrating high resolution images into an interactive experience will slow it down unnecessarily.

The common practice of lowering the resolution of a bitmap image is called downsampling. It's always better to capture more pixels than you need because having an excess of pixels gives you the flexibility to crop out a certain area of that image and still have enough resolution left in the resulting image for your intended end use. The opposite of downsampling is upsampling. Upsampling is the process of adding more pixels to a bitmap image. There's never a good reason to upsample because, even though the software uses the best algorithms to guess what those pixels should be, the resulting image will likely look muddy.

Image resolution is not the only factor that affects the quality of an image. In the previous chapter, you also learned about bit depth: the number of possibilities each pixel in an image can be. Lowering the bit depth of an image is one way to decrease the file size, and the one image format that allows you to do so is the GIF format. This type of compression works well if the image contains only a few colors, such as in a cartoon or a logo, because only a few bits are needed to describe all the colors.

How They are Made

There are a number of ways to create digital images. Digital cameras or even smart phone cameras have allowed companies to take their own product pictures, a task that was once outsourced to professionals at service bureaus. (The suggested image size for an Etsy product picture is 1000 × 1000 pixels at 72 dpi. The iPhone X captures images up to 4000 × 3000 pixels.) The key to taking successful product pictures is to have good lighting and a clean background.

Scanners are an essential tool to convert printed images into a digital format. Some even have extra hardware that allow you to scan slides and negatives. Scanners can also be useful in scanning items other than photos; I've created weird textures and effects by scanning objects like vegetable slices and fabrics.

Realistic textures and unusual effects can be generated as bitmap images in programs like Photoshop by running a series of commands. For example, if you wanted to create a bitmap image that looked like wood grain, you could do so by applying different filters, reversing colors and making a few adjustments.

5.3
Wood grain texture
created in Photoshop

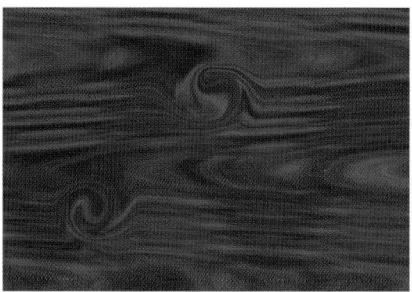

Several books and videos demonstrate these techniques which are very useful to a 3D artist who wants to create a specific texture for a 3D object.

Sometimes the photo you need for a project isn't easily obtainable. Let's say, for example, you need images of healthy-looking, smiling children for an interface design you are mocking up and a very tight deadline. Fortunately, royalty-free stock image sites offer these types of images, and the cost per image is inexpensive or even free, e.g. istockphoto.com or unsplash.com. Just pay attention to the terms of use.

Screen shots are another way to obtain digital imagery and are absolutely essential for showing something on a computer screen. You can use specialized software or built-in shortcuts to take a screen shot. On a PC, simply press the "Print Screen" button on your keyboard, and an image of what's on your screen will be saved on your clipboard (a temporary storage buffer ready for you to paste it). The corresponding functionality on a Mac can be executed with the key combinations of Command + Shift + 4.

File Formats

Pixel-based images can be saved in a variety of file formats, all offering different pros and cons.

- PSD files are the Photoshop native format that maintain editable layers and effects.
- TIFF files are a common (primarily print) image format with lossless compression that can be opened in software other than Photoshop.
- JPEGs are the most prevailing image format because most digital cameras automatically create JPEGs, and they use lossy compression which means the file size is small. JPEGs can also be viewed natively within a web browser.
- GIF files can also be viewed in a web browser. But, unlike JPEGs, they offer transparency, meaning that a portion of the image can be invisible, allowing the background to show through. GIFs also support animation (without sound), but can only be saved in 8-bit color (256 colors maximum).
- PNG files are also commonly used on the web. Like GIFs, they support transparency but do not have a limited bit depth. They are unlike JPEGs in

■ Media Content

that they use lossless compression. PNGs would never be used in a printed piece because they do not support CMYK color.

Software

Adobe Photoshop is the leading pixel-based image editing program and would mostly likely be found in professional environments where image editing is done regularly. However, there are some alternatives. GIMP, for example, is a free and open source program much like Photoshop. There are also some web-based tools and even apps that allow you to create and manipulate bitmap images.

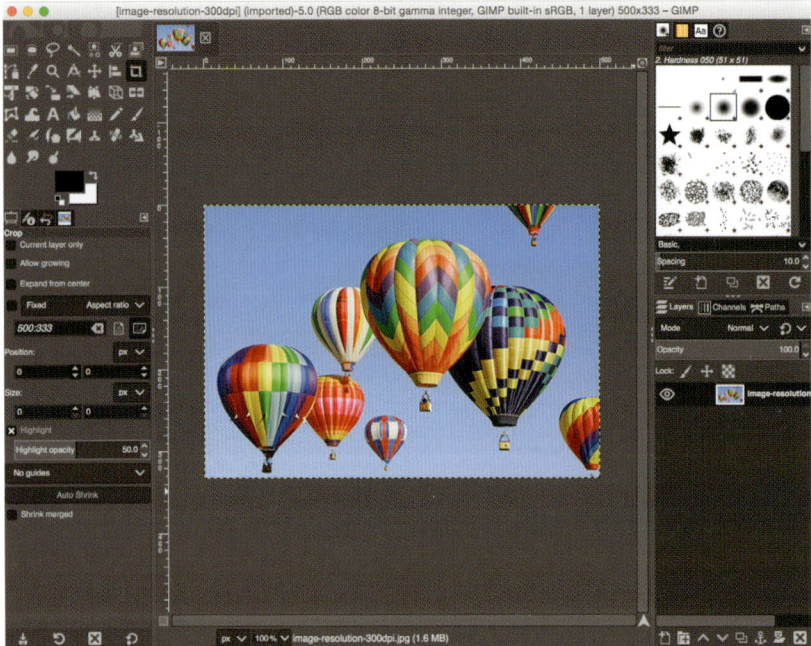

5.4
GIMP: the free, open source image manipulation software

VECTOR-BASED IMAGES

What They Are

Vector graphics are comprised of vectors which are lines with a length, curvature and direction. Programs that create vector graphics are called draw or illustration programs, with the industry leader being Adobe Illustrator.

Technical Details

There are a number of different drawing tools in a vector-based drawing program like Adobe Illustrator. The star, oval and rectangle make it easy to create different type of shapes. The brush, pencil and line tool allow you to create different types of lines. The pen tool facilitates the creation of Bezier curves which are shapes controlled by anchor points (which can be curved or corner) and handles.

Media Content ■

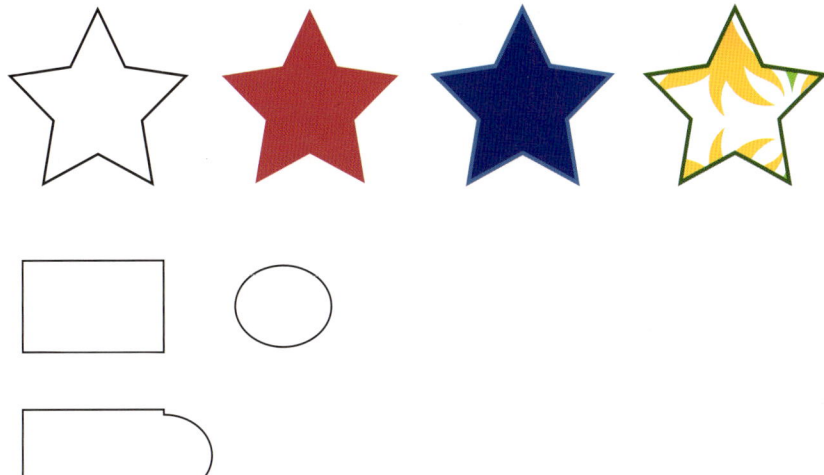

5.5
The same shape with different strokes and fills applied

5.6
A rectangle and an oval unioned create a bullet.

Although they take practice to master, Bezier curves allow you to have very precise control over the type of shape that you're drawing. Editing tools within Adobe Illustrator allow you to manipulate the vector lines and shapes irrespective of the tool you used to create them, and you can apply different strokes and fills to the lines and shapes you make.

In vector-based drawing programs, more complex shapes can be created with Boolean operations. For example, you could make a bullet shape by applying a Union to an overlapping rectangle and oval. Other Boolean operations include subtracting one shape from another, or getting the intersection or non-intersection of two shapes.

There are a number of pros and cons associated with vector-based graphics. One advantage is that a vector graphic will look sharp at any size because it's just a set of commands that regenerates the graphic. And because they are saved as commands, the file size is quite a bit smaller than comparable bitmap graphics. The nature of vector graphics, however, makes them unsuitable for representing photo-realistic effects; they tend to have an inherently cartoony look to them.

While older web browsers only displayed pixel-based images, now, vector-based graphics saved in SVG format can be displayed within a browser. It's an exciting development for web developers, because although their file sizes tend to be small, their graphic impact can be quite powerful.

Vector to Bitmap and Bitmap to Vector Conversion

It's quite simple to convert a vector-based image into a bitmap, but not as easy in reverse. When converting a vector graphic to a bitmap, you are simply asking the software to generate pixels in the color of the vector shape. Adobe Illustrator makes it easy to do so; you can simply choose "export as a bitmap" and specify the resolution and format you need. Keep in mind, however, that once you convert

■ Media Content

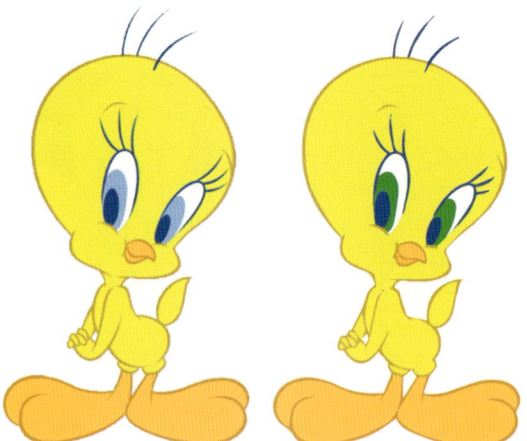

5.7
The image on the left is a bitmap image. I imported into Adobe Illustrator and used the Auto Trace tool to convert it to a vector. Since this image contained larger blocks of color it was suitable for converting to a vector shape. After the conversion I was able to select the eyes as a vector shape and change them to green.

a vector-based graphic into a bitmap, it is no longer scalable and will not look crisp and clear at all sizes.

Converting a bitmap graphic into a vector-based graphic is not as straight-forward because anything photorealistic doesn't lend itself well to being described by vectors. With that said, there are some bitmap graphics (such as ones with large areas of solid color) that would convert well. To do so, you would place the bitmap into Adobe Illustrator and use the Auto Trace tool which will detect the greatest areas of contrast within the pixels to determine where the vector shapes should be. The quality of the resulting vector shape is dependent on the type of bitmap you are working with and the settings you associate with the tool.

File Formats

Vector-based files don't have quite as many common file formats as bitmap graphics.

- **AI** is the native Adobe Illustrator file format and has very limited use outside of Adobe Illustrator.
- **EPS** is a generic vector-based file format and is more readily imported into other programs.
- **PDF** files were developed by Adobe as a software-independent vector-based format that would retain page layout information, but the format is now open-source. Since PDF files can now be opened by almost anyone, they are a good choice for files with a designed layout that need to be downloaded or printed.
- **SVG** files are the only vector graphic format that can be viewed within a web browser. They are also more readily imported into other software.

2D ANIMATION

Anyone who has watched cartoons is familiar with 2D animation. However, the type of 2D animation used within interactive media is not always character-driven. It can be subtle or dramatic and serve a variety of different purposes.

Where It's Used

The first type of 2D animation that was viewable on the web were animated GIFs: a series of 8-bit bitmap images played in succession. Animated GIFs do not support sound, but they can be looping or non-looping and the timing between each image can vary. Because they are GIFs, portions of each image within the animation can be transparent. Animated GIFS were wildly popular in the early days of the web because they were the only type of motion graphic supported within a web browser. They are now used more as a novelty, such as for memes, because they are easy to make and their small file size makes them suitable for sharing.

2D vector-based animation exploded on the web in the early 2000s thanks to Macromedia's Flash software, a popular interactive authoring program at the time, because it allowed the developer to easily integrate animations and sound into an interactive experience that could be viewed through a web browser with the appropriate plug-in installed. Because it was vector-based, the file sizes could be small and load quickly. Many Flash sites fully exploited its animation capabilities yielding websites that would almost make you motion sick.

Websites made entirely in Flash have mostly disappeared due to the lack of plug-in support within mobile browsers and the fact they were terrible for search engine optimization. The demise of Flash curtailed the extreme use of 2-D animation on the web and made it much more subtle and functional. You click on a menu item and new content smoothly swipes in. Image carousels gently rotate in a new set of products for you to review. Animated motion graphics are frequently used as a background on a website home page, infusing cinematic energy into a web page. Animation is also commonly used in web and app advertisements to draw eyes away from the content proper and to encourage users to click. 10–15 years ago this type of animation would have been made in Flash, however it can now be created programmatically using JavaScript and HTML 5.

2D character animation isn't altogether absent from interactive digital media. Many casual games contain animated characters and backgrounds. What would Angry Birds be without the animated, snarling, blinking, flailing little red angry bird? Animated avatars are often incorporated into training applications to serve as a friendly guide.

How It's Made

Traditional animation techniques form the basis of many 2-D animation programs. For example, many animation programs allow the animator to see the previous frame(s) while drawing the current one which is analogous to a traditional animator drawing over the previous frame while using a light table. Animation programs also incorporate layers which operate like cellulose in traditional animation. Cellulose (or a cel) is a transparent sheet on which the animator draws her character, allowing a background image to show through. If the background is to stay consistent in an animated sequence, it prevents the animator from having to recreate it for each frame.

■ Media Content

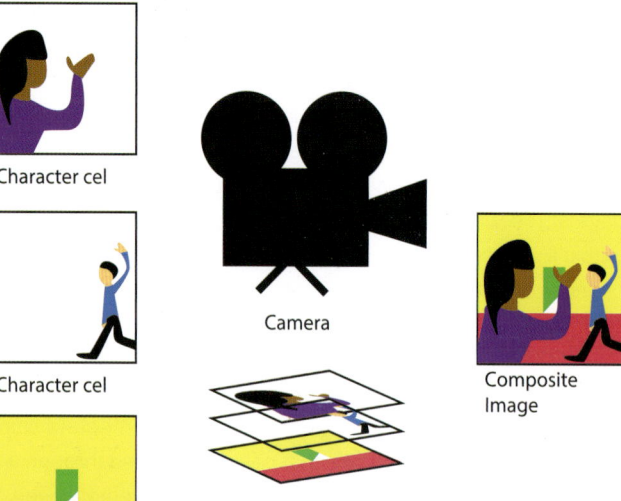

5.8
2D animation software allows you to place objects on separate layers similar to traditional cel animation

Traditional animators would shoot their sequence of drawings by mounting a camera overhead and taking a picture of each one. When animations were shot directly onto film, the animator would often "shoot in twos" meaning that each drawing would be shot two times and therefore of a second as opposed to of a second (due to the standard film frame rate of 24 frames per second) saving the animator a lot of work. Now that sequences of images can be imported into video editing programs, the length of time each image is displayed can be decided once the sequence is imported into the editor.

Software
2D animation can be created within almost every authoring application and game engine. In many cases, the animation is embedded in the application. The following programs allow for the creation and exporting of a stand-alone 2D animation.

- **Adobe Edge Animate** is the newest incarnation of Macromedia/Adobe Flash. The rebranding was intended to disassociate the program from the Flash SWF format which is no longer supported in mobile browsers. Edge Animate has such a robust set of animation tools, it is even used to make popular television cartoons. Content made in Edge Animate can be exported in JavaScript/HTML for display within web browsers.
- **Web-based HTML/JavaScript animation programs, including TinyAnim and HTML 5 Maker** allow you to create animated content that is displayable within a web browser.
- **Adobe After Effects** is a video compositing tool with 2D animation capabilities. Because of its basis in video compositing, After Effects animated content is typically exported as a video file.

- **Harmony by Toon Boom** is a 2D animation software widely used in character-driven animated series, but typically exported as a video file.
- **Adobe Photoshop** (and many other inexpensive alternatives) allow you to build 2D animated GIFs.

File Formats

- **SWF** files were once commonly exported from Flash and incorporated into a website. SWFs are rarely used anymore because they require a browser plugin that is no longer supported by mobile browsers.
- **MOV** and **MP4** are two digital video formats that animation is often exported in, making it suitable for standard digital video editing and distribution.
- **GIF** is the format for Animated GIF files.
- **HTML 5/JavaScript** is now the most common way of integrating animated content into web-based experiences.

3D GRAPHICS AND ANIMATION

3D objects, graphics, environments and animations play a big role in video games, virtual reality, and augmented reality experiences. When you build a 3D object, your objects are not only in the X–Y plane, they also extend into the Z axis.

Where It's Used

When you think of 3D, perhaps 3D animated films may come to mind. While this is a common use of 3D software, and portions of 3D animated content or 3D static images may be integrated into an interactive application, these are just images and video files.

A 3D environment is a collection of three-dimensional textured objects in a space. When you are building an interactive 3D experience, you need to import the entire scene of objects, because user interaction requires the computer to render out images on the fly. Overly complicated models will take a while to render and slow down the experience, so the 3D artist must simplify models whenever possible.

How It's Made

The 3D production process has four distinct phases, all of which can be accomplished within a 3D animation program.

1. **Model the 3D shape(s)**. Modeling is specifying the surface of the 3D object, and there are many different methods. Some objects lend themselves really well to being modeled with geometric objects or the combination of them. For example, a trash can might be modeled by combining a cylinder and a sphere. Polygon modeling allows you to pull polygons in different directions to make more complex shapes. Spline modeling facilitates an extrusion of a surface. Metaball modeling involves pushing blobs together. The techniques

■ Media Content

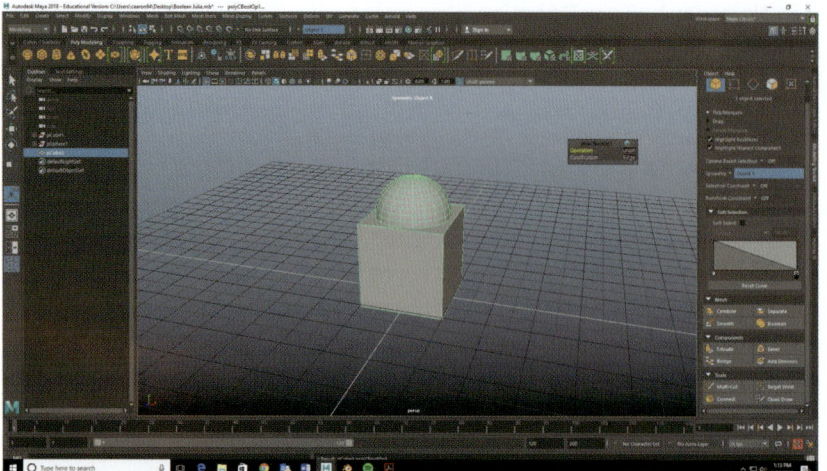

5.9
Modeling with 3D primative shapes is a simple way to build more complex objects. Source: Chris Aaron; www.treetopmedia.com

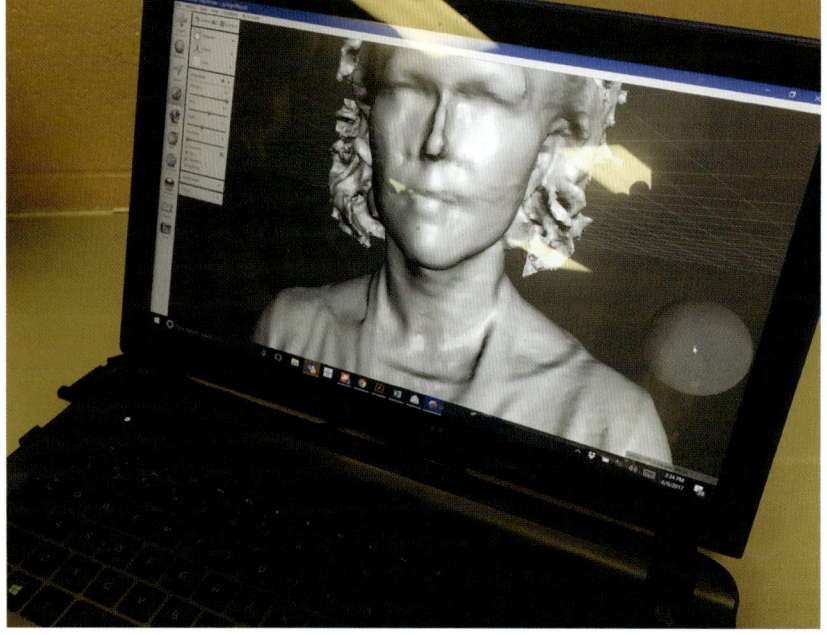

5.10
We used a 3D scanner to capture the surface of my head

or combination of techniques used to make a 3D model should be dictated by the characteristics of the object.

One way of "capturing" a 3D surface is by using a 3D scanner. The scanner detects the 3D coordinates of the physical object in space and generates a model based on the data it captures. 3D scanners are useful for model development when the object is organic in nature and can't easily be modeled with techniques provided in the software.

2. **Surface definition**. Defining the surface means specifying the look of the 3D object. You can select built-in colors and textures for your object or

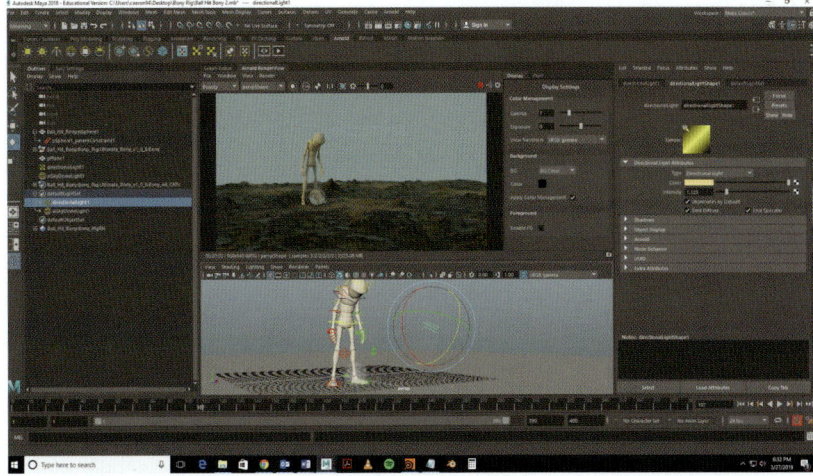

5.11
Building a 3D environment involves placing 3D objects in space and applying textures to those objects.
Source: Chris Aaron; www.treetopmedia.com

"wrap" a bitmap image around it. Images that are intended to mimic real textures are commonly used as surface maps to create realistic looking objects.

3. **Scene composition**. The scene composition is like creating a diorama, because you are positioning 3D objects, lights and cameras in an environment. If the end use is a video game or virtual reality experience, the process ends here; the artist exports the 3D file and imports it into the game engine.

4. **Final render**. A render is needed if the final format of the 3D project will be an individual image or a video. Rendering is taking a picture or pictures of the scene from the camera you positioned within it. If you were creating a 3D animation, you would define a motion path for your object(s) and/or camera and render out a series of images that would be played in rapid succession to create the 3D animation.

Software

Many applications allow you to create 3D objects, environments, images and animation. The software you choose should be dependent on the type of 3D object(s) you need to build and your intended end use.

- **Autodesk Maya** is the most well-known, robust, popular and expensive 3D modeling/animation program. Many of the most well-known Hollywood 3D animated films were made in Maya.
- **Autodesk 3DS Max** is a 3D modeling/animation program that grew out of AutoCAD (an architectural drafting program). Therefore, its strength is in creating dimensionally and numerically dependent 3D models and animation.
- **Blender** made by the Blender Foundation is a free and open-source 3D modeling/animation program.

■ Media Content

3D File Formats

- **OBJ**: Universally accepted 3D format.
- **IFFb**: The native format used by Maya.
- **3DS**: The native file format for 3D Studio.
- **BLEND**: The native format used by Blender.

3D graphics and 3D animation can be exported in any of the common image or video formats.

AUDIO

How Sound is Made

Sound is created by vibration of air that travels to the ear in a wave-like pattern. When the wave reaches the ear, it causes the eardrum and subsequently the bones in the ear to vibrate at the same frequency. The vibration in the ear sends a signal to the auditory nerve which tells the brain to interpret it as sound.

The speed of vibration of a sound wave is called its frequency and is measured in Hertz (Hz). 1 Hz equals one cycle per second and is one up and down of a sound wave. Therefore, a 20 Hz sound means that the sound wave oscillates up and down 20 times per second.

Sounds at very low frequencies and sounds at very high frequencies are not audible to the human ear. Therefore, just because a sound is made doesn't necessarily mean that we hear it. Humans can hear sounds in the range of 20 Hz (on the low end) to 20 kHz (on the high end) which is a pretty broad spectrum considering a piano's range is 27.5 Hz – 4 kHz.

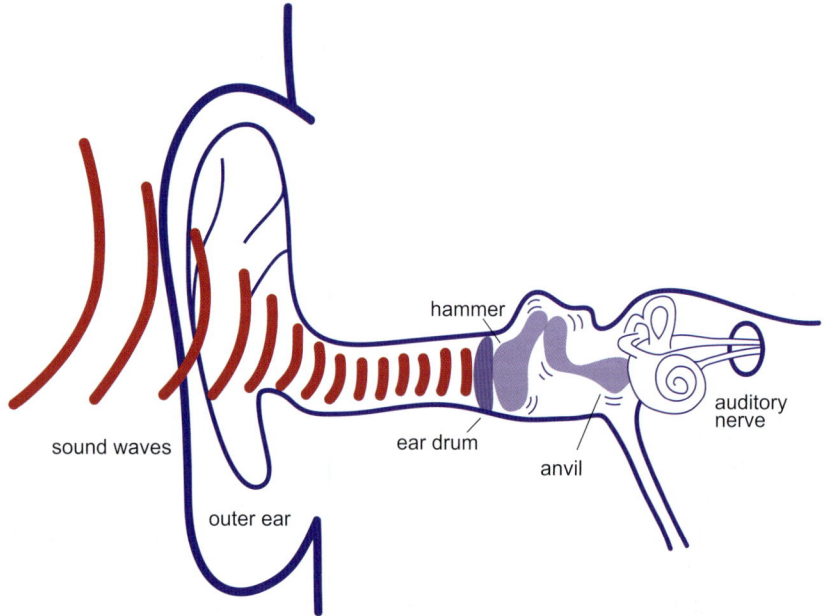

5.12
How sound works

5.13
The colored areas of this diagram are ones that are audible to humans

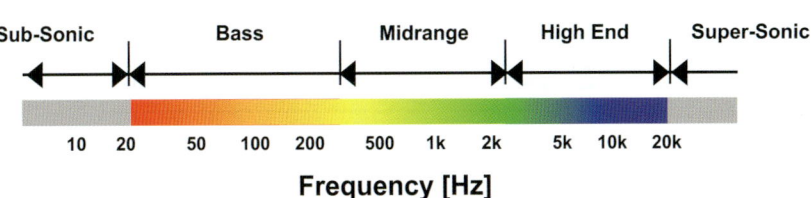

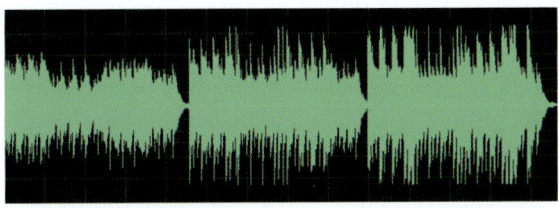
Sound wave of music

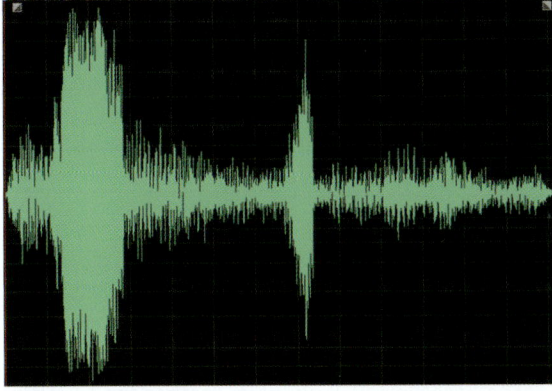
Sound wave of speech

5.14
A sound wave representing speech looks quite different from a sound wave representing music

How Sound is Represented

Most sounds change frequency over time and can be represented in a waveform which can tell you a bit about the sound itself. For example, by examining the sound wave in Figure 5.14, I would conclude that this sound is probably something that's more organic in nature and not necessarily a piece of music because it has such an irregular look to it. If it were Western music, the wave would have more consistent heights and a more regular pattern since Western music tends to have repeating musical phrases and a beat.

In order to "read" a waveform, you need to understand what the waveform is telling you. The wave captures three features of a sound: the volume, the pitch and the duration. The volume of the sound is represented by the amplitude (or height) of the sound wave: the higher the amplitude, the louder the sound. The

■ Media Content

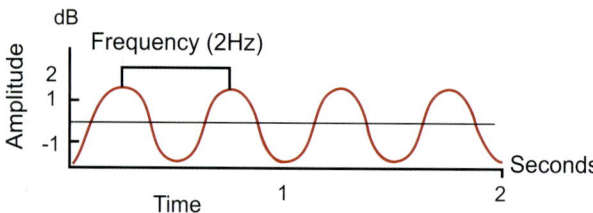

5.15
Note that the frequency of 2 Hz means that there are two repetitions of the sound wave in 1 second.

frequency of the sound (or the pitch) is represented by the number of oscillations (ups and downs) you see in a given amount of time. If you see a lot of oscillations in a short amount of time, that sound has a higher frequency (and consequently a higher pitch). Conversely, fewer oscillations over a period of time produces a lower pitch. The most obvious quality communicated by a waveform is the sound's duration, which is the waveform's length.

There are clear differences between the two waveforms below. The top waveform represents a piece of Western music and the bottom waveform represents speaking. Notice how the top one has more of a regular pattern to it and consistent amplitude throughout. But, the second waveform has more prolonged bursts and varied amplitudes. In both examples, there are moments where there is no height to the waveform, which are moments of silence. Being able to identify these moments, as well as other traits of sound such as volume and pitch changes, can be helpful if you are trying to sync a sound with visual effects.

Audio Recording

A little bit of extra preparation can go a long way to achieve good quality when recording sound. Use a decent microphone and keep it away from your computer to avoid picking up noise from your computer fan. Also, remove as much ambient noise from your environment as possible and, if possible, dampen the sound by hanging soft blankets on the walls.

You should also take the time to adjust your audio levels which is specifying the range between the highest level and the lowest level (noise floor) of sound that can be captured. Ideally, when recording, the levels should be within the high part of the green range while hitting the yellow range occasionally, but not the red range. Recording a sound with a level too close to the noise floor will result in a poor signal to noise ratio with hisses and hums being evident. But, recording a sound that exceeds the range you are specifying results in clipping and distortion. A sound wave that has been clipped has a flat top as opposed to a curve.

File Formats

In every audio editing program, you have the ability to export sounds in several different formats, all of which offer different pros and cons.

Media Content

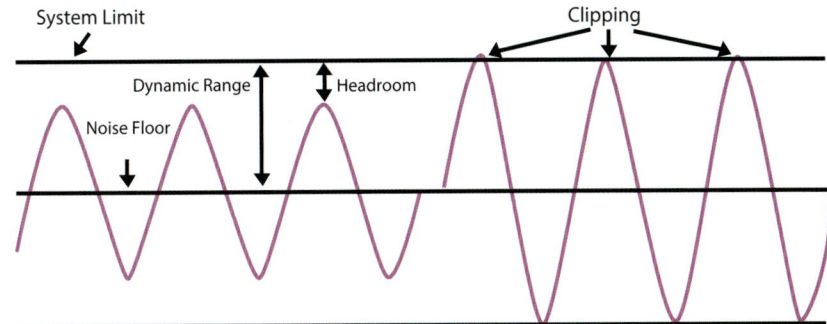

5.16
Ideal recording levels will encompass the sound wave, but if the sound wave exceeds the capture levels, clipping will occur and result in distortion

- **WAV and AIFF** are high quality uncompressed audio formats. They have no decrease in quality at higher or lower frequencies. AIFF is slightly higher quality than WAV.
- **MP3** is a highly compressed audio format that is ideal for online audio and streaming.

Audiophiles are quick to point out the limitations of the MP3 audio format. As a non-musician and non-audio engineer, most MP3 files sound great to me, but most audio professionals would be quick to disagree. Because a lot of interactive media is delivered over the Internet, the MP3's high level of compression is valued. In addition, a great deal of interactive media is experienced through the speakers of computers and hand-held devices that are not capable of delivering the highest quality auditory experience anyway.

Manipulating Sound

When preparing sound to be part of an interactive application, it is often necessary to make a few edits. Fortunately, there are a number of applications that will allow you to do so. Marketed as "digital audio workstations," these programs allow you to record, edit and mix sounds.

- **Apple's GarageBand**
- **Adobe Audition**
- **Sony Sound Forge Studio**
- **Avid Pro Tools**

In addition to these professional-grade programs, there are several free and online tools that allow you to create, edit and mix sound files such as Audacity, Dark Wave Studio, and Soundation.

Even if audio is not your area of expertise, it is helpful to know how to make some basic edits within these programs.

- **Splitting and trimming** are ways of extracting parts of an audio track. These are useful tools when combining different pieces of audio or removing undesirable sounds in the track.

105

■ Media Content

- **Noise removal** involves sampling the hiss (by itself) in your audio, then "negating" it from the rest of the audio file.
- **Normalization** is often done when a group of audio files with different volumes are in sequence on a timeline. Normalization will make the volume range more consistent throughout the entire sequence.
- **Time stretching** is slowing down or speeding up the sound.
- **Frequency adjustment** is making the pitch higher or lower.

Audio in Interactive Digital Media
Audio is used in a number of different ways within interactive media.

- **Ambient sounds** are often used to create a mood such as in a video game.
- **Sound effects** help emphasize an important moment within the experience. Sound effects are often used in video games or virtual reality experiences to add realism and help propel a story.
- **Auditory feedback** is used quite a bit within functional interactive media applications to communicate the user's action was received. For example, the click you hear when you successfully unlock your iPhone helps you understand that the phone is ready for use. Integrating auditory feedback can boost the usability of an application.
- **Music** of different types is occasionally needed within an interactive media application. For example, an e-learning application might integrate a bit of lead-in music to signify the start of a new module and reinforce the brand.
- **Speech** is commonly used within interactive applications. However, in situations where the content of the speech is crucial to user understanding, be sure to caption it, as many people turn off the sound on their devices.

In the early days of the web, it was not uncommon to land on a website and have music play. Developers and website owners were excited to use sound online because it was new and novel. Eventually though, most development teams learned that users generally found sound on websites annoying, and the trend went away. Ironically though, just as the integration of sound within a website has become less popular, the support of sound natively within HTML has improved. In HTML 5, the audio tag allows you to load, play, and pause sounds, as well as set duration and volume.

Sound and the User Experience
Sound can have a significant impact on a user's experience of interactive media. Auditory enhancement of interactive media permits a "more natural human-computer communication." (Bombardieri et al., 2003) which boosts usability.

Sound can also be used to manipulate the user. In video games, "background music improves the narrative experience and can guide the player through the game." It has also been shown to have had an impact on cognitive control (Zhang & Fu, 2015) and promote deeper engagement. For example, researchers found that electronic slot machines that produce more winning sounds are preferred over ones without, arousing the participants both "psychophysically and psychologically" (Dixon et al., 2014).

Composing Sound with MIDI

All of the types of digital sound (WAVs, AIFFs and MP3s) that we have discussed so far fall into the category of sampled sound, where the data within the file is stored as a description of the sound. MIDI files, however, are different from sampled sounds because they are stored as a series of commands. Within the MIDI file, there are codes for specific instruments notes and direction about their force and duration. A MIDI file is much like a musical score.

MIDI systems are often used by composers who "record" their compositions in MIDI format. The simplest MIDI system is a keyboard, a synthesizer and some speakers. The keyboard is used for composition, the synthesizer records the composition, and the speakers play the sounds. The benefit of recording the composition in a MIDI format is that the notes can easily be assigned to different instruments and adjusted over many iterations. A MIDI file is analogous to a vector file as both are stored as a set of commands. For integration within most interactive media, a MIDI file would need to be exported as an MP3 file or one of the other common sampled sound formats.

VIDEO IN INTERACTIVE DIGITAL MEDIA

Film and Video Convergence

Film and video have been around for a long time but were based on very different technologies. Analog film was invented in the late 1800s. To make film, images were recorded on a transparent medium and then projected onto a screen. Until the late 1920s, film was a silent medium, and viewings were accompanied by live musicians. Film remained the only type of moving picture for several decades until analog video was invented in the 1950s. Analog video stored continuously varying electrical voltages on a magnetic tape that produced images on a cathode ray tube monitor or a projection screen.

In the 1990s, digital video emerged. Digital video is a series of bitmap images synced with digital audio. Like images and audio, digital video is stored on the computer as 1s and 0s, albeit a lot more 1 and 0s than a still image or an audio file. Initially digital video cameras stored media on magnetic tape, but now most are tapeless and the digital information is simply stored on a memory card in the camera.

Digital video is comprised of images played in rapid succession, just like a flip book you might have made as a kid. Each image captures an instance of motion, and when those images are played in rapid succession, our eyes are tricked into seeing continuous movement. This phenomenon is called the "persistence of vision theory," but in order for it to work, the images must be displayed fairly quickly, at least 15 images per second. If the images are displayed any slower, the eye is not fooled and the viewer will see the individual images as opposed to motion.

■ Media Content

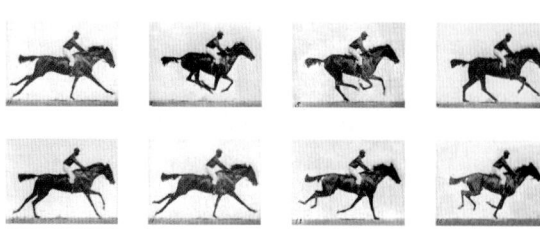

5.17
Images displayed in rapid succession create the illusion of movement.
Source: Edited image of Muybridge Animation © User Waugsberg; original available from Wikimedia Commons.

Quality of Digital Video

There are three factors that contribute to the quality of digital video.

- screen resolution
- frame rate
- compression method

The screen resolution refers to the number of pixels captured in each frame: the higher the resolution, the higher the quality and the larger the file size. High-definition TV broadcasts in 1280 × 720 pixels. But video used in other contexts does not necessarily need to be of such high resolution.

Frame rate also affects the quality of digital video. The standard frame rate for digital video is 30 frames per second. When you reduce the frame rate, you reduce the file size because fewer frames are needed throughout the duration of the video. However, if the frame rate is too low then the persistence of vision theory will no longer apply.

Compression is a third factor that affects the quality of digital video, and can have a dramatic effect on file size. The look of the video should dictate the type of compression used. There are many different video compression codecs, but most can be categorized as either intra-frame or inter-frame. Intra-frame codecs create compression similar to JPEG compression, summarizing runs of similar pixels frame by frame. Inter-frame codecs are different because they achieve compression by finding similarities between frames and summarizing that information. Inter-frame compression would be ideal if you were compressing a documentary with a lot of "talking heads" because a large number of pixels would not change between frames. Another type of compression is variable bitrate encoding where you can opt to use fewer bits to describe the colors in your video. It would be a good type of compression for video content with a limited color palette, like a cartoon.

Working with Digital Video

Working with digital video has become easier over the past 20 years. When digital video was stored on tapes, the content would need to be captured into the computer. Newer, tapeless digital cameras are easier to use: the footage on the camera's memory card can be easily copied onto a hard drive. Tapeless cameras were made possible due to advances in solid-state memory which is the same type of memory used on a flash drive. It has no moving parts and is resistant to movement and shock.

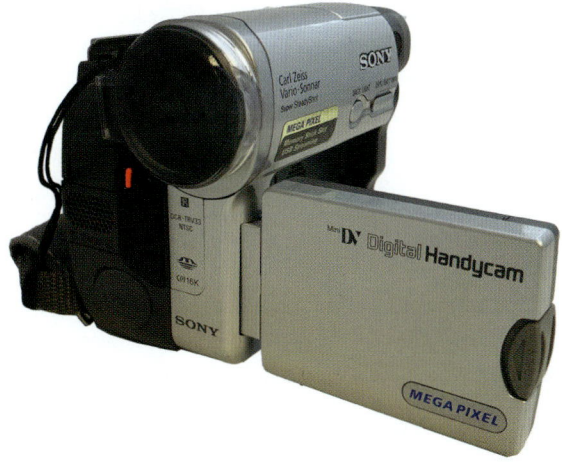

5.18
Mini DV (digital video) camera recorded onto Mini DV tapes

Additional challenges early digital video presented were large file sizes, long rendering times and a lack of processing power. Also, limited bandwidth and a lack of standards prevented much video from being shown online. Fortunately, many of these challenges have become less so within the past few years. Better compression algorithms have made video file sizes smaller, and portable hard drives for video storage have become a lot less expensive and more durable. Improved computer processing power allows for real-time previewing while editing and shortened rendering times. Delivery of video content over the Internet has become more feasible as well, since Internet bandwidth has improved.

Obtaining Digital Video

Video content can come from a variety of sources such as TV stations, personal collections, academic archives, or stock footage sites and formats, both analog and digital. If your source material is analog, e.g. a Super 8 film, you can digitize it by projecting it and filming the projection. If your material is on a video tape, you can often connect the VHS machine directly into a digital video camera and play the VHS tape while recording with the digital video camera. Content on DVDs can be extracted using specialized software. Generic footage, such as an overhead shot of a specific city, can often be obtained from a stock video site. In any of these scenarios, however, make sure you understand copyright law and whether you have permission to use it.

Shooting Digital Video

Sometimes the simplest way to obtain digital video is to shoot it yourself. A video shoot requires planning and preparation. Before shooting, you should have a list of shots you need and the order in which you plan to get them. You should also scout out the shooting environment and know what the weather will be like. It's a good idea to shoot your video on more than one camera and capture more than one source of audio so that you can be sure that you have more content

■ Media Content

than you need, especially if the event you are filming can't easily be recreated. Usually a video shoot will involve people other than yourself (i.e. your subjects and crew), so you want to use your time efficiently.

Part of planning your shots is to think about what types of shots you need. Certain types of shots lend themselves well to communicating your intended message.

- **Pans** (when you move the camera from side to side) help give perspective to a scene.
- **Zooms** can be used to communicate an important detail or help convey an emotion. For example, if you wanted to show that a character was upset, zooming in on the character's teary eyes would help convey this idea.

There are many other types of shots (e.g. establishing, cutaway, point of view, reverse angle, over the shoulder, etc…) that serve distinct visual communication purposes.

The framing of your shot can also benefit or impede your communication objective. The "rule of thirds" is widely embraced as a guideline for framing a video shot. The way to apply the rule is to look at your frame and divide it into nine equal segments then line your subject up on the intersection of lines facing the empty area in the frame. This technique helps to ensure adequate side and headroom and establishes asymmetric balance.

It's often tempting to shoot your video without a tripod, but video content is rarely acceptable when shot without a tripod, as the resulting footage is often shaky and jittery. There are some techniques that you can use to stabilize your camera if you have to shoot without a tripod, but, again, these should be avoided at all costs unless the shaky camera movement is the intended effect.

Editing Digital Video

Editing digital video is quite different from editing film and analog video. Editing film was a physical process where the editor literally cut apart film and taped it back together to make a final piece. This process destroyed the original footage, so an editor had to be very judicious when making any edits.

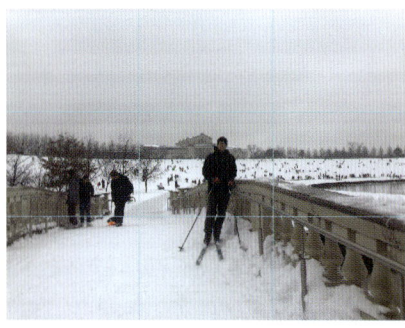

Rule of thirds not applied

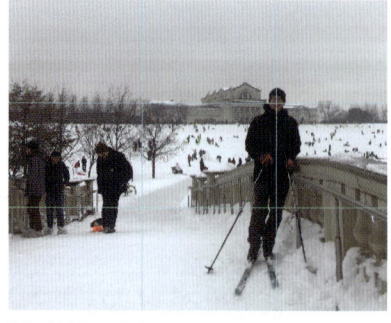

Rule of thirds applied

5.19
Applying the rule of thirds can improve your composition

Editing analog video was done by copying portions of one tape onto another in the desired sequence. The editor would swap out the source tapes in one of the two side-by-side connected video players after recording the desired piece. The problem with analog video editing was that each time you copied the copy, the quality diminished.

Digital video editing programs offer a huge leap ahead of film and analog video editing processes. The biggest benefit was the ability of the editor to work nonlinearly and be able to go back and make changes. Another benefit is that the original source footage does not get destroyed as it would in film editing. And finally, unlike in analog video editing, there is no degradation in quality when copies are made of copies.

There are many digital video editing applications that share similar traits: consumer-grade programs like iMovie that comes installed on every Mac computer, prosumer applications like Final Cut Pro and Adobe Premiere and professional level editing programs like Avid's Media Composer. While they all offer different features, they all have a pretty similar interface. Each of them has a Library window where your source video clips, images and audio are stored, a preview area to view your edited footage and a timeline where you sequence and sync your video and audio tracks. Tools for splitting clips and adding transitions are similar across these applications as well.

When editing is done, you need to render out the finished video, specifying frame rate, frame size, and compression type that best suits your end use. Rendering can take a while because the software needs to create all the frames that make up the final video file.

File Formats

Video editing programs allow you to export your video files in a variety of formats.

- AVI is one of most universally accepted and the oldest video formats developed by Microsoft.
- FLV are videos encoded by Adobe Edge Animate (formerly Flash Video), and are used on many online platforms because they are highly compressed while retaining good quality.
- WMV is a video format developed by Microsoft with dramatic compression.
- MOV is the Quicktime format developed by Apple. It is a fairly universal file format and tends to be high quality and large in file size.
- MP4 is short for MPEG4. Like the MP3 audio format, MP4 is highly compressed while retaining good quality. It's supported natively in HTML.

Video in Interactive Digital Media

Video has been integrated into interactive experiences since the early days of multimedia. But because video files were so large, they were not suitable for playback over networked interactive media. Until the mid 2000s, the web remained mostly video free.

■ Media Content

In addition to limited bandwidth, the lack of standards for how to integrate the video kept it from being used in many websites. Now, however, video is supported natively in HTML 5. You simply save your video as an MP4 file, reference it in your HTML using the VIDEO tag and upload the video and your HTML file to your web server.

The advent of YouTube in 2005 revolutionized online video and its ability to be integrated within a website. Once a content creator uploads a video to YouTube, it can easily be integrated on a website by copying the code provided by YouTube into the HTML code. The benefit of displaying a YouTube video on your website is that the video resides on the YouTube server (and not yours) and the method of display is universally supported. And, as YouTube has evolved, it has become more generous with the size of videos it allows you to upload and better at compressing them.

YouTube has done more than revolutionized how we integrate video on our websites, it's also become an amazing tool for the entrepreneur. It has allowed content creators to build followings by showing off a talent or expertise which can then become a foundation for a business and/or earn advertising revenue.

TEXT

Writing is important in many disciplines and interactive digital media is no exception. Different styles of writing (often used in combination) are needed for production of documents as well as in the interactive applications themselves, including:

- persuasive writing
- instructional writing
- efficient writing
- writing to show personality and build connections
- search engine friendly writing

Audience, context and objective should dictate which of these styles you use.

Persuasive Writing

Persuasive writing is text intended to convince someone to do something and can be found in the following contexts.

- **Proposals**. Most projects begin with a proposal, where you, as a developer, are proposing a solution to a client's problem. To increase your chances of landing the project, your writing should be crafted to convince the client to choose you.
- **Audits**. An audit is a document often created by an outside consultant who assesses a company's interactive application (typically a website) and offers advice on what should be altered to better achieve its goal. In an audit, the writer should make observations, and explain the effect—good or bad. The

audit should not contain opinion statements to downplay personal bias. And, every critical statement should be backed up with some type of rationale. As the author of the site audit, it's beneficial to be encouraging and persuasive because you might get asked to actually do the redesign project.

- **Ads**. Ads are integrated on websites, apps, games and before, during and after videos. For any ad to be effective, it has to be succinct, eye-catching and persuasive. Google is a popular ad network in which ads have a very prescribed structure: three lines, with the title of the ad on the first line, the URL below it and then two additional lines of text. Because characters are so limited, the ad writer needs to be extremely efficient and persuasive to encourage the user to click.
- **Social media posts**. Social media marketing posts are often intended to persuade a viewer to take action, but must commence by engaging the viewer. A common strategy is to start by asking a question that speaks directly to their needs, wants, or interests, then providing some enticing information without disclosing everything. Finally, provide a link. The most effective methods to persuade a viewer to take action, are somewhat platform dependent. In other words, the methods you use to engage people on Twitter might be very different from how you engage users on Facebook. Generally, though, a positive post is going to engage visitors more than a negative one. Posts with a picture get more attention than ones without. And posts that request the user to do something tend to get more clicks than ones that don't.
- **Game scripts**. Persuasive writing is critical in a gaming script as the objective is to get the player to engage more deeply within the game.

Instructional Writing

Instructional writing is writing that's designed to teach someone how to do something, and it can be found in almost all forms of interactive media. Many games, apps and kiosks incorporate help screens or at least simple instructions explaining how to use them. Think about the first time someone checks in at an airport kiosk. How do they know how to interact? In these scenarios instructional writing takes center stage.

Some of the challenges in writing instructions within interactive media include:

- **Using universally understood language**. Even people from different parts of the United States interpret words differently. For example, New Englanders call their groceries "bundles," where a Midwesterner may think they are referring to hay or a bundle of joy.
- **Fitting it all in**. On a smartphone, there is limited screen real estate so you don't have a lot of room for text.
- **Limited attention spans and low frustration tolerance**. If an application is not intuitive enough to be immediately understood and visitors are reading instructions, they are probably already frustrated.

■ Media Content

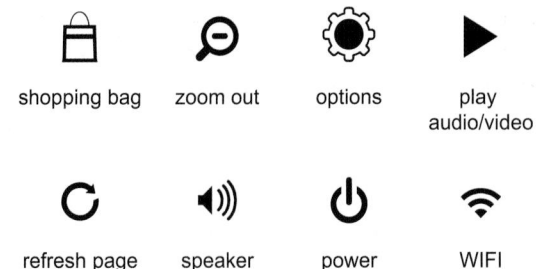

5.20
Many icons can take the place of words

Instructional writing should be clear and concise. But, sometimes instructive writing shouldn't actually be written. It's often more efficient to use an icon to provide directive, especially if the icon is universally understood.

If users access help screens, they are usually trying to get a question answered. But sometimes they don't find the desired answer on the first try. Therefore, help screens should be searchable as well as highly indexed with a rich system of cross links to allow visitors to easily click to get to a related topic if they land on information that isn't quite what they want.

Writing for Efficient Communication

Efficient communication is important in almost every context because readers have a limited attention span. This is especially relevant when writing website copy and social media posts for marketing purposes. Always consider how you can make it as easy as possible for your visitors to get your point.

Web copy needs to be written for scan-ability. When your website is text heavy, it should be broken up with headings and subheadings so that a visitor can scan through the document and get a sense for what each section is about. Anchor links (links that take you to a lower place on the page) are also very helpful for breaking up large chunks of text and communicating more efficiently.

Efficiency is key when it comes to writing social media posts. People typically scan their news feeds really quickly, so it's imperative to deliver concise messages. Compare the following social media posts.

"Come visit Nationwide furniture this weekend and check out our sale going on at all locations. All sofas are on sale for up to 50% off the regular price. Sale period: 8/28–9/1"

"Need a great deal on furniture? Shop Nationwide furniture: 8/28–9/1. S-A-L-E"

These posts essentially say the same thing, but the one on the right is written more efficiently and tells the reader exactly what to do.

Writing to Show Personality and Build Connections

When you write with a distinct voice, it allows people to better understand and connect with the brand you are representing. If there's no personality or flavor to a brand, then there's nothing for a visitor to identify with. The key in writing with personality is to use a style appropriate for the brand and the target audience and be consistent across all platforms.

Consider the following two social media posts and their different tones. What does the tone tell you about the brand and the target audience?

"See Who Reads Your Tweets! Amazing Disney Princess Facts! Vanessa Hudgens Surprises! FanCeleb Body Image Quotes!"

"Colorful kicks, friendship bracelets, personalized backpacks—these crafts are a blast to make and even more fun to rock on the first day of class."

In the first example, every word has the first letter capitalized, and every short sentence ends with an exclamation point. In the second example, the writing still has a fun tone but is more relaxed. The writing on the left was written for a tween demographic, as it's a little bit more upbeat, excited and fun. It was actually taken off of the Seventeen Magazine website. The second example is definitely positive but more sophisticated. It was copy from the Martha Stewart website whose readers are a bit more mature.

Blogging is a platform where it's often beneficial to show personality. If a customer falls in love with the personality of the blog, they will likely fall in love with the brand. For example, the site Young House Love was built by a young couple who blogged about remodeling their house. The writing has a fun DIY tone which has garnered a lot of attention, followers and traffic. Now they earn advertising revenue and sell products on the site. The personality of the blog is what readers have connected with and made it so popular.

Writing for Search Engine Optimization

Search engines scour text-based content and rank websites for various keywords based on several factors including the relevance of the keyword to their text. Almost everyone wants their website to be found by search engines, and writing strategically can help.

The first step in "search engine optimizing" a website, is to first decide what terms you are optimizing for. Start by brainstorming a list of keywords and phrases that your target audience might be using that relate to your site. Then you should use a keyword planning tool to find related search terms with high search volume and low competition. These are good ones to target.

Once you identify your target keywords, you should structure your site around them. Naming pages after your targeted keywords tells search engines that the page is relevant to those terms. You should also strategically integrate those search terms on your page. Search engines deem copy in certain areas of your page such as your title, headings, alt tags and links more relevant for categorization than others. Therefore, it makes sense to integrate your target keywords in these areas.

■ Media Content

Since search engines love text, adding a blog to your site is a great strategy for search engine optimization. Since most blogs contain a lot of text, it should capture searches, especially if it is optimized well. Many bloggers base their posts around key phrases they are targeting. The power of search engine optimization has made it possible for anyone to be perceived to be the most relevant to almost anything.

PRACTITIONER INTERVIEW

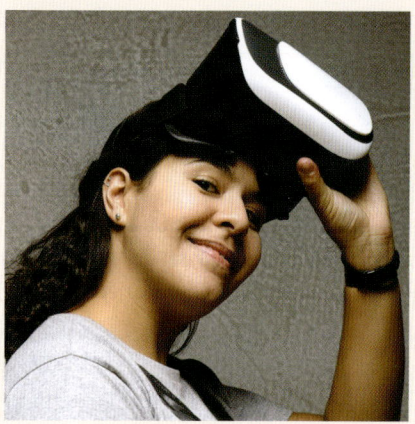

Ana Monte

Sound designer and co-founder of DELTA Soundworks, Sandhausen, Germany
Ana Monte is the co-founder of DELTA Soundworks, a sound design company based in Sandhausen, Germany that does audio post-production for virtual reality and other immersive experiences. One of their recent projects has been to create sound for the Stanford Virtual Heart, an innovative, interactive virtual reality training tool that takes the medical trainee inside and around a virtual heart, helping them to better understand pediatric heart problems and learn how to treat them.

What's your background and how did you get into this industry?

I studied music industry and technology in California for my Bachelor's degree. In my last semester, I actually took a class called "audio for video" and I just fell in love with Foley techniques and manipulating sound and creating stuff out of noise, not necessarily [making] music.

I ended up in Germany because I did an internship at a theater in Berlin and I just fell in love with the city. While I was doing the internship, I met someone from Film Academy Baden-Württemberg, and [I learned that] I could study there for free which was amazing, because it is really great. They get nominated for student Oscars almost every year.

What type of projects do you like to do?

I've been doing [audio for] traditional formats [of media] like movies for about five years, but I got into immersive audio when we founded DELTA. The application and approach is a bit different than [creating audio for] traditional media because the workflow is non-existent. I jump from software to software because virtual reality is kind of swimming in between game and traditional media. [Once we create the sound,] how we implement it in the platform in the end is very different depending on what the experience is going to be. I often work in Unity and Unreal Engine.

When did you start DELTA Soundworks and how did you land the Stanford virtual reality pediatric heart project?

In June of 2016 we started DELTA on paper. [My partner and I] did our contract between the two of us and then we applied for some startup awards. In Germany, [there is a program called] "Kultur- Und Kreativpiloten Deutschland," and they give an award to the 32 most creative startups in Germany every year. We ended up winning that award about two months after we founded the company.

Shortly after getting started, we attended a really huge tech IT tradeshow. They had an area for VR where we met David and David, the Stanford guys [who were working on the pediatric heart virtual reality experience]. One David is the top pediatric surgeon at Stanford and the other David is the 3D expert. They were just there with their laptops and asked if we would like to check out their experience. We were blown away! It's really an amazing experience. But then we were like "oh there's no sound, you guys need sound!" And that's how the journey started with them, actually.

Initially we thought [the sounds would be] user interface sounds like "clicky-clicky " [Then we learned that] sound is the first thing that a doctor uses to diagnose a patient by listening through the stethoscope. Medical students train their ears [to listen] for the different sounds that the heart makes [to diagnose different problems].

How did you record the heart sounds?

That was a very long process. Initially we wanted to record original heart stuff, but, obviously we're talking about babies and that's super difficult to find. With some of the diseases, there's only like a thousand kids in the whole world that even have this.

■ Media Content

So, we [created the sounds ourselves from] reference sounds. They call [the sound made by the heart] "lub dub" which the doctors think is the sound of two valves that are closing, one valve is the "lub" and the other valve is the "dub." [To make these sounds we needed to figure out] what does a lub sound like? What about a dub? And what does this murmur that happens when there's a hole [sound like]? We analyzed the frequency characteristics of each element and then rebuilt them from scratch actually using synthesizers and recording random stuff. Some sounds were real recordings of healthy hearts because the "lub dub" is always the same. It was very important that that it was medically accurate because that's what the students will be using to learn the sounds. Measuring how many milliseconds are between them can tell you if there's a certain problem. We used the numbers [provided by the doctors to help us with the timing].

In some conditions, a new sound is introduced. For example, one heart problem with kids is called VSD (ventricular septal defect) when there is a hole between the two chambers of the heart. So besides also doing the "lub dub," there is also a sound like a garden hose. So instead of hearing "lub dub lub dub," it sounds like a "lub murmur dub, lub murmur dub." It's really freaky the first time you hear it.

The other challenging part was to make the sound spatialized because in the virtual reality experience you can teleport yourself inside the heart and hear and see the heart from the inside. When you are inside the heart, you may hear the "lub" from here and the "dub" from there. You need to be able to determine where a hole is based on where the sound is coming from.

What are some of the challenges in creating sound for VR?

Sound is always considered after the images are made and that stays true for VR. Unfortunately, people know sound is important, but when it comes to paying the price, they don't want to. It's hard enough to explain to people what is stereo, and what is surround. When you get into the spatial audio realm, that gets even more complicated. People don't get it.

As far as VR goes, immersive audio is a must. You need to be in that space 100 percent, and you need the sound source to come from where the thing is. But, it's still a challenge to convince people that sound is important.

What are some of the biggest mistakes people make integrating sound into an interactive experience?

I think there's a lot of projects where there's one dude doing everything and we're just delivering the assets instead of actually having control. That gets really tricky because they don't have the [spatial] sound experience. They're just focused on integrating the sound at the end. But there's still a lot to be done once you put sound in the experience. You need to spatialize the sound. We've had [to fix] a lot of projects where [the sound was integrated wrong], for example a church bell that should be on the right but it's actually coming from back left. People don't know what you're talking about [when you point this out]. It's just not something people pay attention to.

What's the weirdest thing that you've done to generate some kind of a sound effect?

[For a project in college], I needed to give voices to some aliens. So, I asked my friend to say some weird German things. She said something like "pork ribs don't taste well if you don't eat salad with it." I then reversed it and added some sound effects and it sounded so bizarre. We laugh about it all the time. I have recorded my cat many times to make monster sounds. I also record myself making weird noises with my mouth.

What's the most fun thing about doing sound for interactive media?

[Working on virtual reality experiences], sound has gotten a little bit more attention than in traditional media. I think people know from the beginning they want good sound and they budget for it. So the sound team is involved from day one. When doing sound for traditional media, you're usually the last one involved and are there to solve problems. A good VR experience needs to be immersive, so we work together from the beginning and, as the sound person, you feel more a part of the team.

DISCUSSION QUESTIONS

1) Where have you seen 3D graphics integrated into interactive applications? In what context do you think these types of graphics would be most effective?
2) Give a *specific* example of a project where you would choose to create a vector graphic or a bitmap graphic. Why would you make this choice? Explain.
3) Have you experienced audio in interactive media? If so, where? Did you find it to be distracting? Annoying? Helpful?
4) Why do you think video has become increasingly integrated into interactive digital media applications?
5) How do you feel about video content creation being so accessible to anyone with a camera? Do you see this as an opportunity or an annoyance? Can you imagine ways in which posting YouTube videos on a niche topic could benefit you in your career and entrepreneurial endeavors?

■ Media Content

REFERENCES

Bombardieri, E., Aktolun, C., Baum, R. P., Bishof-Delaloye, A., Buscombe, J., Chatal, J. F., Maffioli, L., Moncayo, R., Mortelmans, L., & Reske, S. N. (2003). FDG-PET: Procedure Guidelines for Tumour Imaging. *European Journal of Nuclear Medicine and Molecular Imaging*, *30*(12) B115–B124. Online. Available at: <https://doi.org/10.1007/s00259-003-1355-2>.

Dixon, M. J., Harrigan, K. A., Santesso, D. L., Graydon, C., Fugelsang, J. A., & Collins, K. (2014). The Impact of Sound in Modern Multiline Video Slot Machine Play. *Journal of Gambling Studies*, *30*(4), 913–929. Online. Available at: <https://doi.org/10.1007/s10899-013-9391-8>.

Zhang, J., & Fu, X. (2015). Background Music Matters: Why Strategy Video Game Increased Cognitive Control. *Journal of Biomusical Engineering*, 3(105). Online. Available at: <https://doi.org/10.4172/2090-2719.1000105>.

6 Aesthetics in Interactive Digital Media

INTRODUCTION

What makes interactive media "aesthetically pleasing?" It depends on who you ask. We all have different biases and preferences, so there is no right answer. However, interactive media is a visual medium with a goal of facilitating efficient, effective and enjoyable communication between the user and the device. If the aesthetics work against these goals, it is problematic; if it supports them, it is good.

While media elements play a supporting role, the interface of an interactive application is usually the more dominant factor in defining the overall look and feel. Type, color and layout of the interface elements are the key tools at a designer's disposal that influence the overall aesthetic.

TYPOGRAPHY

Almost every form of interactive digital media contains some type of text which makes it an integral and powerful element in the overall design. Typographic choices can have a radical effect on how it is perceived, affecting usability and readability. Once you start to recognize the unique characteristics of typefaces, you will be able to make more informed type-related choices.

The Power of Typefaces

Looking at the following four restaurant signs below, do you get a different impression about the food and atmosphere in my restaurant? When I show this example to my students, they almost always unanimously respond: 1—barbeque, 2—sports bar, 3—vegetarian restaurant or café, and 4—upscale Italian. When I ask them which one is the most expensive, it's always number 4. It's amazing that they can draw such distinct conclusions from these signs even though the name on all four is exactly the same. Clearly, the typography is communicating more than the text itself.

Because the style of type can immediately evoke a feeling, it important that it conveys an appropriate tone. Good typography can be very powerful, enhancing your intended message; bad typography can undermine it.

■ Aesthetics in Interactive Digital Media

❶ **Julie's Restaurant**

❷ JULIE'S RESTAURANT

❸ Julie's Restaurant

❹ *Julie's Restaurant*

6.1
The typeface used for my fictional restaurant says more about the restaurant than the words themselves

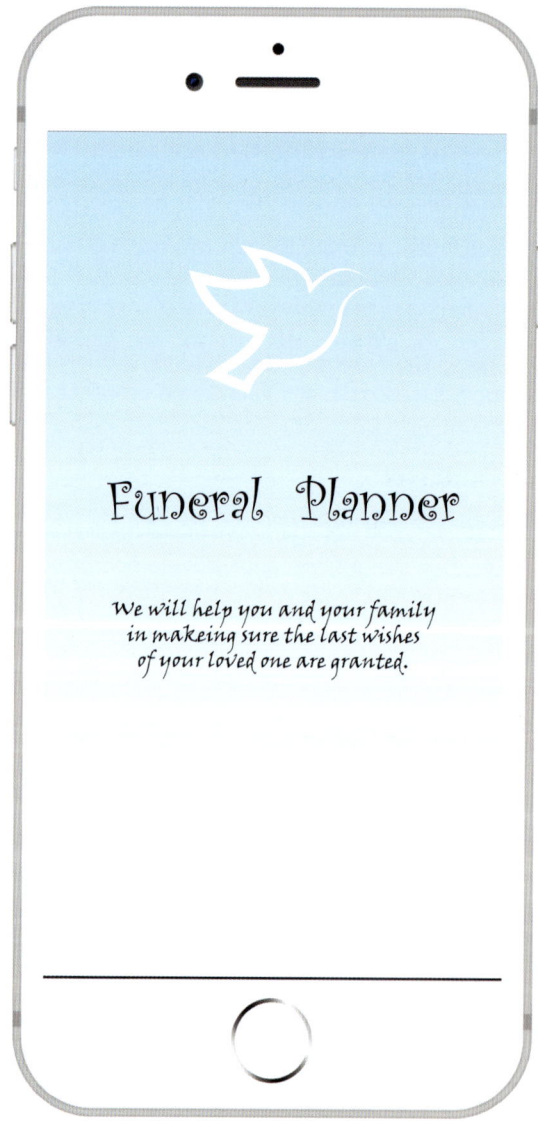

6.2
In this app, the typography style is in conflict with the content and it feels off

Type Properties and Definitions

A typeface is a family of characters sharing a common design. It is different than a font, a more specific term, including weight, size and style of the type you are using. For example, your font might be "Arial," while your typeface could be "Arial 12-point bold."

Many type families have members that are of varied weights and horizontal spacing. The weight of the typeface refers to the thickness of the lines within the letters. An example of a heavier weight typeface would be Arial Black which is thicker and bolder than the standard Arial. Heavier weighted typefaces can be used effectively for emphasis.

Condensed vs. extended text refers to how spaced out or compressed the letters are. A condensed variant of a typeface has less space between letters and extended text has more.

Serif vs. Sans Serif

Two very broad categories of typefaces are serifs and sans serifs. Some common examples of serif typefaces include Times and Palatino. Sans serif typefaces include Arial and Helvetica. To differentiate between serif and sans serif typefaces, look at the words rendered in Times and Palatino. You can see that at the start and end of each of the letters, there's a little foot which delineates the end of the letter form. The word, serif, comes from the Dutch word meaning "line," therefore, serif typefaces are ones with extra lines at the end of each letterform. Since the word sans means "without," sans serif typefaces don't have the lines. Another differentiator is that serif typefaces have varying stroke weights but sans serifs do not. Of course, there are many novelty typefaces that are neither serifs nor sans serifs, but most of the type you encounter within interactive media is either a serif or sans serif typeface.

Serif and sans serif typefaces have inherent stylistic qualities. Serif typefaces tend to look more traditional which makes them an appropriate choice when you want to imply something is older and more established. Conversely, if you want to project a more modern feel, a sans serif would be more appropriate. Sans serif typefaces look more modern because they were invented in the 1920s in the Bauhaus School of Design. Serif typefaces, on the other hand, date

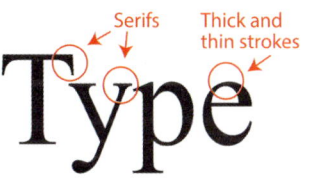
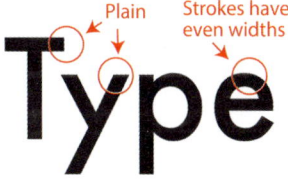

6.3
Differing characteristics of serif and sans serif typefaces

Aesthetics in Interactive Digital Media

back 650 years to the invention of the printing press which is why they look older and more traditional.

Serifs and sans serifs have different levels of legibility in different contexts. Serif typefaces are more legible on a printed page, whereas sans serif typefaces are more legible on the screen. With ink on a page, you can articulate more detail than with pixels on a screen. Have you ever noticed that just about every book you open up has body copy set in a serif typeface? On a printed page, the little serif lines that delineate the end of the letter form are crisp and clear, making it easier to read with optimal comprehension. Sans serifs, on the other hand, are more legible on a screen. Because computer monitors and mobile device screens are lower resolution than a printed page, serifs look muddy and blurry when rendered at a small scale on a screen, and are therefore more difficult to read. For this reason, most body copy on websites and in apps is rendered in a sans serif typeface.

Case

Have you ever received an email or text entirely in uppercase? Did you actually read it or quickly hit delete? Reading text set entirely in caps is uncomfortable because it feels like the author is shouting at you. It also is more difficult to read due to the fact that each word takes on a blocky shape. So, when we encounter a block of text set in all caps, it will take us longer to read—that is, if we read it at all.

Tracking, Kerning and Leading

Graphics programs like Adobe Illustrator and Photoshop allow you to manipulate the tracking, kerning and leading of a block of type for legibility or for stylistic effect. Kerning and tracking both pertain to the space between characters, however kerning refers to the space between two specific characters, and tracking

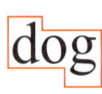
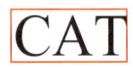
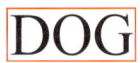

This leading is the default leading.

This leading is is a larger leading.

Before kerning: **W M**
After kerning: **WM**

This is a tighter track.
This is a looser track.

6.4
If the words are rendered in all caps, they take on a blocky shape. But, when they are lowercase, they each have a more distinct shape Setting type in all caps is not always a bad idea. For small amounts of text, rendering type in uppercase is acceptable, especially when the objective is to differentiate the words visually from the ones around it.

6.5
Tracking, kerning and leading can be adjusted for dramatic effect

is the spacing between a group of characters. Tracking is useful when you want to force text to align with something on the left and the right.

The space between lines of text is called the leading, and it is measured from baseline to baseline. Therefore, the leading setting is almost always larger than the type size. Leading can be manipulated in graphic applications, as well as in your HTML/CSS code when you're building a web-based application using the CSS attribute line-height. Increasing your leading improves the legibility of your text, because that extra bit of whitespace can make it easier for a reader to make out the letter forms. However, when leading is too large, it can be visually confusing. Most authoring applications have similar controls for modifying tracking, leading and kerning.

Alignment and Justification

In Western culture, most text we encounter is left aligned due to the fact that we read from left to right. With left aligned text, each line has the same starting point; the eye knows exactly where to go to start reading the next line. With center and right aligned text, each line starts at a different place, so your eye has to search for the starting point after reading each line. This extra bit of effort makes center and right aligned text more difficult to read and left-aligned text more suitable for large blocks of text.

Center aligned text tends to look formal is because we are used to seeing it in wedding invitations and poetry. Some websites like Williams Sonoma and the Knot take advantage of the inherent formal quality of center aligned text and use it extensively in their graphics to associate their brand and products with a wedding or other special events.

Other instances where center aligned text can be effective is when there is a very limited amount of type in the design. Placing the type in the center can make it the primary focus. Consider the interface of the Google website. Everything is centered which helps communicate the singular purpose of Google: to start searching.

Right alignment is used sparingly because it's more difficult to read. However, captions on photos are often right aligned to visually contrast against the body copy which is usually all left aligned. This contrast clues the reader in that the caption text is different from the body copy and thus has a different purpose.

Justification adjusts line lengths to produce straight edges on left and right margins. Newspaper columns are often set in justified paragraphs. The tricky aspect of justification is that in order to have a straight edge along the left and a straight edge along the right then the tracking within each line of text will be inconsistent and you may get some awkward spacing between words and letters. Justified text is not often used within interactive media.

Making adjustments to the text's tracking and kerning can really change the feel of some text. I noticed this after watching a film by Fritz Lang, the German expressionist filmmaker from the 1930s, who integrates his personal logo on

■ Aesthetics in Interactive Digital Media

No text styling

FRITZ
LANG
FILM

After tracking and leading adjustments

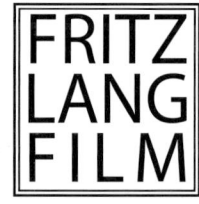

6.6
This distinct logo was made possible by tracking and kerning

the last frame of all of his films. The logo is really simple; it's just his name and the word "film." But the way the type has been manipulated makes the words more distinct. If the words were rendered with default type settings it would have looked like the example on the left, but by manipulating the tracking and the leading and putting a box around the words, the type looks more stylized, like a logo.

Type Within Interactive Media

Typography was somewhat limited on early websites. Web developers used to only choose common typefaces that came installed on Macs and PCs to ensure that the client computer accessing the site would be able to render the correct typeface. If the client computer didn't have the typeface specified by the developer, a random alternative would be used.

One way web developers avoided this problem was to render areas with specialized typefaces as a graphic. Unfortunately, text as an image can't be parsed by search engines, and users can't copy and paste the text. In the early days of the web, however, some designers laid out entire pages as images in order to have precise control over the layout of the type.

Fortunately, HTML technology has improved quite a bit. Now developers can actually package a typeface with the web page and specify that typeface in the code. So, it no longer matters if the client computer has the specific typeface installed. The most common method of integrating a wide variety of unique typefaces in HTML-based interactive media is to incorporate Google Fonts which are freely available, and assure consistency in appearance across browsers. In app and game development the typeface is packaged in the final files assuring that the end user will see the appropriate typeface.

PDF documents are prevalent online, offering the advantage of maintaining the original formatting and typefaces chosen by the designer across all platforms. PDF documents are usually designed to be print-friendly, can be indexed by search engines, and viewed within the browser window. Documents like manuals and resumes are ideal to post as PDFs because people tend to print them, and when they do, they will maintain all type and layout properties.

Aesthetics in Interactive Digital Media

COLOR

Color plays a large role within all forms of interactive media and "can carry important meaning, [having] an important impact on people's affect, cognition, and behavior"(Elliot & Maier, 2014). Colors have different associations across cultures and are preferred differently across generations and sexes.

Part of the interactive digital media design process involves choosing a color palette. It's tempting to start building a color palette based on your own personal preferences, but it's usually not the best choice. Recognizing implications of colors and how they work together will help you make color choices in line with your objective.

The Impact of the Color Wheel

Viewers have different physiological responses to colors based on their position in the color wheel. Warm colors like reds, oranges and bright yellows have more energy, while cool colors like blues, greens, and some purples tend to be more relaxed. In a study comparing performance of warm versus cool colored ads, researchers found that ads with predominantly warm colors received substantially higher click through rates than their cooler counterparts (Sokolik et al., 2014). Perhaps the users deemed the warmer, higher-energy ads more exciting which inspired them to click? In this context, clearly warm colors were a good choice. But, would you create a sleep app that was predominantly orange? Probably not.

The relationship of colors to each other on a color wheel also has an effect on their communication value.

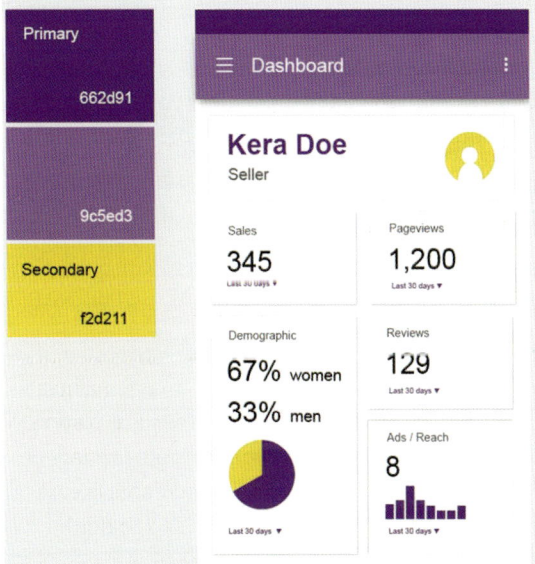

6.7
This app has a color palette comprised of complementary colors

■ Aesthetics in Interactive Digital Media

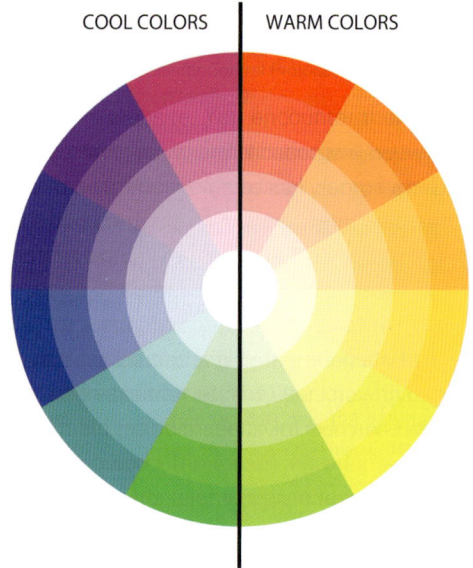

6.8
Warm and cool colors sit on opposite sides of the color wheel

Complementary Colors
Complementary colors are ones on opposite sides of the color wheel. When placed next to each other, they tend to have an energizing feel and can be used to draw attention to an element on the screen. Complementary colors include orange and blue, yellow and purple, and red and green.

Analogous Colors
Analogous colors are ones that sit next to each other on the color wheel, e.g. blue and green. Analogous color schemes tend to have a more relaxed, natural feel.

Triadic Colors
Triadic colors are ones that are spaced evenly around the color wheel, forming an equilateral triangle. The combination of these colors is quite vibrant; therefore, it is recommended to use one color in the triad as the dominant color and the other two as accents.

Split Complementary
Split complementary colors are colors that form an isosceles triangle with their positions on the color wheel. A split complementary color scheme is like a complementary color scheme in that it has strong visual contrast, but with less energy and tension.

Choosing a Color Palette
Like choosing typefaces, defining colors early in the design process makes your work easier because you have narrowed down your options. As you start building

Aesthetics in Interactive Digital Media

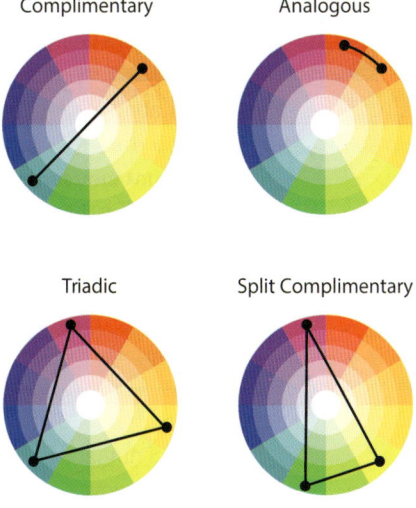

6.9
Relationships of colors within the color wheel can impact their effect when used together

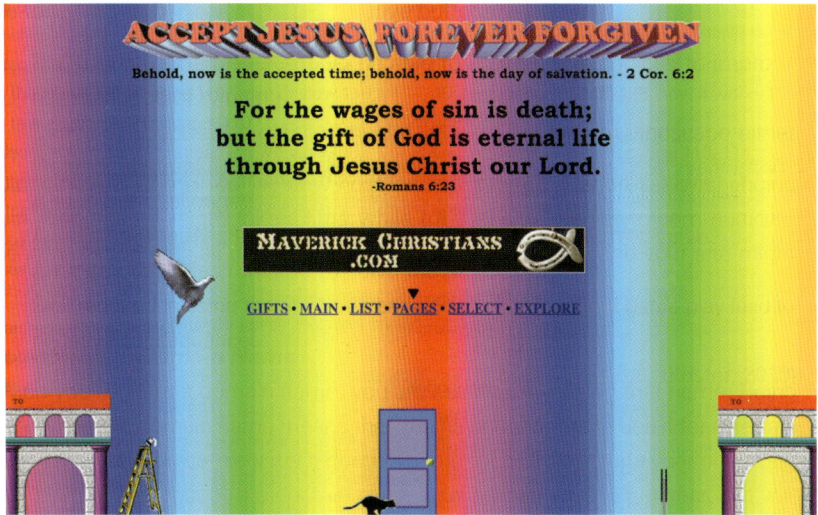

6.10
A lack of contrast between background and content makes it difficult to read.
Source: www.dokimos.org/ajff

mockups of screens, you can focus your attention on applying the colors and typography to your chosen layout.

With the rainbow of colors available to us, it is may be tempting to want to use them all throughout the design. But the results can be disastrous. Flooding a screen with color can be confusing to a viewer because you are not showing them what is important, where to look, and how objects function.

Strong color contrast can be helpful in drawing attention to important elements on the screen, especially when most everything else is neutral. In the following examples, notice how the majority of the screen is neutral, allowing the one accent color to pop, focusing the user's attention on the most crucial elements.

■ Aesthetics in Interactive Digital Media

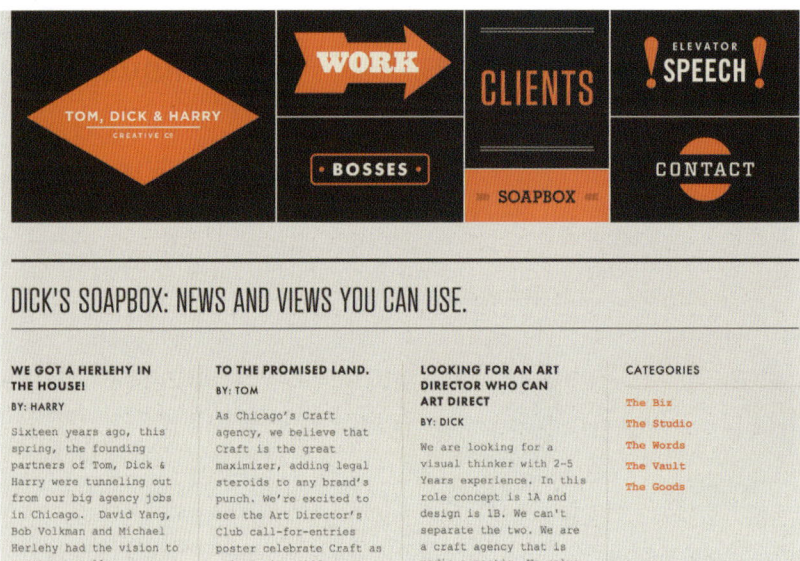

6.11
The Tom, Dick and Harry creative company website. Source: tdhcreative.com

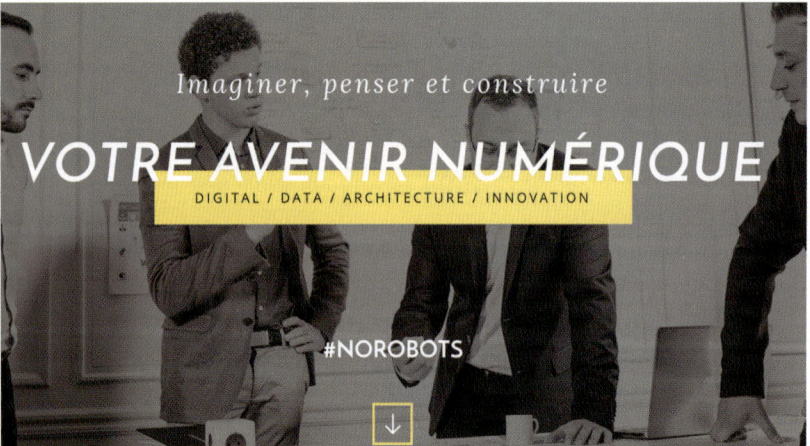

6.12
The Pramana (a French creative services company) website. Source: www.pramana.fr

Picking colors based on their position on the color wheel can be a good starting point for building a color palette. There are also many online resources that help you choose a color palette (e.g. colormind.io, paletton.com, coolors.co). In addition, there are several other factors you should consider such as legibility, branding, meaning, preferences and trends.

Color and Legibility
Poor color contrast can have a detrimental effect of legibility. If there is not enough contrast between the type color and the background color, then it's going

Aesthetics in Interactive Digital Media

6.13
Some color combinations offer higher color contrast than others which dramatically affects usability

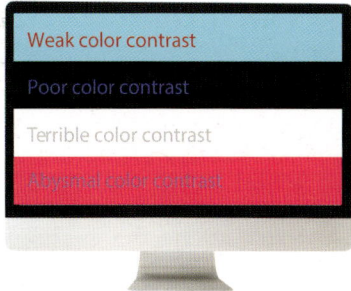

to be very difficult to make out the letter forms. When choosing a color palette, make sure there are colors that layer well. If they are all the same value, they will be difficult to read when applied to type and background.

Color and Branding
Oftentimes color choice is dictated by the existing branding of the company or organization, which is actually helpful because it gives you a place to start building a color palette. If a logo contains very bright colors, it might work best to use the logo colors as an accent with a more neutral color being dominant. You may also consider screening the primary branding color to provide variation and more layering possibilities.

Color and Meaning
Colors have inherent meaning to people in different cultures. In Western cultures, pink is associated with little girls, red is for danger, white is for weddings and black, for funerals. But color associations are not consistent across cultures. For example, in Far Eastern cultures, black is associated with prosperity, and brown with death and mourning. So, if you're going to be creating a cross-cultural

6.14
The Starbucks app uses the brand's signature green as an accent in its app design. Source: © www.starbucks.com

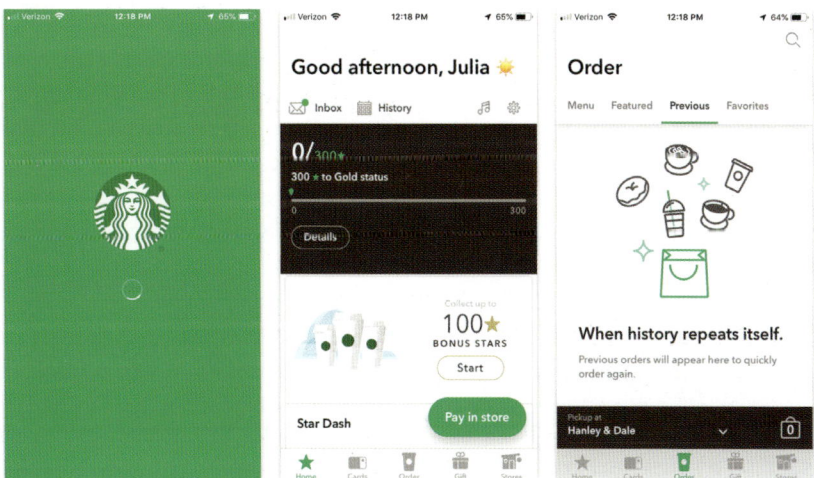

■ Aesthetics in Interactive Digital Media

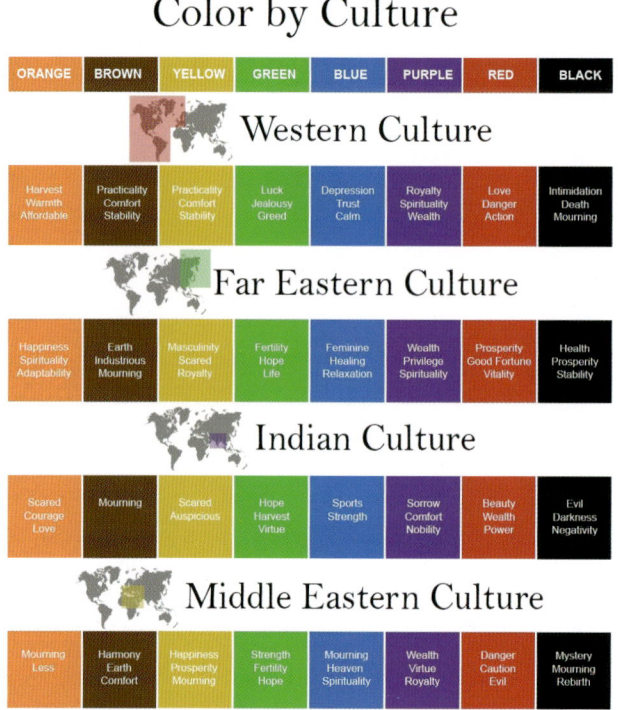

6.15
Colors have different meanings and associations in different cultures

application or developing a piece targeted to a specific culture, you should familiarize yourself with relevant color associations.

Even within your own culture, colors can have different associations within industries. The color green has positive connotations with almost half of the top 20 real estate companies using green in their branding. However, green is not used at all in the branding of the top 20 hospitality companies (Desjardins, 2017). If you're working on a project within an industry you're not familiar with, you should ask your client about colors to avoid and/or research it yourself.

Years ago, I noticed that Monsanto, a multinational agricultural biotechnology corporation, changed the color of their logo from a red, all caps, aggressive looking "MONSANTO" to a lowercase green and brown version. In the new logo, an innocently rendered plant towers over the corporate name which is now rendered in a classic, serif typeface. At the time of this rebranding, Monsanto was under attack for their work in genetic modification which some perceive to be dangerous. Having a red, aggressive-looking logo did not help Monsanto project an image of being concerned about people's health.

I admit I have made the mistake of choosing inappropriate colors by not considering a color's inherent meaning and the context in which I was using it. Years ago, when working on a website for kids with cancer, I mocked up interface designs with a black background. It seemed appropriate since the navigation iconography incorporated colorful bugs, and they really popped on the dark background. It didn't dawn on me how inappropriate my color choice was until my client pointed it out. My black designs with bugs and spider webs were a bit too doom and gloom for a site created as a resource for kids with cancer. After our meeting, I promptly changed the background to a more uplifting shade of blue.

Color Preferences
Always consider the age and sex of your audience when choosing colors, as different colors appeal to each gender and age group. Blue is a universally favored color across all genders and age groups despite its association with depression and glumness, especially with men who favor blue more than any other color. Females, on the other hand, are more evenly divided, preferring both green and blue. Interestingly, sexual orientation does not seem to affect color preferences; homosexual and bisexual males and females have similar color preferences to their heterosexual counterparts (Ellis & Ficek, 2001).

As we age, our color preferences change. Green is more favored by a younger demographic while purple gains popularity with older populations (Hallock, n.d.). Orange is often a least favorite color, and it's liked the least by people between the ages of 19 and 24. Studies have shown that kids have a "preference for intense visual stimuli," which is why designers often choose bright and neon colors when creating products for children (Westerbeek et al., 2004).

Color Trends
When choosing a color palette, it helps to be informed of color trends, especially if the piece you are creating is intended to evoke a specific era. Pantone, a company that makes a proprietary color system used in many industries, reports on color trends. If you would like to determine what colors are very on trend right now, you can find this information on their website (did you know that the color of 2019 is "Living Coral?"; Pantone, n.d.). Resources like Pantone are helpful as it is challenging to look around our environment and know what colors are very "now." On the other hand, looking into the past, it's easier to associate colors with different eras. Old books, catalogs, magazines and films are great resources to identify popular colors in previous eras.

LAYOUT PRINCIPLES

Once you have chosen your typography and colors, the next step is to consider where and how to apply these colors and arrange them on the screen. Understanding some basic layout principles and how they pertain to interactive media will help you make more strategic choices in line with your communication objectives.

Unity

What is Unity?
You may not realize it, but you probably think about unity every morning when you get dressed. If you are wearing primarily one color, you will likely choose shoes and accessories that also contain that color. Most of us want our outfits

■ Aesthetics in Interactive Digital Media

to coordinate and look cohesive, so we choose ensembles that feel unified, meaning that the clothes we put on our bodies have a clear visual relationship to each other.

Why is it Important?
Unity works in a similar manner within the context of interactive digital media. Unifying graphic elements make it feel cohesive and strengthens the brand. It's hard to forget you are using the Target app because of the unified design. The Target red is the predominant color and circle icons are integrated throughout to remind us of the Target logo.

Unity also helps orient the user. Consistent looking screens across an interactive experience tell the user that they are within one environment, which is especially important on the web, where it's easy to get disoriented by clicking on a link and not knowing whether you are still on the same site.

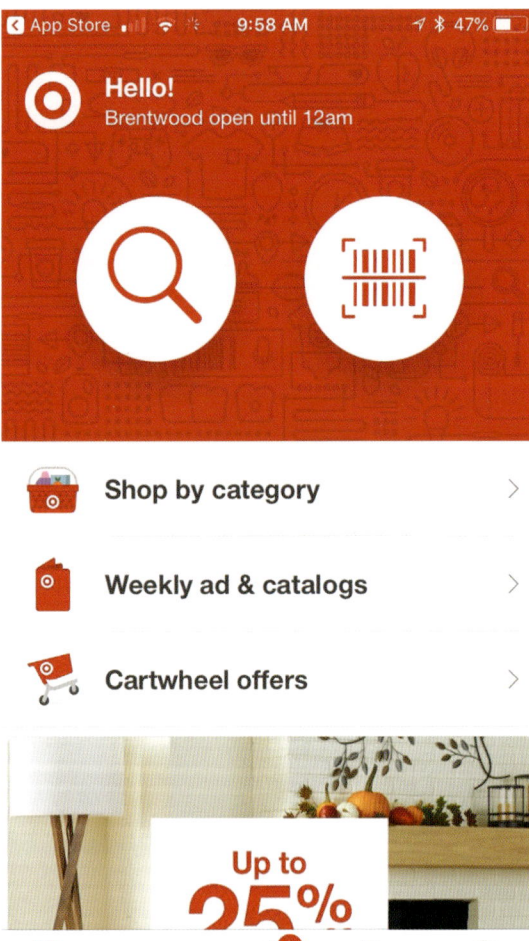

6.16
The Target app has a cohesive design.
Source: www.target.com

Aesthetics in Interactive Digital Media

Unifying elements with similar functions help the user understand the interactive experience. Unifying the look and feel of related controls tell the user that they do a similar thing. Menu bars display unity, as the buttons generally all have the same look and feel, implying they are related in some way.

Best Practices
Unity in interactive design is achieved by limiting the number of colors, typefaces, layouts and image, icon and characters styles across your application. By sticking to a prescribed color palette and two or three typefaces, you are well on your way to achieving a unified design. Unity can be strengthened, however, by applying a consistent style to other graphic elements. For example, you may crop all your photos to squares, or apply a similar filter to them. Or you may integrate a distinct icon or a unique illustration style throughout the application to enhance the unity.

When an application lacks unity, it can sabotage usability. Imagine if the menu bar on an app only appeared on certain pages or the main header on a website kept changing locations. Wireframing helps to ensure unity, as it encourages designers to keep key elements consistent across all screens.

6.17
Icons created from a single continuous line throughout the Panera app have a distinct and unified style. Source: www.panerabread.com

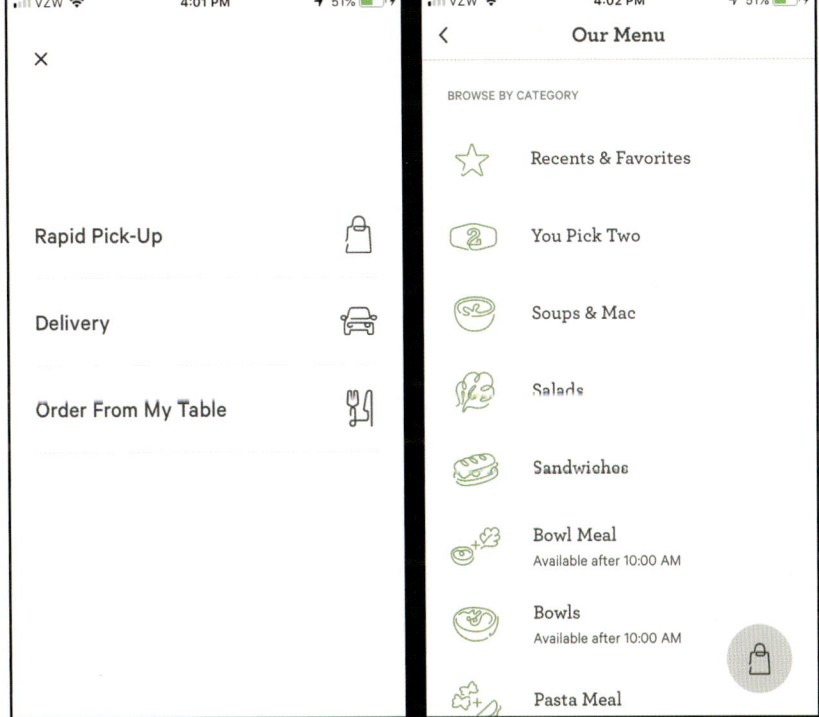

■ Aesthetics in Interactive Digital Media

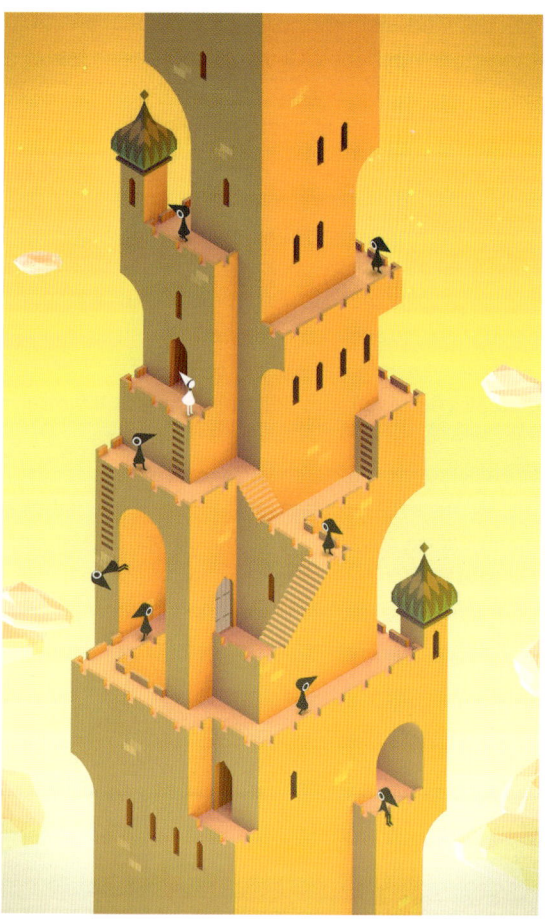

6.18
Characters in the game, *Monument Valley*, have a consistent style. Source: www.monumentvalleygames.com

Differentiation

What is Differentiation?
Differentiation is making elements look different from one another. While differentiation might seem to contradict unity, within interactive media, appropriate differentiation is variation within the unified whole.

Why is it Important?
Imagine you are traveling through different levels of a game and they all looked and felt alike. It would be pretty boring and disorienting. You might wonder, haven't I been here before? Similar confusion can occur within other forms of interactive media. If a user doesn't notice a change on the screen, how will she know the application is responding. While screens should be laid out consistently, uniqueness helps communicate different types of content.

Within the context of one screen, differentiation helps to identify elements with different purposes. The viewer assumes that if two elements look really different from each other, then they probably do something very different.

Best Practices

Wireframing can also help articulate differences between disparate areas of an application with dissimilar objectives. For example, a search results page would have a different look to it than a checkout page.

Differentiation should also be used between typographic elements on a screen as it makes text more understandable and easier to scan. Typographic contrast is the notion that different type styles should be applied to text with differing purposes, and it is used in both print and screen-based media. In a newspaper, the headline of an article is often set in a large, bold sans serif

6.19
Typographic contrast allows a reader to distinguish between different type of content

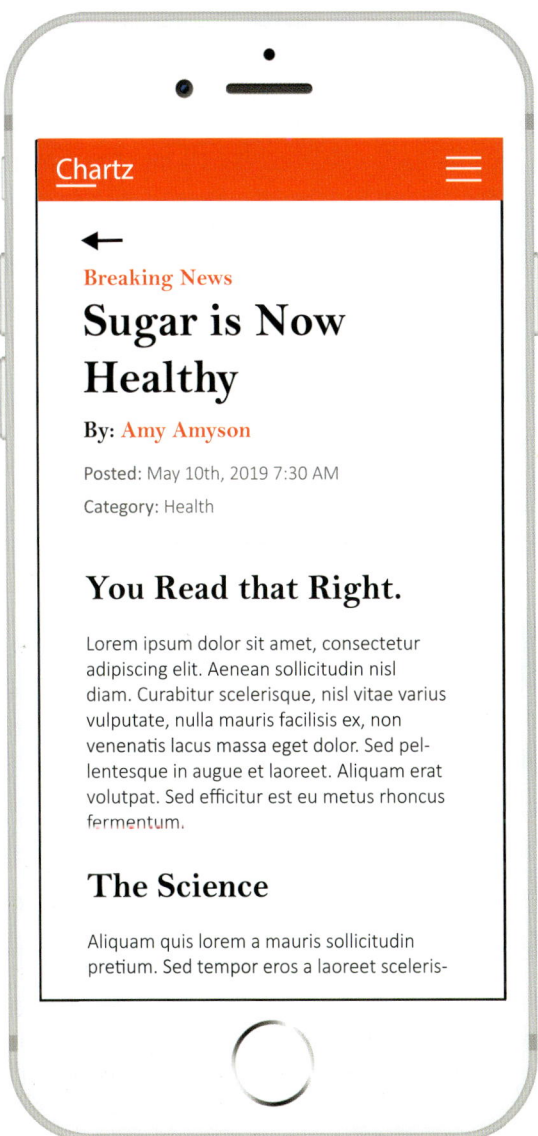

■ Aesthetics in Interactive Digital Media

typeface. The intent is for it to contrast with the smaller serif body copy allowing a reader to quickly scan headlines and read further if interested. Within interactive media, differentiation between hyperlinks and body copy is also vital. If the hyperlink is styled the same as the rest of the text, it is hard to tell what is link and what is not.

Most interactive applications combine at least two very different looking typefaces throughout the application allowing the designer to create contrast by assigning a distinct typefaces/size/style for each type of content. Resources online such as: https://fontpair.co help designers pair Google fonts by providing previews of the typefaces used together.

The example, below, is a responsive web-based application that I built for an exhibit at the Missouri Botanical Garden. Using a QR code scanner in the exhibit or on a mobile device, the user can scan a labeled artifact to access information about it. The content that appears on the screen includes some basic information about the artifact as well as pictures and where it can be found within the Garden. Because each screen contains a lot of content, it was important to use typographic contrast to differentiate headlines, subheads, body copy and links. Each heading is rendered in a bold, large, serif typeface with an orange icon next to it on a light green background. The subhead is smaller, but a lowercase bold green sans serif on a white background. The body copy is also sans serif but black and much smaller. Captions are small, black and italicized, but on a grey background. Links to other sections are associated with icons and the text is white. These stylistic choices are consistent throughout the application and were deliberately chosen to clarify the different purposes of the elements.

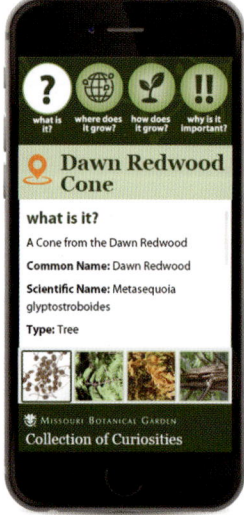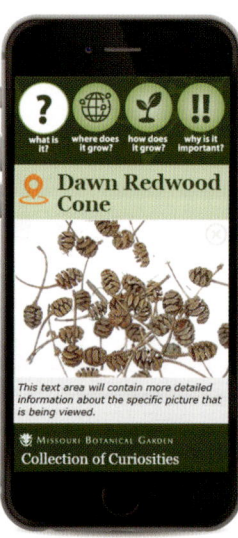

6.20
The screen-based component of the "Collection of Curiosities" exhibit at the Missouri Botannical Garden demonstrates typographic contrast

Aesthetics in Interactive Digital Media

Emphasis

What is Emphasis?
Emphasis is making something stand out. The most important elements on a screen should be emphasized! A viewer should look at a screen and immediately understand what is most important because it is emphasized, then intuitively know where to look next based on the layout of the other components.

Why is it Important?
Generally, people don't spend a lot of time trying to figure out what your message is; they look at things very quickly and want to get the point as fast as possible. If they are interested in learning more, they want to be led to the next most important thing.

Best Practices
Think about what users want to do/learn/buy/play when they launch your application and emphasize it. Place crucial items where the user will look first. On a website, this means what appears when the screen first loads, otherwise known as "above the fold," which refers back to the visible part of newspapers in a newsstand. Content above the fold is the high real estate area of a website and should be reserved for the most important elements.

In the game *Candy Crush*, the "Play" button is positioned right in the middle of the screen and rendered in a large typeface with a three-dimensional looking background to make it pop off the page. It is clearly being emphasized above anything else. The designer of this interface understands that his goal is to get users playing as quickly as possible.

6.21
In a newspaper dispenser, only the content on the front page above the fold is visible, therefore it must catch your attention so that you will buy the paper. © lupungato; 123RF.com

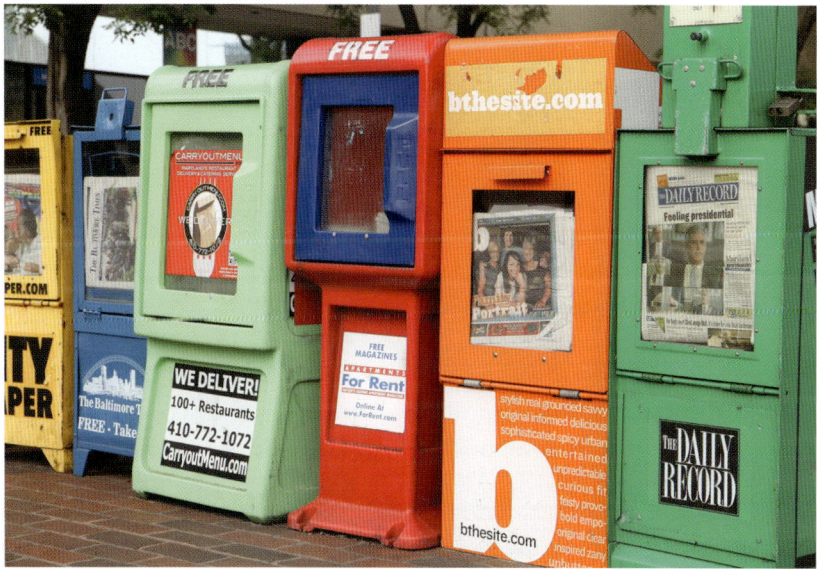

■ Aesthetics in Interactive Digital Media

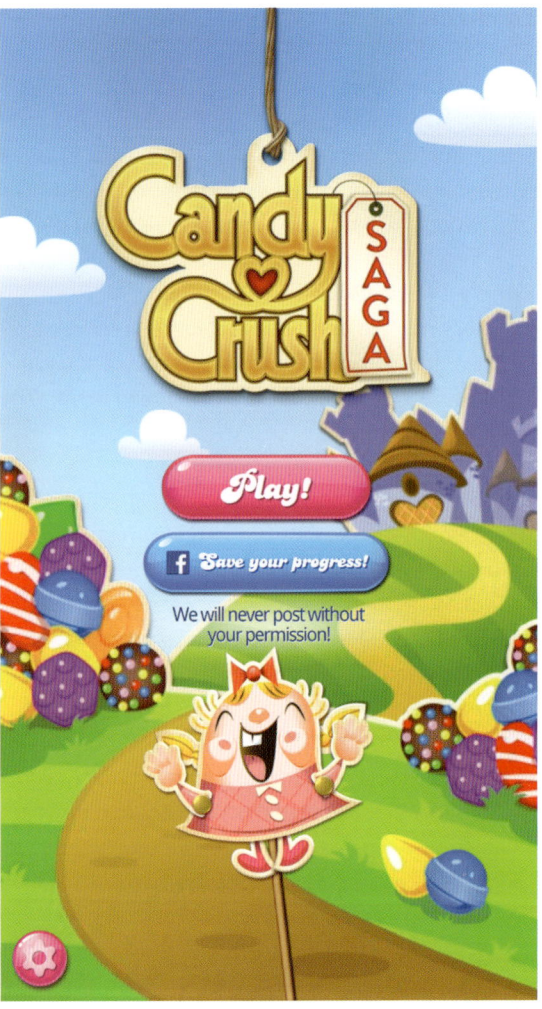

6.22
The *Candy Crush* opening screen

Placing the most important elements in a location that will get a user's attention is not the only way to create emphasis. Contrast, the act of making something look different from the elements around it with scale, color or style, can also be used to generate emphasis.

On the Gift Rocket website, the only elements in color are the icons representing all of the different types of gift cards you can buy. They are in contrast to the neutral background and are different from anything else on the screen. The designer has emphasized this graphic using color, scale and style to draw attention to it. Gift Rocket wants visitors to understand exactly what they can do on their site: buy gift cards.

Once you have gotten the viewer's attention by emphasizing the most important element, show them where to look next by establishing a visual hierarchy: prioritizing information based on importance. Ask yourself, if users looked at this quickly, would they get the point and know where to look if they wanted to learn more? Users will read further, if they are interested.

Aesthetics in Interactive Digital Media

6.23
On this website, the highest contrast element is the graphic which also "points" to the key message.
Source: www.giftrocket.com

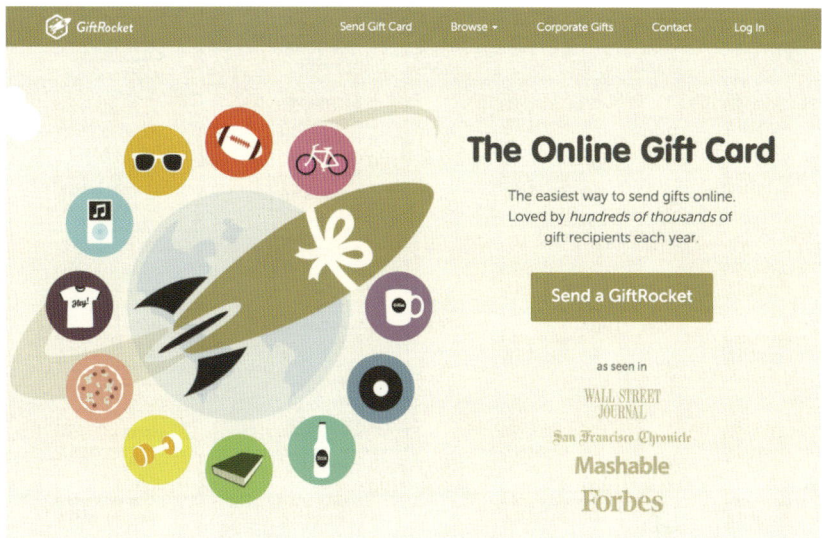

Positioning an element so that it gestures towards another one is a great way to establish a visual hierarchy and lead the viewer's eye to the next most important element on the screen. Looking back at the Gift Rocket website, the rocket is literally pointing to the description of the site. Once they've grabbed the viewers' attention with the colorful icons, they are directing them to the message of the site: buy gift cards here. The use of emphasis and pointing devices in this design helps quickly and efficiently communicate what they want visitors to do.

Whitespace

What is Whitespace?
Whitespace (also known as negative space) is the empty space between elements (graphics, images, text) on a screen. Whitespace isn't necessarily white. The empty space may be filled with any color as long as it is free of any elements like graphics, images or text.

Why is it Important?
Whitespace is important because it clarifies relationships between elements on the screen. Users interpret items that are close together as being related, and ones far apart as not related. The distance or lack of distance implies a relationship.

Best Practices
Improved visual communication and user comprehension can be achieved by making some subtle adjustments with the whitespace between items on the screen. For example, in a menu bar, adding a bit more space between different groups of menu items can help the viewer understand what is a sub menu element of one group and what is a new group.

■ Aesthetics in Interactive Digital Media

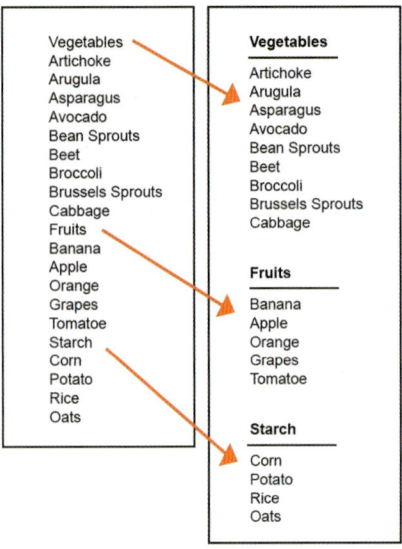

6.24
Use of whitespace can add clarity to relationship of elements on the screen

It is apparent that the designers of the Gingiber website paid close attention to their use of whitespace to help orient shoppers. The amount of whitespace between product pictures and product details is minimal because they are related. Approximately twice as much whitespace is used to separate rows of products to clarify which product the name and price are referring to. The category title is set off with ample whitespace to clearly inform the visitor where they are on the site.

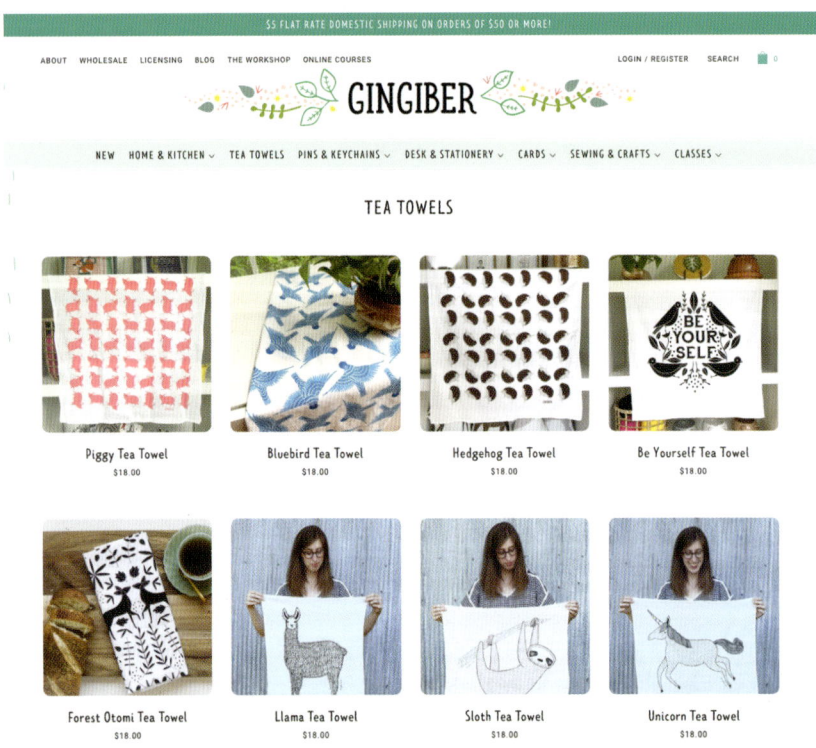

6.25
The Gingiber website is full of disparate product images, but because the interface is so neutral and well organized the content does not feel overwhelming. Source: www.gingiber.com

142

Aesthetics in Interactive Digital Media

Adding ample whitespace around an element can be a means of drawing attention to it. On many high-end fashion websites, there is often copious amounts of whitespace around their images to keep the users' focus on them. The abundant use of whitespace also helps the site project an elegant, uncluttered look.

Alignment

What is Alignment?
Alignment refers to lining up the top, bottom, sides, or middle of text or graphic elements on a page. Visual elements should line up in straight lines horizontally and vertically.

Why is it Important?
Aligning elements along the same horizontal and vertical invisible lines gives a more organized appearance. When elements are placed arbitrarily on the screen, it feels haphazard and disorganized. Consistent alignment also allows viewers to see the difference between elements and make quick visual comparisons.

Good alignment can aid legibility, especially in online forms. If the form fields start at different left alignment points, it takes more effort to figure out where to

6.26
Notice how each product blurb is aligned consistently throughout this product listing page. The result is that it feels less overwhelming and easier for viewers to make quick visual comparisons. Source: hunters.co.nz/shop

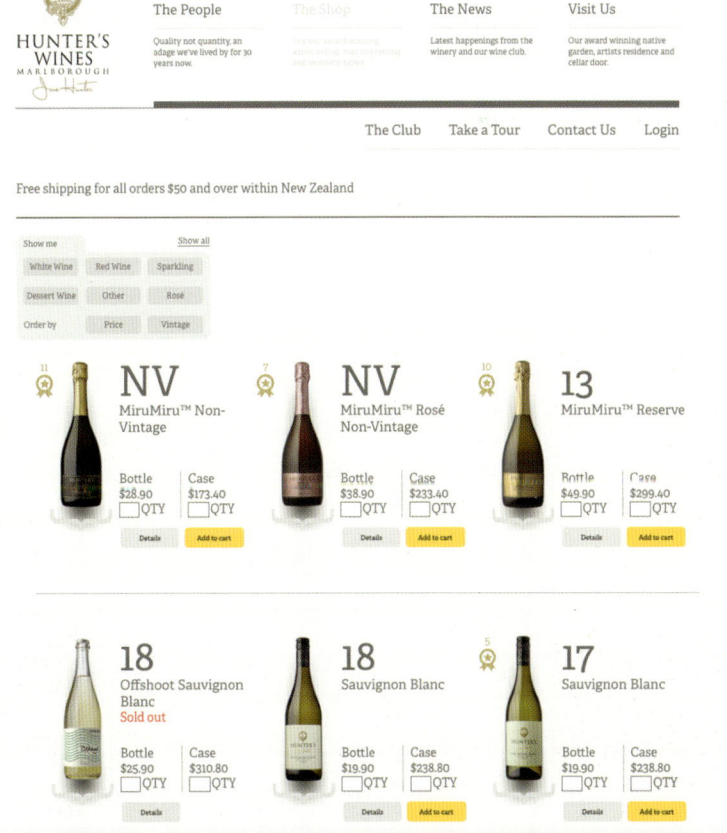

143

■ **Aesthetics in Interactive Digital Media**

go next. If your business depends on extracting information from a visitor, your form should feel effortless.

Best Practices

If you are designing for the web, technologies like the Bootstrap framework (a set of JavaScript files that can be downloaded and included in your web files) are based on a grid. If you avoid varying column padding settings, your alignment will naturally be consistent.

When authoring interactive media in other platforms, use tools like guides and grids to ensure elements are aligned. When designing graphics, use the alignment tools within the graphics applications to help you build images in which content is aligned.

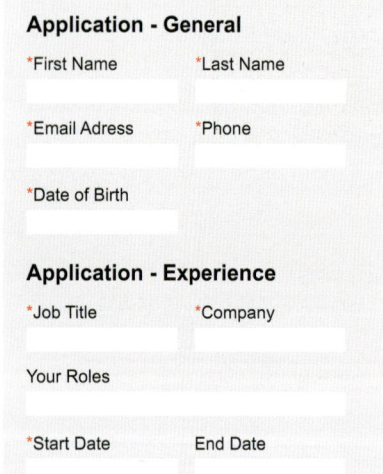 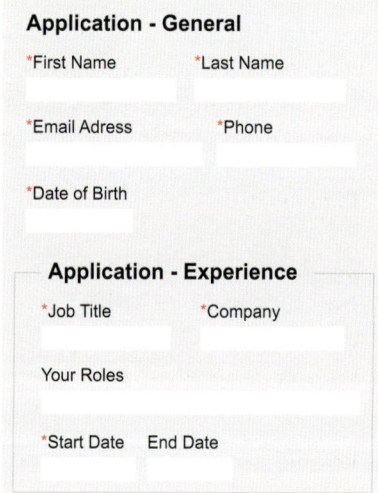

6.27
A form with good alignment is quicker and easier to fill out

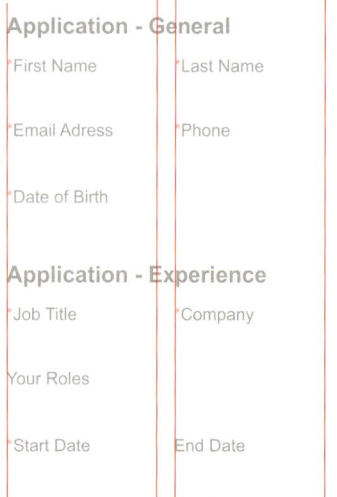 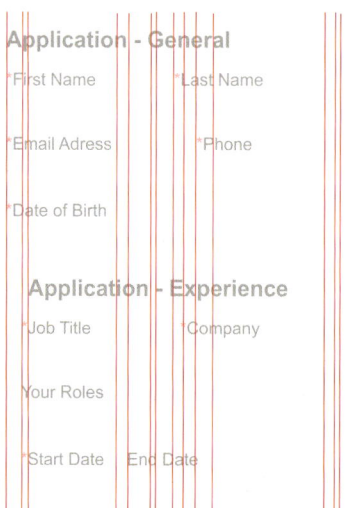

144 □

PRACTITIONER INTERVIEW

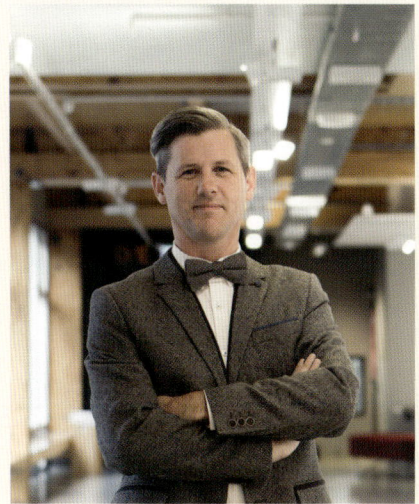

Brian Lucid

Massey University – Wellington, New Zealand
Brian Lucid is a professor of design at Massey University in Wellington, New Zealand. He is also a practicing visual interaction/interface/user experience designer who uses his design skills to simplify complex information and build usable interactive applications.

How did you start your career in design?

I started my career as a type designer and while I love type, I now understand that I was drawn to type because I was actually really interested in building and developing tools for other designers. So, it was a natural evolution for me to move from the drawing of letters into other forms of tools that users interact with. That led to web and app development and the interaction design space that I'm in.

How much of design is talent vs. learned?

I think very little of it is talent. Students often don't recognize that what they see as talent is actually just hard work. Very few students just naturally pick it up and it flows from them. [But,] I think that anyone who has a passion for and an interest in design can absolutely [build design skills.]

What is the design process do you teach?

We have to teach the usability and functionality, the core of data-driven design. But we also want to teach the speculative part. How does this connect to a wider concept? What can it be? How do we push the boundaries of what the expectations are for this as an application?

We deal with a lot of the detail work and the technical work early, like teaching typography. We learn to do spacing and scale and hierarchy first and then we start to learn how to play with it. We start to say, all right, now that we have those tools and we have those skills in our hands, then we can then think about how it's applied.

When the [interactive] product is in development, it's a refinement process. It's much more focused on that really deep feedback loop of making changes, being able to observe how users interact with that work, feeding it back, making more changes, etc. It's an iterative rapid prototyping process.

The majority of design that we have today is generating real-time metrics in terms of usability and so it's not just about designing something and putting anything in front of somebody and saying oh they liked it, but actually being able to develop a trail of use data, and over time, being able to observe that data. The majority of applications that we use on a day to day basis are A/B tested nearly all the time. So, as a designer, you need to be able to understand the results and then know how that transforms into either small or large changes.

I think that it makes design a lot less subjective because you can tell by changing the color of a button how that impacts the number of clicks you get.

You're right! It's a lot less subjective.

A lot of that data-driven flow is very good at identifying some of those smaller aesthetic details but may not get to the level of really deep radical changes. [Exploring] radically different [ways of] doing things are usually done at a much earlier stage.

How do you hone in on a design direction?

From the very core, it has to grow from a human-centered context of design which is very much rooted in UI and UX. This was our big transition from print design into interaction design. We actually had to learn a lot from industrial designers and architects, because all of a sudden, we were creating things for use. A beginning designer needs to understand that before any of that other work can be done, we have to identify what are we trying to do, who is using it, what are their challenges and then that gives us a platform upon which to start telling a narrative of what that use looks like. So, before I'm thinking about what color the buttons are or even what size the buttons are, I have to be thinking about what button needs to exist in that context. It's first and foremost about identifying those needs and those requirements and then allowing yourself to then, in a conceptual way, start to explore how those needs get met.

When we talk about process, and particularly for beginners who may be more familiar with print design, the biggest transition is this integration to sequence. Often, when I work with designers starting out in this space, they very much think of the screen as a singular moment. But we really need to think about narratives. We need to think about what is happening and how did we get from here to the end result through a collection of interactions.

Once we identify the user, we identify the needs, then identify what needs to happen when, then we can start to go in and start to define hierarchy, first in terms of what needs to be seen on this page, what does the user need to know how to do through their sequence, and then finally how does that connect to a certain level of aesthetics. When I'm doing this type of work, color comes last. So almost all of the work that I do initially is in grayscale. I work in hierarchy: typographic hierarchy, and I do use color to create hierarchy.

You started your career as a type designer and now you're not even really talking about your type choices or your color choices.

The thing that taught me the most about human centered design and usability cognition is typography and I would still make the claim that probably 80 percent of my job as an interaction designer is still typographic and that relates to everything, [especially in] thinking about hierarchy. [Questions like] how big does this need to be? How important is this? How do I arrange these elements in a sense of visual importance? All of that I learned from typography. And I would say still probably 60 to 70 percent of [the answers] to those [questions] I still communicate through typography. So obviously, typography is still a core skill.

What would you say in terms of typographic hierarchy — what would be the most important thing for a beginner to recognize when making type choices?

Obviously, typography teaches a great deal of sensitivity to seeing, but what that leads to is an understanding of how visual properties can manipulate meaning and communicate. So, it's not about making type big or small, but why we make type bigger or smaller and what that communicates. Certainly, in my own teaching I focus a lot on that idea of visual property. What are the tools we have at our disposal, and what's the impact of using those tools? The idea is that we have a set of visual properties that our eye is really good at picking up on and then we have the ability of connecting those visual properties to meaning. I can tell a story through color, I could tell the same story through size, movement, etc. These are simply just ways to create contrast and connect that contrast to meaning. It's true in data visualization, storytelling, UX, etc.

So at its core, typography is a really wonderful entry point into recognizing visual properties and how it communicates. [That meaning is] amplified when we're able to connect these visual properties to text that has meaning. There's an amazing manipulative property to that in a positive or negative way. That's where we really start to be able to communicate and it's where the designer starts to learn their power and their influence.

DISCUSSION QUESTIONS

1) Find an example of a company or organization that uses a serif typeface in their logo and one that uses a sans serif typeface. Why do you think these companies or organizations made that choice?
2) What is your favorite typeface? Why?
3) Have you ever found type to be difficult to read? Now that you have read this chapter, why do you think that was?
4) Are there are any colors you see frequently within a particular industry? Why do you think that is?
5) Find an example of a visual hierarchy. Why is it effective?

REFERENCES

Desjardins, J. (2017). Color in Branding: What Does it Say About Your Industry? *Visual Capitalist,* February 20. Online. Available at: <https://www.visualcapitalist.com/color-in-branding-industry>.

Elliot, A. J., & Maier, M. A. (2014). Color Psychology: Effects of Perceiving Color on Psychological Functioning in Humans. *Annual Review of Psychology, 65*(1), 95–120. Online. Available at: <https://doi.org/10.1146/annurev%2Dpsych%2D010213%2D115035>.

Ellis, L., & Ficek, C. (2001). Color preferences according to gender and sexual orientation. *Personality and Individual Differences, 31*(8), 1375–1379. Online. Available at: <https://doi.org/https://doi.org/10.1016/S0191%2D8869(00)00231%2D2>.

Hallock, J. (n.d.). Colour Assignment. Online. Available at: <http://www.joehallock.com/edu/com498/index.html>.

Pantone (n.d.). *Color of the Year.* Online. Available at: <https://www.pantone.com/color-intelligence/color-of-the-year/color-of-the-year-2019>.

Sokolik, K., Magee, R. G., & Ivory, J. D. (2014). Red-Hot and Ice-Cold Web Ads: The Influence of Web Ads' Warm and Cool Colors on Click-Through Rates. *Journal of Interactive Advertising, 14*(1), 31–37. Online. Available at: <https://doi.org/10.1080/15252019.2014.907757>.

Westerbeek, A., de Graaf, C., Liem, D. G., Kok, F. J., & Wolterink, S. (2004). Sour Taste Preferences of Children Relate to Preference for Novel and Intense Stimuli. *Chemical Senses, 29*(8), 713–720. Online. Available at: <https://doi.org/10.1093/chemse/bjh077>.

7 Authoring Interactive Digital Media

INTRODUCTION

Authoring interactive media is all about making the interactivity work, and can be done one of two ways: via writing code or using an authoring application or doing a combination of both. Different tools and techniques are used to author the various forms, all of which have evolved significantly over time. Authoring web-based content presents an additional set of challenges as the developer must register a domain name, establish hosting, integrate content management systems, and upload files to a web server.

MULTIMEDIA AUTHORING

Early experimentation with interactive media began long before the web and the personal computer. In the 1970s NASA scientists built a "Virtual Interface Environment Workstation" (VIEW) and other instruments that would allow you to move around in the virtual space. In this same decade, programmers authored video games and other types of interactive applications, although the experiences were primarily text based with rudimentary graphics (if any). It wasn't until the mid 1980s that the era of multimedia authoring was born. The Macintosh's built-in software, Hypercard, kicked off the multimedia revolution, allowing anyone to build an interactive audio/visual experience. In fact, the first version of the game, Myst, was developed using Hypercard (Scott, 2017). Another early authoring application for interactive media was Authorware. Its strength was for developing e-learning content.

The real juggernaut for professional interactive digital media authoring, however, was Macromedia Director which was released in 1988. Director was the dominant program used to build stand-alone interactive experiences that would run off of a CD or in a kiosk. Several popular CD-ROM-based adventure games were built with Director in the 1980s and 1990s. It even allowed for the integration of video within the experience. But, just as Director started hitting its stride, along came the world wide web offering the potential for networked interactive experiences.

■ Authoring Interactive Digital Media

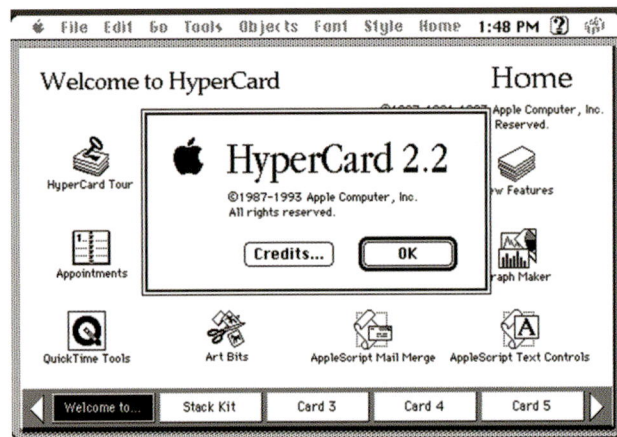

7.1 Hypercard multimedia authoring application. © Bill Atkinson. Online. Available HTTP: https://www.macintoshrepository.org/2328-hypercard-2-2

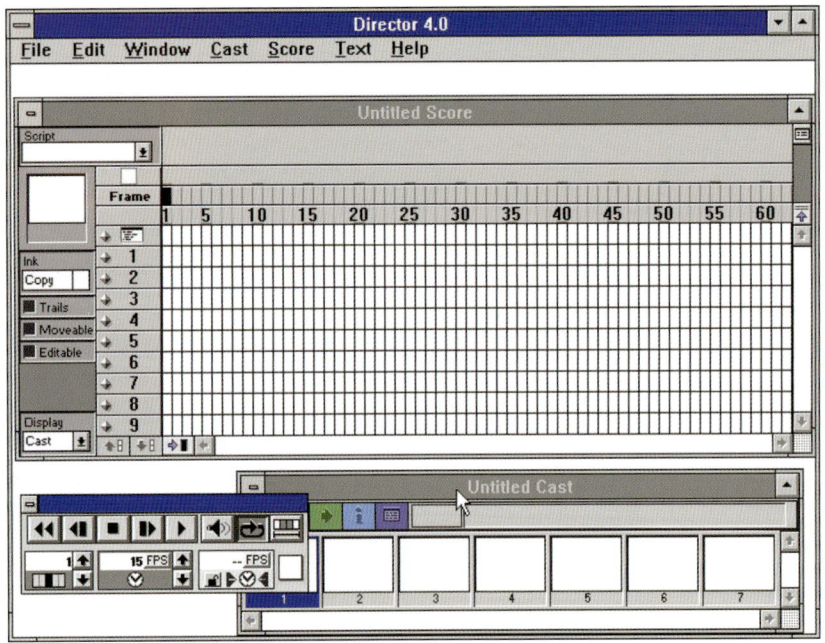

7.2 Macromedia Director running in Microsoft DOS circa 1994. © Anatoly Shashkin

The development team behind Director responded to the Web by inventing the Shockwave plugin which would allow a file made in Director to be viewed through a web browser. It was a great idea in theory, but not in practice. The problem was that the applications made in Director were quite large and not suitable for delivery over the Internet which was still in its infancy with very limited bandwidth. Nevertheless, Director maintained its dominant position as a multimedia authoring tool, because unlike with early HTML, the author could precisely control the look and feel of elements on the screen.

150

Macromedia was quick to recognize that the files made with Director were too bulky for the web and released a new product called Flash that quickly became the darling for interactive media authoring. Flash was similar to Director in that it allowed the developer to precisely control the position of elements on the screen and easily integrate audio and video, but was unlike Director in that it offered the benefit of smaller file sizes since the graphics created in Flash were vector and not pixel-based. Many websites in the late 1990s and early 2000s featured content built in Flash. It was also used to create web-based games, and because of its superior animation tools, many popular cartoons on broadcast TV. As Flash became more widely used, Director became obsolete.

The emergence of the smartphone in the late 2000s marked the decline for Macromedia Flash (which at that point had been acquired by Adobe). Apple would not support Flash-based content within a browser window on iPhones and iPads, because Steve Jobs argued that Flash content was too bloated for mobile devices and drained too much power (McNichol, 2010). As a result, any site that incorporated Flash content would not show up in the iPhone or iPad Safari browser. Jobs encouraged users to develop interactive content with new HTML/CSS/JavaScript capabilities, specifically the Canvas element which allows vector graphics to be generated on the fly. While Flash content was still supported for a while within browsers on Android devices, it is now no longer the case.

Adobe responded to the situation by rebranding Flash as Adobe Edge Animate and adding some new features. Developers can now author in Edge Animate, but export files as HTML and JavaScript so that the resulting application can run natively in a browser, even a browser on a mobile device. Developers can also build stand-alone interactive experiences that can be made into apps for iOS and Android devices as well as desktop applications.

MAKING VIDEO GAMES: CASUAL AND CONSOLE

Casual games are ones designed to be played in short spurts on the go and are not overly complex. Adobe Edge Animate is actually a popular tool for building these types of games. In fact, it was actually used to make Angry Birds (Helander, 2012). However, software like Edge Animate is not required to build a casual game; a developer can do so by typing HTML and JavaScript into a text editor and previewing the resulting game in a web browser. Or, the developer can use one of the many JavaScript game engines, e.g. Phaser, Babylon.JS, or GDevelop, that provide some drag and drop functionality, shortcuts and previewing capabilities to make the game development process quicker. Some of these programs are even free and/or open source.

Another popular free and open source game engine is Twine. Originally a tool for authoring interactive fiction, Twine has since been extended with HTML, CSS and JavaScript enhancement possibilities. Some game narrative designers use Twine as a planning tool. But full-fledged apps can be made in the program as well. Any casual game built in core web languages can be packaged as a game for the app marketplaces using a tool like Adobe Phonegap.

■ Authoring Interactive Digital Media

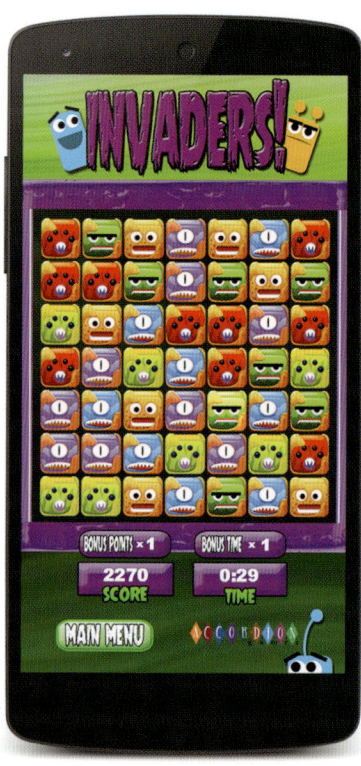

7.3 The mobile game, *Invaders*, was made in Construct 2, a HTML/Javascript game engine. © Joshua Yates

More robust, complex games that incorporate immersive three-dimensional environments and are played on a PC or home gaming console are typically not made in JavaScript, but instead programmed in (typically) C# or C++, which are true object oriented and compiled languages. Object oriented languages are essential for writing complex programs because they have a modular structure where objects can be reused across the application. A compiled language is one that must be run through a complier (a program that translates programming language into machine code) before it can be executed. The benefit of a compiled program is that it runs quickly, which is essential for complex games.

To help game developers build their games, most use a game engine software. Essentially game-engines are code compilers with a graphical user interface that provide previews of graphics, functionality, coding shortcuts, animation tools, and previewing of functionality. They are much like the aforementioned Adobe Edge Animate or one of the JavaScript engines, albeit much more robust. Game engines are also used to create virtual and augmented reality experiences.

Common game engines include:

- **Unity**, developed by Unity Technologies, is a popular cross-platform game development engine used to make "half of the world's games" (Unity, n.d.). It supports the creation of both 2-D and 3-D games for the Android, iOS as well as all of the major gaming consoles. It's known for being easy to use

Authoring Interactive Digital Media

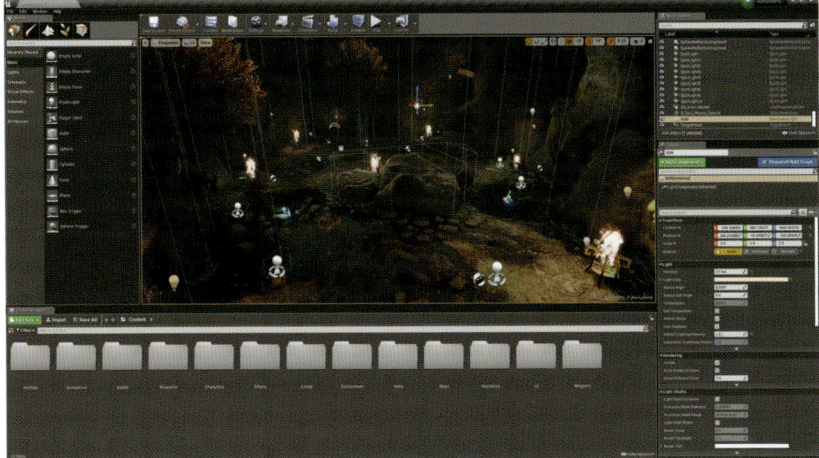

7.4 Game development in the Unity game engine. © Joshua Yates

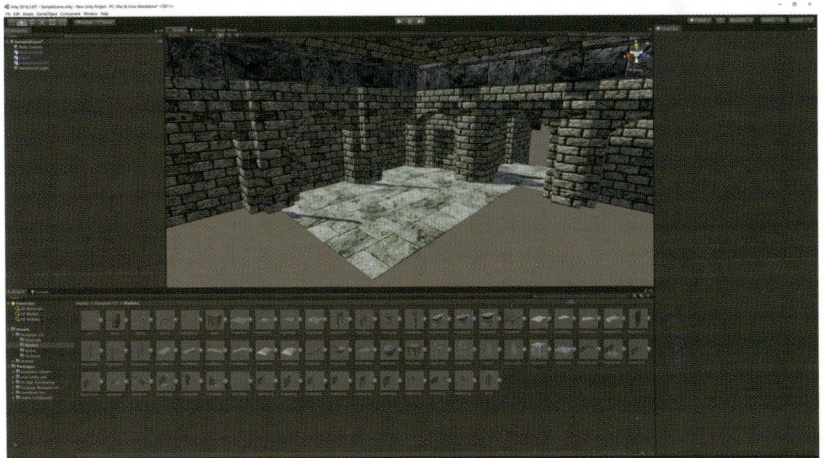

7.5 Game development in the Unreal game engine. © Joshua Yates

and free. It also includes a platform embedded in the software that facilitates sharing of code and other assets among developers.
- **Unreal Game Engine**, developed by Epic Games, is also free for developers to use, however Unreal takes a 5 percent royalty for any games made from it. It too, provides a platform for developers to share code and assets and even a marketplace where developers can sell their games. The Unreal Game Engine is known for its superiority in rendering detailed graphics.

BUILDING APPS

Apps are one of the newest forms of interactive media, having been around only a little more than a decade. However, with over 2 million apps available for download in both the Apple and the Google Play store, there truly is an app for

■ Authoring Interactive Digital Media

everything (Clement, 2019). Because apps can be so useful, informative and entertaining, and with us wherever we go, app addiction is a new concern. Studies have shown that app addicts are more likely to be injured because they become oblivious to their surroundings while using their smartphones (Kim et al., 2017). There now even apps to help use apps less (Löchtefeld et al., 2013).

App culture was started by Apple in the late 2000s. In June, 2007, as they were launching the first iPhone, Apple announced that developers would be allowed to create apps that looked and acted just like the ones that came installed on the device. These apps would be able to take advantage of the built-in iPhone services such as the phone, GPS and camera. A little over a year later, in July of 2008, the Apple App Store was launched, offering iPhone users 552 different apps that they could install on their iPhones. In October of 2008, the Android marketplace (later rebranded as the Google Play store) opened (Strain, 2015).

There are a number of different methods you can use to build an app. Initially, iPhone apps needed to be built within the editor provided by Apple called Xcode using the Swift programming language. Android apps were made in Android Studio and primarily written in the Java programming language. If you wanted to develop an app for both platforms, you would have to make the app twice in these two different development environments. While these methods are still used, it is also now possible to develop an app using any of the aforementioned editors that export content in HTML, CSS and JavaScript.

As you are developing the app, you can install it and preview it on your own device. But getting it into the app marketplaces requires a few extra steps. First, you need to obtain a digital certificate to sign your apps. Then you upload the app to the respective app stores. Both app stores require you to provide keywords and a description pertaining to the app. The Apple and Google Play stores both require developers to register and pay a fee to submit apps. Apple charges $100 and Google Play charges $25. For both stores, there is a bit of a waiting period until your app is approved and made available to the public.

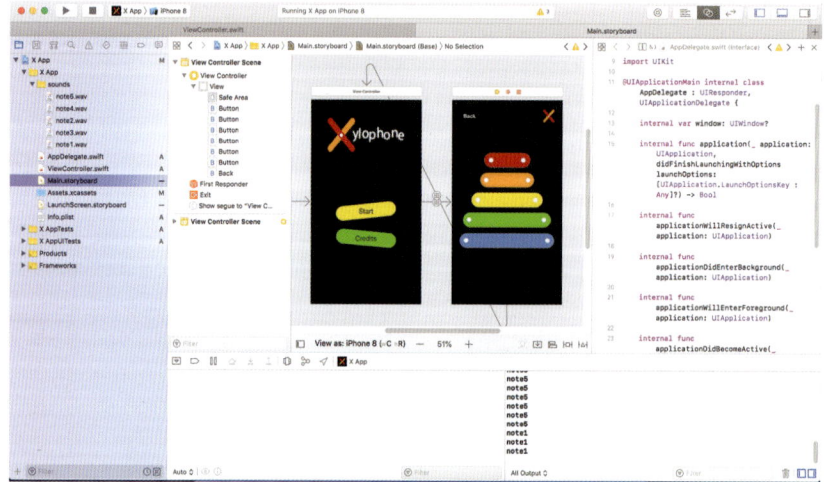

7.6 App development in Xcode. © Joshua Yates

BUILDING INTERACTIVE MEDIA FOR PERFORMANCE AND PUBLIC SPACES

Interactive media can often be found in public spaces, either for functional purposes (like a grocery store kiosk) or in a more experiential context (like in a museum). For more straight-forward, screen-based interactive experiences, the development may be done in a multimedia authoring application, a game engine or native Web languages. There are also specialized programs designed specifically for kiosk application development, e.g. SureFox, SiteKiosk, etc.

For experiences that are more physical in nature, a different approach is required. First, the developer must consider the input. Is the system responding to a user's movements or to the position of the users in the space or the volume of noise in the environment? Specialized sensors can track these variables and feed input to a computer which can then react (producing sound, visuals) based on the input.

Since typical computers are not equipped with input for these specialized sensors, inexpensive stripped-down, credit-card sized circuit boards, such as the Arduino microcontroller motherboard or the Raspberry Pi general-purpose mini-computer, are used to build these types of physical, interactive experiences. Both devices are built to accept sensors, motors, etc., communicate with a monitor or a standard computer, and can be programmed to respond to the data they are sensing in the environment.

Interactive physical experiences can be written in different languages and built in different authoring environments. The following languages and applications can interface with the Arduino and Raspberry Pi.

- **Pure Data** is a free and open-source programming language which is also visual, making it easier for a non-coder to author interactivity.
- **Processing** is another free and open source programming language that interfaces easily with the Arduino.
- **Max** is actually an earlier version of Pure Data that was further developed and commercialized by the company, Cycling '74. It, too, is a visual programming language. Unlike Pure Data, it is not free and open source. But the company provides many tutorials and help.
- **Touchdesigner** by Derivative is a robust authoring environment to create real time, physical, interactive experiences

Physical, interactive experiences built with the aforementioned tools can take on various forms and purposes. For example, developers used Touchdesigner to create a wall of screens that animate based on the conditions in the room at the Microsoft Theater Lounge in Downtown Los Angeles (Derivative, 2017). Another more didactic physical interactive experience (made with Max) can be found at the Zaans Museum in the Netherlands: hundreds of miniature windmills spin based on the visitors' location and movement in the space (Cycling '74, 2014).

■ Authoring Interactive Digital Media

BUILDING WEBSITES

Websites are built on the foundation of HTML, CSS and JavaScript. While these languages can be used to build games, apps and even kiosks, they are rooted in web development. For these reasons, a solid foundation in HTML, CSS and JavaScript is a versatile and practical skill set. But, to develop websites, a developer must also know how to register a domain name, set up web hosting, integrate a content management system, and transfer files to the web server.

How the Web Works

The web is built on a client-server model, with your computer acting as a client and the server, of course, the server. It works just like ordering at a restaurant: the computer is the patron and the server is the waitress. When you type a web address in your browser, you are making a request to the server, telling it exactly what you want it to serve up.

When requesting web content, the browser automatically prefaces the address you type with a http://or a https://. HTTP stands for Hypertext Transfer Protocol which indicates you are requesting content in the form of hypertext (meaning a web page). The extra "s" in "https:" indicates that the website is secure, a necessary measure a website owner must take in order to facilitate financial transactions.

Core Web Languages

HTML, CSS and JavaScript are the three core web languages used in conjunction to build websites. While you could technically build a web page without CSS and JavaScript, you definitely need to use HTML. JavaScript and CSS code are either included within the HTML page or referenced as external files within the HTML. Typically, web pages have the file extension "HTML," even when they include JavaScript and CSS. The reason why all three languages are used together is because each language is concerned with a different aspect of the site's functionality.

HTML, which stands for hypertext markup language, is focused on the meaning of the page. It describes what things are on the page, for example, this is a heading, this is a paragraph, or this is a list of items that goes in a particular

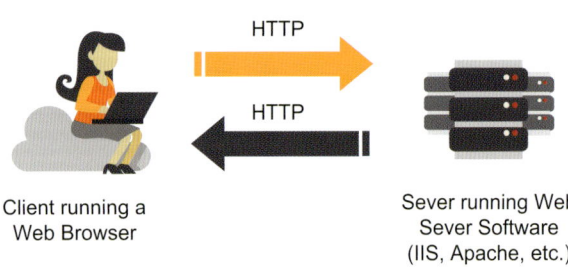

7.7 The web is based on a client-server model

order. So, just by looking at the HTML, you could understand the structure and the meaning. That's how Google can read a page and understand what the most important keywords are.

CSS, short for Cascading Style Sheets, is concerned with the presentation of the page. Within the CSS, developers describe the colors, fonts and how blocks of content relate to one another. Even spaces between paragraphs and line breaks are all controlled by CSS. Without CSS, a web page would all be one unbroken block of text on the page. Typically, all of the HTML files that are part of a website reference the same CSS file or files, which facilitates consistency in look and feel across all pages.

JavaScript is concerned with the behavior of elements on a website. JavaScript allows you to create interactive effects within the web page after it loads. A common use of JavaScript includes hiding and revealing areas on a page based on the user's mouse click. JavaScript is known as a "client-side language" because it doesn't communicate with the server. All of the interactivity occurs after the site is loaded on the client's computer.

Responsive Websites

Not long after smartphones made their debut in the late 2000s, it became exceedingly clear that it was not easy to see an entire website within the confines of the smaller screen. Reading text on a website required a lot of pinching and expanding. It also became evident that users were needing different types of content when accessing a website from their smartphone. For these reasons, developers started building sites that "responded" to the device that would access it. So, if a smartphone requested a website, the mobile version would be displayed, but if a desktop computer requested the site, typically a more robust version would be served up.

One of the most common methods of building responsive websites involves using the Bootstrap framework. Bootstrap is a set of open source JavaScript and CSS files that, when included within a website, allow the developer to design the page in a 12-column grid structure. Using Bootstrap syntax, the developer can specify how many columns an element should span in different contexts. So, for example, on a desktop computer screen, the corporate logo may be constrained to the top left corner and only span 2 of 12 columns, but on a mobile device, it might span all 12 columns. Bootstrap has made it much easier for developers to build responsive sites.

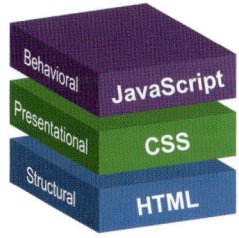

7.8 HTML, CSS and Javascript are the core web languages

■ Authoring Interactive Digital Media

Web Server-side Languages

Oftentimes, websites require functionality beyond the scope of HTML, CSS and JavaScript. In instances where content must be read or written to a database, a server-side language must be used. An e-commerce website is a perfect example of a website that depends on a server-side language because they are comprised of a product list, customer information, and past orders which are all stored in a database that can only be read from and written to by a server-side language.

One of the most common server-side languages is PHP, but there are many others. PHP is popular because it is open source, unlike Microsoft's server-side language ASP and ASP.NET. Like JavaScript code, blocks of PHP are inserted into the HTML page. However, unlike JavaScript, the PHP is interpreted by the server prior to returning the resulting page to the client. For example, the PHP code may request information about a particular product based on its ID in the database, but the resulting web page simply displays that product name, image, etc., that it has pulled from the database. Server-side languages cannot be seen when you view the source of a website within a browser because by the time it reaches the client computer, the language has already been interpreted by the server and the resulting HTML is displayed.

Content Management Systems

In the early days of the web, to change a web page required a change to the source code and re-uploading of the file. If a client had hired a web developer to build a website, they would have to contact the developer to make even a minor text change. From this conundrum, content managements systems were born. A content management system (CMS) is software that resides within your hosting

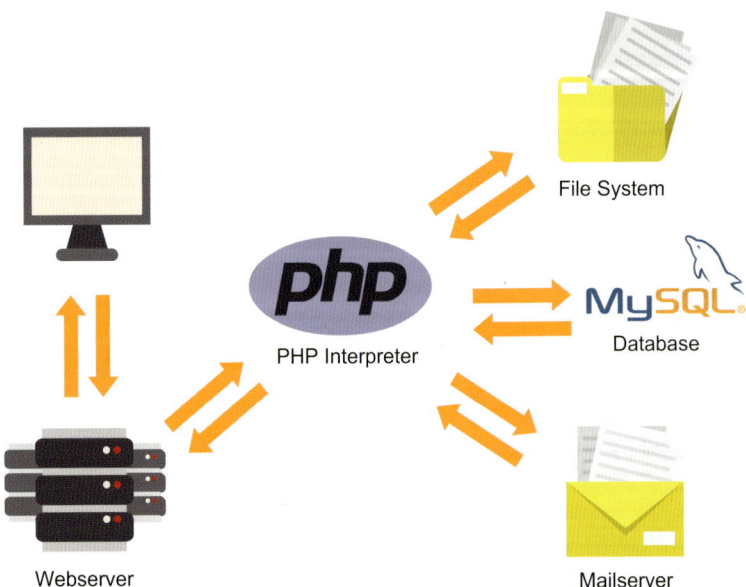

7.9 PHP is a server-side language that extends the capabilities of a website

Authoring Interactive Digital Media

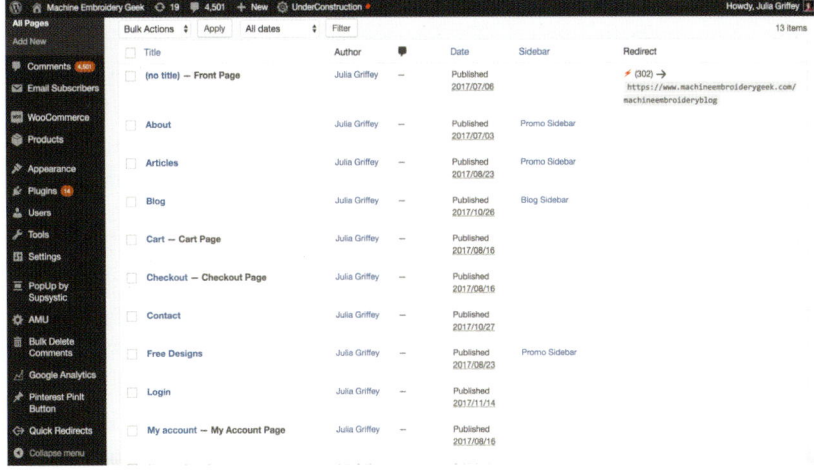

7.10 I use Wordpress to manage one of my websites. You can see in the dashboard that all of my pages are listed and I can easily edit the contents of that page

environment that allows an administrator to easily make changes to a website without having to know any code.

In order for editing and updating to work properly, however, the developer of the site would need to build the site in conjunction with the CMS. WordPress, despite the fact that it is known primarily as a blogging platform, has become the most popular content management system on the web with 30 percent of all websites running on it (Sawers, 2018). WordPress is widely used because it is free, open-source and written in the popular server-side language, PHP. Because it was developed for bloggers (and not coders) it's also very easy to use.

The Domain Name System

One of the most important steps that you need to take before building a website is to choose and register a domain name. Of course, if you build a site on a free

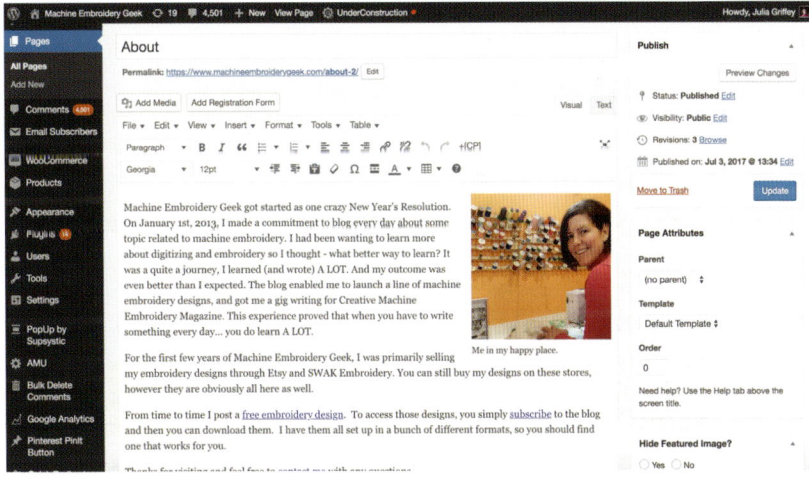

7.11 I use Wordpress to manage one of my websites. You can see in the dashboard that all of my pages are listed and I can easily edit the contents of that page

Authoring Interactive Digital Media

platform, you don't have the option to choose your own unique domain name. But if you are building a website with a more professional goal in mind, you should register your own domain name.

A domain name is the name of a website. You encounter them frequently in your everyday life: www.google.com, www.whitehouse.gov, www.craigslist.org, etc. They are fairly easy to remember and are usually somewhat intuitive since they often incorporate the company or organization they represent in the domain name. Domain names are actually aliases to numerically addressed Internet resources, which are called IP addresses. IP addresses are a string of numbers separated by periods, for example, the IP address of my website is: 107.180.50.232. (Note: this IP address will not pull up my website because the host has blocked requests via IP addresses for security reasons. If you type this IP address in the browser address field, you will see a GoDaddy branded landing page because it is where my site is hosted.) The reason why domain names are used instead of IP addresses is because it's a lot easier to remember a domain name than its associated IP address.

Every domain name has an extension which are the last characters of a domain name. For example, the extension for Yahoo is .com because the domain name is www.yahoo.com. Domain extensions were established by the Network Information Center in the early days of the Internet, and new ones are created all the time. These were intended to tell you a little bit about the website that resides at that domain. Websites for schools, school districts and universities have a .edu extension because they are educational institutions. Other common extensions include .mil for military sites, .gov for governments sites, and .org for non-profits. The .com domain, which is short for commercial is the most common, most desirable and usually most expensive domain extension. There are also many domains that are country specific. You can buy a domain with the .us extension to imply that your site is U.S. based, however this is not as common in the United States as it is in other countries. Almost every country has an associated domain extension, for example .fr is a French company, .mx is Mexican, etc.

You may wonder, if a domain name is actually an alias for an IP address, how do computers know what IP address refers to what domain name? In other words, if a user types www.yahoo.com into their web browser, how does your browser know the associated I.P. address for this domain? It must first ask a domain name registry, a table that stores domain names and associated IP addresses.

In the early days of the Internet, there was just one domain name registry, however, as the Internet grew, decentralization and redundancy were needed. The Domain Name System (DNS), launched in the mid 1980s as a network of servers throughout the Internet containing tables that match IP addresses to domain names. DNS servers are constantly checking each other and updating their tables based on the most recent information they find in other DNS servers. Once you register a domain name and associate it with a web server's IP address, it gets recorded on a DNS server that communicates with other DNS servers throughout the Internet so that they all have the same information. So, if

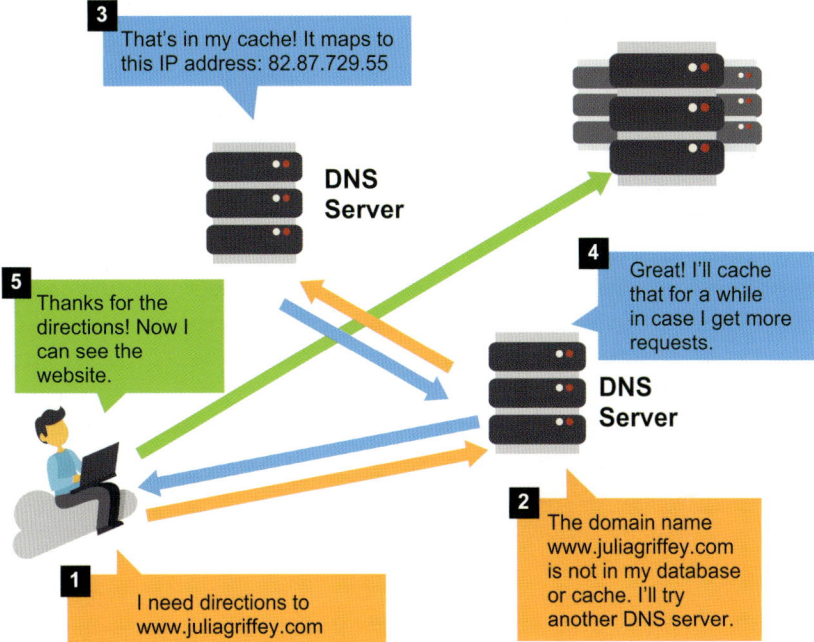

7.12 How DNS works

you point your domain to the new host (and associated IP address) by changing your web host, it might take a little while for that DNS server to communicate the information with all the other DNS servers in the world, and your site might be down for an hour or so.

Registering a Domain Name

When you register a domain name, you are essentially leasing that name. Being the owner of a domain name means that you have the rights to use it for a certain period of time. You can register a domain name for as little as one year or as long as 10 years. The cost of the domain name is usually about $15 per year, but varies depending on the desirability of the domain name. You can register a domain name from a number of companies called domain registrants, including Network Solutions, Register.com, 1and1.com, GoDaddy.com, Dreamhost.com, etc. Pricing varies from site to site but has gotten less expensive since the domain name registration business became decentralized in the mid 1990s.

While there are many options, it's a good idea to register your domain name when you purchase your hosting. First of all, it's a lot easier to have your domain registry and your hosting with the same company so that you receive just one bill. And, it's easier to point a domain name to an IP address within the same company.

Oftentimes people falsely assume that a domain name is available if they go to a web browser, type in the domain name and no website appears. However, it is possible for someone to register a domain name and not point it to an IP address where a website resides. In fact, some people buy domain names speculatively, never intending to build a website. Savvy entrepreneurs buy domain names of phrases and ideas that emerge in popular culture. Domain names have sold in the hundreds of millions of dollars and have only gotten more expensive (Styler, 2019). When Facebook wanted to change their name from "The Facebook" to "Facebook" and obtain the facebook.com domain in 2006, it was already taken. But they were able to purchase it for $200,000 from About Face Corp. who probably registered it for $15 per year. Their next major domain acquisition was even more expensive: in 2010, Facebook purchased fb.com for 8.5 million dollars (Drobnjak, 2017).

If you're curious about who owns a particular domain name, you can easily look it up on any domain registrant's "Whois lookup," where you can enter any domain name and learn who owns that domain. Even if the domain name was not registered with that particular registrant, you can still obtain this information because DNS information is shared among registrants.

If you really want to buy a domain name that is owned by someone else, like Mark Zuckerberg of Facebook, you can contact the owner and offer to buy it from them. Or you can look at the expiration date of the domain and hope that the owner forgets to renew it which will allow you to have the rights to purchase it. In the early days of the world wide web, this used to happen a lot more frequently than it does now. In the late 1990s, one of my clients forgot to renew their domain name and had to scramble to buy it back. And they weren't the only ones. Many large, respectable organizations like the Dallas Cowboys, Regions Bank and even Microsoft forgot to renew their domain names, lost control of them and had to buy them back (Duskic, 2018). Failing to renew domain names happens a lot less frequently now as most registrants have auto renew features so that you must take action to let your domain name expire.

Choosing a Domain Name

There are several factors consider prior to registering a domain name, which include:

- **Branding**—If you have an established brand, the domain should match. But, sometimes that's not easy because the most obvious domain name may not be available. If this is the case, sometimes getting creative can work to your benefit. For example, when my friend, Alix Henry founded Henry Architects, the domain name henryarchitects.com was not available. So, she registered the next best option: www.henryarchitectstaos.com, which turned out to be a good choice. If someone was searching for an architect in Taos, her site might show up in the results since her domain name contains both "Taos" and "architect."
- **Future directions**—If you have a company that currently offers one type of product, you may not want to put that product name into the domain name. Imagine you own a candle company, but later decide to branch into soaps and other personal care products. If your domain name is www.awesome-

candlecompany.com, your domain no longer represents what you have to offer. Fortunately, it is possible to buy multiple domain names and point them to the same IP address. So, www.awesomecandlecompany.com and www.awesomepersonalcare.com could point to the same website.

- **Length and spelling**—A common school of thought is that domain names with fewer characters are more valuable than longer ones. In fact, as of 2000, there were no three-letter .com unregistered domain names (Friedman, 2000). While shorter domain names are usually more desirable, one that is created at the expense of removing key letters can be confusing and hard to remember. For example, I have a friend named Zellie who owned a web design company and the corresponding domain name, zdsign.com which is a combination of the first letter of her first name and the word design with the "e" omitted. I always found it hard to remember because I couldn't recall which vowel was left out.
- **Other extensions available**—In some instances, it is important to have a variety of extensions available for the domain name you want to purchase. For example, if a company has both a charitable and a for-profit arm, it might be important to register both the .org extension and the .com extension.
- **Opinions of others**—Since there are no spaces in domain names, people might group the letters in a way that you had not expected. Pen Island (a company that sells pens) set up a website under the domain: www.pen-island.com and Speed of Art (a site for art enthusiasts) is: www.speedofart.com (Shontell, 2011). Ask your friends what they think of your potential domain name before proceeding with registration.
- **Previous ownership**—A domain name is only owned by a person/company or organization for fixed a period of time. But the web has been around since 1991, so a domain name might have been used by a company 10 years ago and then given up, and the domain's history could either be good or bad. If it was associated with a really popular site, it may result in residual traffic. Googling a domain name might lead you to sites referring to that domain, which may tell you what the old site was all about.

Setting up Web Hosting

If you want to set up a website, you will need to find a server on which to host your site. Most of the same companies that provide domain name registration also provide hosting. A web hosting company provides space on a web server (that they own or lease) with a continuous Internet connection so that the sites they host can be accessed at any time. Web hosts also provide access to this space so that the developer can build and update the website. A shared hosting account is the least expensive option, but you share server space with others. Dedicated hosting means you have your own dedicated web server which you could configure as you wish. If you were a web developer with many clients, you could sublease space to your clients and generate some ongoing revenue by billing your clients for hosting.

■ **Authoring Interactive Digital Media**

Anyone with a computer can be a web host, although it probably is not a great idea. If you did want to host your own website, you could turn your computer into a server by installing web server software and connecting that computer to the Internet. The problem with being your own host is that if your home loses power, or Internet access, your website will go down. You also open your entire home network to hackers.

In about 2000, a friend of mine decided that he would host all of his clients' sites out of his house on his own web server. Easy money, right? Just keep the computer running and connected to the Internet and send the client a bill each month. The only problem with this plan was that his Internet connection (DSL, which was new and spotty at the time) would go down periodically and bring down all his clients' websites. He would get calls from panicked clients at all hours wondering why their websites were down. Needless to say, he very quickly stopped acting as a web host.

Web hosting companies offer the benefit of having several continuous high-speed connections to the Internet so that if one line goes down, a backup is in place. Also, servers are cloned so that if one fails, the websites on it will still be accessible. Nonetheless, major hosting companies still have service failures from time to time (Warren, 2012).

The cost of hosting varies quite a bit: from a few dollars per month to hundreds of dollars a month depending on how much space you need, what kind of technology you need to support and how much traffic you plan to get. You can get web hosting for free, however, it comes with either advertising, very limited space, and/or restricted bandwidth. Free hosting also prevents you from registering a domain name and pointing it to a site you build in that space. Nevertheless, it will suffice for practicing your web development skills.

Other factors you should consider when choosing a web hosting plan include:

- **Reviews**—Many sites review web hosts, offering valuable insights.
- **Bandwidth limitations**—Bandwidth is the amount of data that can travel into and out of your website. Anytime someone requests a page on your site, it uses bandwidth.
- **Technical support**—Being able to speak with technical support can be very helpful, but not all hosts offer this service. Some tasks such as transferring a domain name or installing an SSL come up fairly infrequently, so it's helpful to be able to get some one on one guidance.
- **Email accounts**—Email accounts often come with a hosting package. For example, if you set up a website for a business www.yourbusiness.com—how many emails can you associate with the domain, e.g. sales@yourbusiness.com, info@yourbusiness.com, etc.?
- **CMS support**—If you plan on using a content management system for your website such as Joomla, Drupal or WordPress, make sure the hosting environment will support it.

Authoring Interactive Digital Media

- **Server-side language support**—If you will be programming in any server-side language, you will need to make sure that it will run on the web server. A Windows server supports ASP, but an Apache web server supports PHP.
- **Database support**—If you plan to build a website that communicates with a database, you will need to know the type and size of a database you can build.

Uploading a Website

After you build your website, have your domain registered and your hosting set up, you need to get your website files onto your server. The most common method of transporting files to the server is via FTP which stands for File Transfer Protocol. Some web hosts allow you to upload your files via a web-based interface, but FTP is still the preferred method of file transfer for most web developers. There are many different free or low-cost FTP programs available. In general, they all work very similarly: on one side, you see the files on your computer and on the other side, the files within your hosting space, and you just drag and drop your website files from your computer to the server and your website is visible to the world.

PRACTITIONER INTERVIEW

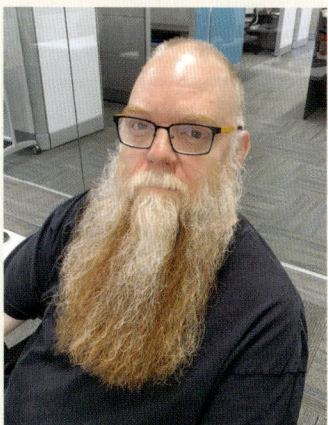

Jans Carton

WebSanity St. Louis, Missouri, USA
Jans Carton has been building websites for almost as long as the web has been in existence. In 1995, he founded one of the first web development firms in St. Louis, Missouri. Since 2002, Jans has been a principal of WebSanity, a St. Louis-based web development firm with a diverse clientele including large non-profits and Fortune 500 companies. Jans does UX

design, manages client communications, and writes all the display layer coding (HTML and CSS) for the sites WebSanity builds.

What's your background how did you get into this field?

I have a BS in photography. As I transitioned into manipulation and enhancement of digital imagery on computers, [it was] right at the cusp of the Internet, and I got distracted by this thing called the world wide web. So, I'm essentially self-taught.

How would you describe the beginning of the web?

I was introduced by a friend to the web. He pointed out some web pages and said, "Hey, check out this new publishing platform." At that time, it was very easy to look under the hood, so we just viewed the page source to learn how to build web pages. At that point in time it was very basic compared to web development today. I had the advantage of entering at a time when it was much simpler to pick up and learn on the go.

Why has web development gotten so much more complicated?

Now you have a lot more JavaScript involvement with websites, so if you just take a look at the source [code] it might not be what ends up actually being rendered on the page because the code could be modified via JavaScript [based on user interaction].

Did you do any Flash development and if not, why?

Well, we didn't do Flash development because we felt it had a short lifespan.

Wow, that was pretty good foresight.

We did do some Flash stuff back when it was FutureSplash [circa 1997], and then it was purchased by Macromedia, and it was renamed to Flash, and then Adobe bought them. We ran into lots of problems with it because of the kinds of websites we were building. They were very informational websites, and since Flash was not native to the web, all the information that was inside of any kind of Flash element on the page was a black box to Google and [other search engines]. They made efforts to make it more transparent later on, but it was never a true native thing, and we were like "this is definitely not the future of the web." So, we didn't want to develop expertise in something that we felt wasn't going to last.

What type of hosting and CMS do you offer your clients?

We use an open-source content management system that we've extended with some proprietary add-ons. Our major motivation in choosing it was the business model of providing web services.

So, instead of building a "love them and leave them" site, we felt it was best to provide those services of maintaining the server environment, updating the software, monitoring for security, and providing ongoing support. We had been in companies that had tried the previous method [of building a site and letting the client maintain it], and it always ended in tears. They would have a change of personnel, and then have no idea what to do with the site. So, typically, after a period of time it got thrown away and completely replaced. We find with providing web services, they come back to us, and when they want changes, and we can evolve the site, and it lasts much longer and they're happier and get better services through it.

It seems like a smarter business model too, because it's ongoing revenue.

It is great. But you never get rid of a terrible client, and it's not scalable. So, we are always going be a fairly small company. It's not something we can get rich on. We are always going to have a limited number of people that we can support.

What about any mistakes along the way? Any epic fails?

The craziest idea was to use frame sets for layout purposes. Way back when, we had very little control over the layout of the web page. You had tables, or nothing. Then frame sets were introduced, and I said "hey, you know, you can have independently scrolling parts of the page. Let's use this for actual framing and layout purposes." [The problem was,] it got massively complex. It worked, but it was it was just a nightmare to try to maintain.

Have you had any domain mishaps?

Yeah, there were a couple of lost domains. We'd have clients that were hesitant to have us maintain and update the domain. But sometimes clients want to do it themselves, for whatever reason, and will fumble the ball and just not renew it. And we don't get any notifications because we're not listed as a contact. Then we'll get a panicked phone call [from the client] saying "my website's down!" And we'll have to tell them, "oh, your domain has expired."

It's been some time since a domain has been lost because they've added a grace period. Now you get a 90-day period to renew the domain even after it has expired, preventing anyone from registering it right out from under you. [That would happen] back in the day where [the domain would expire], and then—boom—it [would get] snaked!

What do you what do you think has been the most exciting evolution in terms of web technology?

Well, just the newer layout mechanisms. I'm talking about flexbox and grid layout. Many developers still don't understand that the web is a document oriented infrastructure. It was designed to display text on the page that's

■ **Authoring Interactive Digital Media**

hyperlinked to other text. There was no layout method built in to the web until flexbox. Before that, the closest thing you had were floats which were intended to simply get text to wrap around an image. Up until flexbox, everything that you did for layout was a hack. Previously, we used tables for layout, but tables were never intended for layout, they were intended to present tabular data. Then we switched to floats. I mean even Bootstrap 3 uses floats for creating a grid. Floats were never intended for that purpose. But now we have flexbox which is definitely intended for layout. It's mind-blowing that it hasn't come up until now.

What web evolution are you excited to see in the future?

One of the things that I've seen coming up in the future is the ability to have compiled apps running natively in the browser which is called web assembly. What that means is that you could have a full-fledged app like Photoshop running inside the web browser.

Also, Scalable Vector Graphics (SVG) format is really huge which provides an image/drawing format that can be manipulated via JavaScript (because it's text-based). This means you can do really cool visualizations and animations without depending entirely on JavaScript [and the HTML element], Canvas. It also brings resolution-independent graphics to the Web.

Virtualization is a super biggie from an infrastructure standpoint. We used to have to house, configure, and maintain a web server computer in a data center to serve websites. Now we can create virtual servers on the fly. We're moving toward "server-less" hosting where we simply access web server services instead of configuring and maintaining an entire virtual machine.

DISCUSSION QUESTIONS

1) Are there any web domain names that you find difficult to remember? If so, why?
2) Do a Whois lookup for your domain name (e.g. mine would be www.juliagriffey.com). Is your domain name available? If not, who owns it? Does it lead you to a website? What would it cost for you to buy it?
3) Does the interactive media authoring process seem more or less complex than what you had anticipated? Why or why not?
4) How did Apple manipulate the interactive media authoring tools and processes? Was this fair or unfair to developers who invested in building expertise in a specific area?
5) How has video game production changed with the introduction of game engines? Is it a positive or negative change?

REFERENCES

Clement, J. (2019).The Statistics Portal: Number of apps available in leading app stores as of 2nd quarter 2019.*Statista*. Online Available at: https://www.statista.com/statistics/276623/number-of-apps-available-in-leading-app-stores.

Cycling '74 (2014) Interactive Windmill Installation for Zaans Museum Exhibition. Online Available at: https://cycling74.com/projects/interactive-windmill-installation-for-zaans-museum-exhibition.

Derivative (2017) VolvoxLabs Meticulously Animates Engagement at Microsoft Theatre Lounge DTLA. *Derivative*, October 17. Online. Available at: http://derivative.ca/events/2017/MicrosoftDTLA.

Drobnjak, A. (2017). From TheFacebook.com to Facebook.com to FB.ME to M.ME. *Domain.Me*. Online Available at: https://domain.me/how-thefacebook-com-became-facebook-com.

Duskic, G. (2018). 9 Famous Domain Expirations in Internet History. *WHOAPI Blog*. Online Available at: https://whoapi.com/blog/5-all-time-domain-expirations-in-internets-history.

The Franklin Institute (n.d.) *History of Virtual Reality*. Online Available at: https://www.fi.edu/virtual-reality/history-of-virtual-reality.

Friedman, S. C. (2000). No 3-Letter .Com Names Left. *New York Post*, April 17. Online Available at: https://nypost.com/2000/04/17/no-3-letter-com-names-left.

Helander, D. (2012). Mobile Gaming Gets a Performance Boost: Adobe AIR 3.2 with 2D and 3D Hardware Acceleration Announced. *Adobe Blog*. Online Available at: http://blogs.adobe.com/flashplayer/tag/angry-birds#sthash.qrDG4auK.dpbs.

Kim, H.-J., Min, J.-Y., Kim, H.-J., & Min, K.-B. (2017). Accident Risk Associated With Smartphone Addiction: A Study on University Students in Korea. *Journal of Behavioral Addictions*, *6*(4), 699–707. Online Available at: https://doi.org/10.1556/2006.6.2017.070.

Löchtefeld, M., Böhmer, M., & Ganev, L. (2013). AppDetox: Helping Users with Mobile App Addiction. In *Proceedings of the 12th International Conference on Mobile and Ubiquitous Multimedia* (p. 43: 1–43:2).New York: ACM. Online Available at: https://doi.org/10.1145/2541831.2541870.

McNichol, T. (2010). How Adobe is Battling the Flash-Bashing. *Bloomberg Businessweek*, (4185), 28–29. Online. Available at: https://www.bloomberg.com/news/articles/2010-06-24/adobe-battles-the-flash-bashing.

Sawers, P. (2018). WordPress now powers 30% of websites. *Venture Beat*, March 5. Online. Available at: https://venturebeat.com/2018/03/05/wordpress-now-powers-30-of-websites

Scott, J. (2017). HyperCard On The Archive (Celebrating 30 Years of HyperCard). *Internet Archive Blogs*, August 11. Online. Available at: https://blog.archive.org/2017/08/11/hypercard-on-the-archive-celebrating-30-years-of-hypercard

Shontell, A. (2011). 15 Unintentionally Inappropriate Domain Names. *Business Insider*, June 28. Online. Available at: https://www.businessinsider.com/20-wildly-inappropriate-sounding-domain-names-2011-6#whod-have-thought-nycanalcom-had-historical-value-9.

Strain, M. (2015). 1983 to Today: A History of Mobile Apps. *The Guardian*, February 13. Online. Available at: https://www.theguardian.com/media-network/2015/feb/13/history-mobile-apps-future-interactive-timeline.

Styler, J. (2019). The Top 25 Most Expensive Domain Names. *GoDaddy*, June 18. Online. Available at: https://www.godaddy.com/garage/the-top-20-most-expensive-domain-names/.

Unity. (n.d.). Online. Available at: https://unity.com.

Warren, C. (2012). GoDaddy's DNS Servers Go Down, Along with Thousands of Sites. *Mashable UK*, September 10. Online. Available at: https://mashable.com/2012/09/10/godaddy-down/#2u0j.NKdSuqB

8 Usability

INTRODUCTION

Put simply, usability is an interactive application's ability to function in a manner that accomplishes what it was intended to do in an efficient, learnable, memorable, error-free and pleasurable manner (Nielsen, 2012). If the application has poor usability, then interaction cannot occur and the product will not do what it was intended to do. Even when the concept is great, if usability is bad, games aren't played, products aren't purchased and apps are deleted.

Think about the last time you installed a new app on your mobile device. What criteria did you use to decide whether or not you would keep it? If I can't get the app to do what I want it to do in a few minutes, it's gone. My experience is not unique. A massive percentage (80–90 percent) of all downloaded apps are removed from smart phones after their first use (Abhishek, 2016). If you want to build a popular app, usability matters!

Good usability has a direct correlation to revenue. More usable games lead to longer play times and higher rates of transactions (Duran, 2017). On e-commerce sites, good usability has been shown to enhance trust with the user, and in turn, generate better online sales (Aubert et al., 2001).

WHY GOOD USABILITY IS IMPORTANT

In 1982, Atari was at its peak. The Atari 2600 home console was one of the hottest products on the market and consumers gobbled up new games as soon as they hit the stores. That summer, *E.T. the Extraterrestrial* was a blockbuster hit. Looking to capitalize on the success, Steven Spielberg approached Atari about making a game to be released in time for the holiday season. The catch was that Atari needed to produce the game in 6 weeks which was quite a bit shorter than the typical game development timeline of at least 6 months.

Atari game developer, Howard Scott Warshaw, took on the task of building the game and completed it within the outrageous timeline. However, with such a tight development schedule, he had no time to learn more about his audience and their expectations or get much feedback on the game. Despite the fact that it featured the hottest movie character at the time, the game was a compete

Usability ■

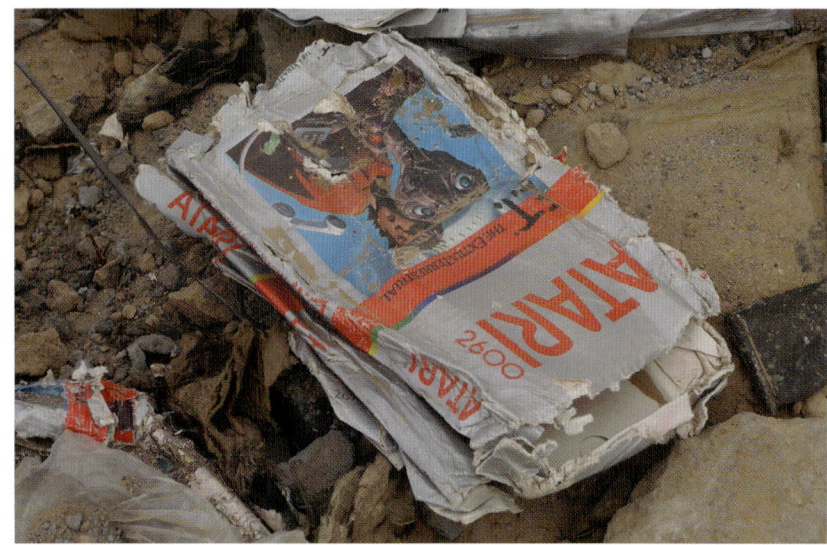

8.1
Atari's E.T. game recovered from the landfill.

Source: Wikimedia Commons. Online. Available HTTP: <https://commons.wikimedia.org/wiki/File:Atari_E.T._Dig-_Alamogordo,_New_Mexico_(14036097792).jpg>

flop. In fact, it's often referred to as "the worst video game ever." It was incredibly frustrating to play because E.T. kept getting stuck in a ditch. As a result, many copies were returned or unsold, and Atari buried almost a million *E.T.* games in the New Mexico desert. *E.T.*, the video game, marked the beginning of the end for Atari's dominance in the home video game industry (Kent, 2001).

What could have prevented the *E.T.* video game disaster from happening? One bad decision before the project even began (truncated development timeframe with one primary developer) had a cumulative negative effect on the final product. Had the production process been executed with usability in mind, would the outcome have been different? What would have happened if extensive user testing had occurred? Would the game have been released? Now that the industry has matured, common practices have been established that begin in the pre-production phase, continue throughout the production phase, and are carried on even after the product is released, that improve the usability of an interactive product.

ACHIEVING GOOD USABILITY IN EVERY PHASE

What is the point of making any interactive media application if it is reviled by users/players? No development team wants to build an application with poor usability. But designers and developers are not users, so it's easy for the team making the product to miss the mark. Fortunately, strategies exist throughout the development process to improve the usability of the final product.

Discovery Phase
Learning about users should commence prior to any design or production. The more you can learn about your users, the easier it will be to make decisions about what direction the project should take.

■ Usability

A common way user experience designers get to know the future users of an interactive project is through surveys, interviews and focus groups where users reveal their likes/dislikes, frustrations, needs and wants. Oftentimes users' responses are not what you expect. Don't make assumptions about users. Be open to what your research is telling you.

When asked about problems or issues with an application, users have a tendency to offer a solution, which is oftentimes not the best one. Focus on creatively solving users' problems instead of putting too much weight into their proposed solutions. Henry Ford said that before the invention of the automobile, if you were to ask people what they wanted, they would have said "faster horses." They had no idea that a car would be a possibility. In a similar way, users may not be aware of alternative designs and technologies that could solve their problems.

The different types of users for an interactive application are often different to what you initially expect. It has been well documented that gaming studios believed the majority of their players were adolescent men. Surprisingly, women gamers are now outnumbering men, and studios are beginning to respond, albeit slowly, including female protagonists in their games (Jayanth, 2014).

One exercise that helps development teams put themselves in the users' shoes is to write user personas. User personas are short narratives about representative users and what they would be looking to accomplish or expect by using the application. This exercise helps to ensure that the needs of every type of user are met.

Design Phase

A user-centric design approach can also improve usability. In content-rich applications, users can help with the organization and labeling of information through the use of a card sort. A card sort is a method in which all of the topics within the application are written on individual cards. Representative users are given the cards and are asked to group them into related topics and label each group. Based on how the testers sorted the topics, designers create a taxonomy for the content and then test their assumptions by performing a reverse sort. A reverse sort is like a card sort, however, users are asked to place topics or questions under given category names. Reverse sorts allow an information architect to test her organizational structure she built based on the first sort.

Optimal Sort (www.optimalsort.com) has great tools that facilitate web-based card sorts and reverse sorts. You simply set up all the content to be sorted and send out invites to representative users through the Optimal Sort website. The site then keeps track of the results and generates visualizations to help you understand the data.

Developing a hierarchy of categories and subcategories that users understand makes a content-rich application more usable. Presenting too many options upfront can overwhelm a user. While this may seem counterintuitive, think about how you feel when trying to order off of a really long menu at a restaurant. My gut reaction is to tell the server to just bring me anything, because I don't want to try to sort through it all. In a similar way, some applications have a lot of options and information. Grouping and categorizing helps guide users through all of the content and prevents them from feeling overwhelmed.

Many information-rich websites not only categorize content, but also prioritize it. For example, if you visit Yahoo, you can see that information is categorized and prioritized so that the viewer is guided through the information. There is a main dominant image which is generally a big news story, but users can easily access all of the categories down the left-hand side to find what we came to Yahoo for. If we want to get further in-depth news, it's still readily available. Sites like Yahoo employ other design techniques to keep it from feeling overwhelming. For example, the use of color is kept to a minimum. The intention is to prevent color from detracting from the content and overwhelming the user.

Users' existing knowledge can help guide the layout of elements on the screen. Most users who visit your website, use your app, or play your game will have had some previous experience interacting with similar applications, and designers can take advantage of this knowledge to expedite understanding of your application. On a website, an established convention is to locate the logo at the top left corner. For example, visitors generally look to the footer of a website for general information about the organization such as the address and contact information. Underlined text is generally perceived to be a link. Menu bars are usually placed on the left-hand side of the website or across the top. If you put your menu bar in other locations or you spread out in different locations, it can be confusing.

Even though apps have only been around for a relatively short amount of time, conventions have been established around their design as well. On an app, branding is usually in the top center of the screen. There are also usually a few icons in the bottom bar that take you back to the different functions of the app. By following these conventions, your app will be easier to learn.

Visual metaphors can also boost usability. You may recall from English class that a metaphor is a comparison between two items using "like" or "as." Metaphors are incredibly useful for boosting comprehension because the definition is based on something your audience already knows. For example, if you had never tried frozen yogurt, I might tell you that it's like ice cream, but a bit lighter.

A visual metaphor works in a similar way. Consider a right-pointing triangle within an interactive experience; it alludes to the play button on a media player. Since we are familiar with it in one context, we can immediately understand that if you click on it, you're going to play some form of media. The trash can is another great example of a visual metaphor. It's easy to understand that

■ Usability

the trash can is for throwing away a file because we get rid of stuff in a real trash can. Folders are another good example of a visual metaphor. We know that folders are for organizing things, because we know how to file papers in a folder in the real world. While these visual metaphors have been incorporated into our computers' operating systems, these and others are frequently integrated throughout any interactive application for the purpose of aiding usability.

After designers have made some decisions about layout of key screens, preliminary usability can be tested. Specific tasks are defined that would likely pertain to different types of users. Then, designers can use programs like Axure, Sketch and InVision to rapidly develop wireframes and prototypes that can be tested by representative users. Observing user interaction with wireframe prototypes can help identify any usability issues prior to development of the final product.

Good usability goes beyond the functionality of an application, it also matters if the application is enjoyable to use. Fun and enjoyment are the most important attributes of many interactive applications, especially games. Understanding the users' abilities, preferences and needs should guide design decisions to make the application pleasurable for the users. For example, the homepage of PBSkids. org reflects the development team's understanding of their target audience: kids. Even pre-school aged kids who are not yet reading can still use the application. The interface design relies on very few words; it's playful and simple. All of the interactivity happens via clicking on pictures. There is also a large wheel that the user can turn by putting the mouse on one of the large arrows around it. It's fun to use as well as very forgiving. The designers understood that some kids don't have great fine motor control and would likely have trouble interacting with traditional dropdown menus. So, to get to a specific game, the kid just needs to put the cursor over a large picture of the character in the game. The color scheme also contributes to the fun, as the interface is filled with bright colors, especially neon green which is a favorite with kids.

Development Phase

The goal of building a usable product does not end after the design phase is complete. To ensure good usability, the development process should be agile, where work in progress is continually tested and assessed, with the user experience designer(s) working hand in hand with programmers and even the client in some cases. Some of the principles of agile development include valuing users, welcoming changes and working collaboratively (Beck et al., 2001).

An agile development process is the antithesis of Howard Scott Warshaw's experience building the *E.T.* video game back in 1982. Warshaw isolated himself for 6 weeks to finish the doomed game. There was no time for prototyping, collaboration, reflection, iteration and making modifications which explained why the game had such poor usability.

GUIDELINES FOR GOOD USABILITY

While user research and feedback guide the design and development of an interactive product, following some guiding principles can boost usability.

When the web was emerging in the late 1990s, Jakob Nielsen was working as an engineer at Sun Microsystems, hired to make their software easier to use. With a PhD in human-computer interaction, he was well-qualified for the task. However, as he was working on Sun software, he also noticed an explosion of new websites, especially really bad websites, and was inspired to write some guidelines for building more usable ones (Muiseum, n.d.). Since his time at Sun, Nielsen has written several articles and books on the topic, and has been called the "king of usability" (Nielsen Norman Group, n.d.).

While Nielsen's guidelines were inspired by the web, many of his ideas can be applied to all forms of interactive media as a checklist to avoid pitfalls that lead to poor usability. The following principles are endorsed by Nielsen as well as other usability experts.

Be Explicit

What will the user experience/learn/do with this application? Before anyone tries to use your application, they will want to know a bit about what to expect. For this reason, video games often commence with a cinematic opening that provides players with a preview. Even on websites, a visitor should know right away what the site is about and the value it might provide.

Be Consistent

Consistency enhances learnability. For example, once the user discovers that a certain option lives within a particular menu, it's easy to find again. Changing colors, location of controls and visual treatments can be confusing to a user.

Be Flexible

Allow the user to skip features. Think about any e-commerce website. Let's say you enter all your shipping information but then you realize you want to add one more thing to the cart. It can be annoying to have to go back and fill out all that information again if you just want to make one little change to your shopping cart. Designing interactive applications with flexibility in mind makes them more usable.

Be Forgiving

Don't assume users will do the "right" thing. Users tend to do things in a way a developer does not expect. What happens if the user tries to check out before adding any products to the cart? What happens if a user tries to return to a previous challenge in a game? The developer may wonder why anyone would want

■ Usability

to do these things, but users are unpredictable. Don't punish users for their unexpected behaviors.

Be Helpful
Despite your best efforts, not everything in your application will be self-evident. Provide easy access to help in various forms. Tool tips can clarify functionality of icons and statements. Helpful tips in a game might motivate a player to keep trying. Accessible help in various forms will reduce user frustration.

Provide Feedback
Let users know when they have done something. Integrating a bit of auditory feedback when the user has clicked on a button lets the user know that their input has been received by the computer. Simple animations are also used as feedback to help the user understand that the computer is working on a task, e.g. after checking out on an ecommerce site or when elements are loading.

Minimize Memory Load
Minimizing memory load means not asking users to recall a great deal of information in order to accomplish a task. Having the links change colors after the user has clicked them prevents the user from having to memorize where she has gone. On a checkout kiosk at a grocery store, users should not have to memorize codes for various fruits and vegetables. Thumbnail images of the produce allow the user to quickly identify and scan the object.

Provide Closure
Provide users with assurance that they have done what they set out to do. For example, at Southwest Airline check-in kiosk, the final screen features a "finished button." It isn't necessary for the users to click it because at that point the user has everything he needs: bag tags, boarding pass and instructions on where to go next. However, clicking the finished button provides reassurance to the user that he has completed all the required tasks and the next person who uses the kiosk won't be accessing their information.

Provide Motivation
Progress bars in a game remind the user how far they've come and what they have left. On the training website, Lynda.com, you are motivated to complete a course with visual reminders of how much you have left to complete. Vacation home booking sites motivate both owners and guests to contribute knowledge to their database. If you are a host, Airbnb won't let you see how your guest reviewed your place until you leave a review of your guest.

Reduce effort
Make it as easy as possible for the user to do what they need to do. Keep related controls together and important features accessible. For example, on an

e-commerce site, users should be able to see their shopping cart and checkout from any page.

It probably sounds like there's a lot of rules to follow to ensure good usability, but there are occasions where you can break them. For example, if you know that your target audience has a common knowledge base, then perhaps you don't have to be as explicit in some areas. Innovative designs and new navigation schemes that don't adhere to known conventions could be far superior to their predecessors but should always be tested to determine their usability.

GUIDELINES FOR FUN

For task-oriented applications, usability is a paramount. But when it comes to video games, fun is equally as important. A game of tic tac toe is a lot less interesting once you figure out how not to lose. A game's fun factor can be assessed prior to production based on a set of heuristics, such as ones outlined in Ralph Koster's book, *A Theory of Fun*. In it, he states that successful games that have the following traits "hit the right cognitive buttons to be fun."

- Preparation—the player should be able to make some choices to improve her likelihood of winning.
- Sense of Space—the game should exist in some type of landscape either literal or abstract (e.g. a checkerboard).
- A range of challenges.
- A solid core mechanic—some type of interesting problem to solve.
- A range of abilities required to solve the encounter.
  Skill required in using the abilities—bad decisions throughout game play lead to negative consequences.

(Koster, 2013)

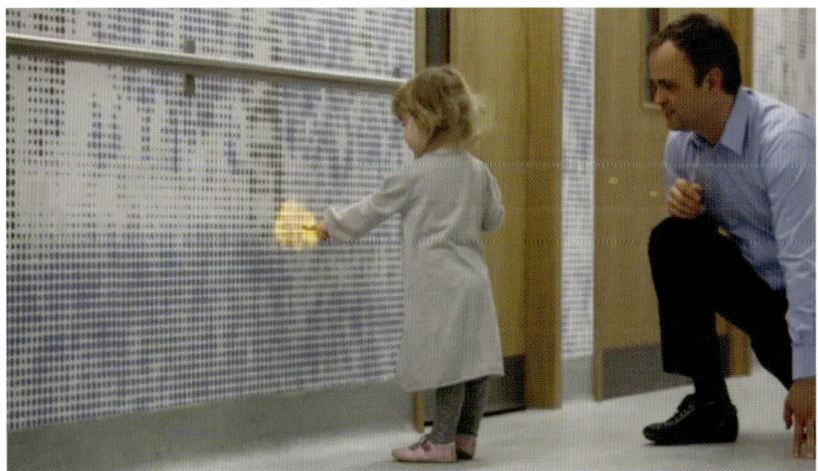

8.2
The Nature Trail exhibit reveals moving animals "inside" the wall when touched

■ **Usability**

Interactive, physical installations are not at all task focused; their reason for existing is to inspire playful experimentation. Successful installations require a user to learn how to interact with the system while incorporating an element of random surprise. For example, the "Nature Trail" installed along the walls of the Mittal Children's Medical Centre in the UK requires a visitor to discover that the wall responds to touch and that moving animals will appear "inside" the wall based on the user's location. Because the projection changes over time, there is always an element of variability.

USABILITY AND PLAY TESTING

Even if the team has followed a user-centric development process and abided by all of the principles of good usability, usability testing should be performed after the product is built. Usability testing is designed to answer the question "is the application easy and pleasurable to use?" The goal of the testing is to identify and fix as many problems as possible.

One challenge of usability testing is that clients tend not to value it the way they should and do not budget for it. So, it puts you in a tight spot as a developer knowing that it's in the best interest of the application to do some usability testing but not having the budget to do so.

There are two different types of usability tests you can do: expert usability tests or user usability tests. Or, you can do a combination of both. The experts would be professionals familiar with usability pitfalls, and they then report on problems. User usability testing involves getting together a group of representative users and having them try out the application while you document the experience.

Common types of expert usability tests include:

- **A heuristic evaluation**. Experts go through an application to see if it violates any rules contained in a short set of design heuristics.
- **A guidelines review**. Like a heuristic evaluation but focused more on technical issues.
- **A cognitive walkthrough**. Experts go through a series of tests that the user would perform and assess the functionality.
- **A consistency inspection**. An expert reviews all parts of an interactive application to ensure that the layout, terminology, colors, design, etc., is the same.
- **Formal usability inspection**. Designers justify and defend their design choices to expert reviewers, screen by screen.

The process of user usability testing begins with finding representative users. If you're making an application for doctors, you wouldn't want college students to do your usability testing. People that participate in user testing are either paid or are people who are really enthusiastic about testing out the product who will do it for free. For example, software companies like Adobe will contact instructors or heavy users to test out the latest version of Photoshop before it's released. The benefit to the software company is that bugs are discovered before the software is released on a larger scale.

When you do a usability test, you want to mimic the actual use setting. For example, if you are testing an app that is intended to be used while exercising, you should have someone test it while exercising.

Some companies that do a great deal of usability testing actually have usability labs which contain computers, cameras, audio recording devices and a one-way mirror to observe the users. An alternative to testing in a lab is to bring a "lab in the bag" to your users. It is also possible to conduct a web-based usability testing where you can observe user behavior through the web.

The following user usability testing methodologies can be done independently or in combination with others.

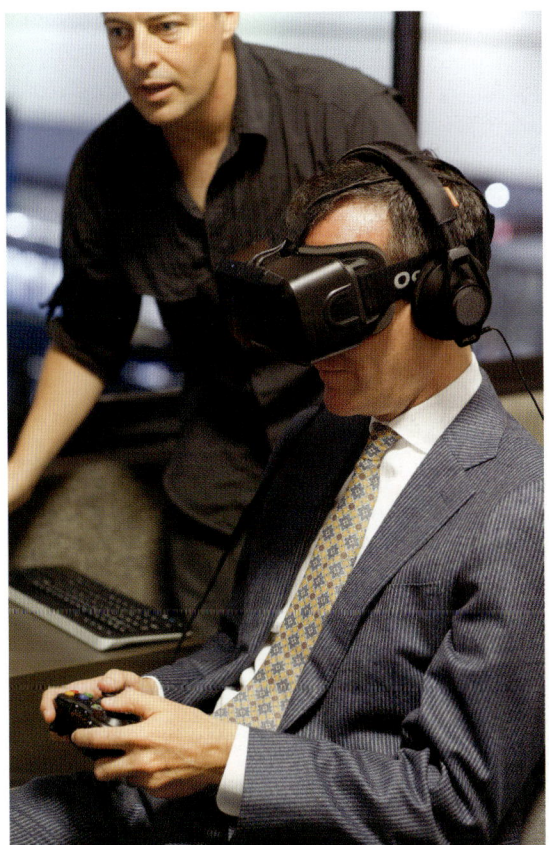

8.3
User testing a virtual reality experience. Source: Wikimedia Commons. Online. Available HTTP: <https://upload.wikimedia.org/wikipedia/commons/0/0d/E3_Gaming_Conference_%2814518761733%29.jpg>

■ **Usability**

- **Performance Measurement**—users are asked to perform a list of critical tasks within the application and are scored based on their performance.
- **Thinking Aloud**—users are given tasks and encouraged to verbalize their thoughts as they attempt to complete them.
- **Coaching**—users are assisted by the evaluator in the execution of various tasks while the evaluator is assessing the user.
- **Questionnaires**—users are asked to perform some tasks with the application and the tester asks for feedback on their experience.

After an application is launched, the usability of specific features are often assessed via A/B testing online. For example, if a website contains a sign-up form and the goal is to maximize conversions, the development team may roll out one form style for a week and then a different one for another week and see which one leads to the most conversions. The winner of that test might be tested against another version until the team is satisfied with the results.

Game companies often have an entire quality assurance department dedicated to testing their games. While playing video games all day, every day, might sound like a dream job to some, it's actually quite time-consuming and repetitive. The game tester has to come up with as many different ways to play the game with the intention of finding bugs. For example, if a game has 20 different characters and 20 different levels, a video game tester would have to play as each character vs. each character on all levels which would be 8,000 different matchups. After a while it would probably get a bit monotonous. For this reason, quality assurance (QA) testing in the video game industry is an entry level position taken to springboard one's career into the industry.

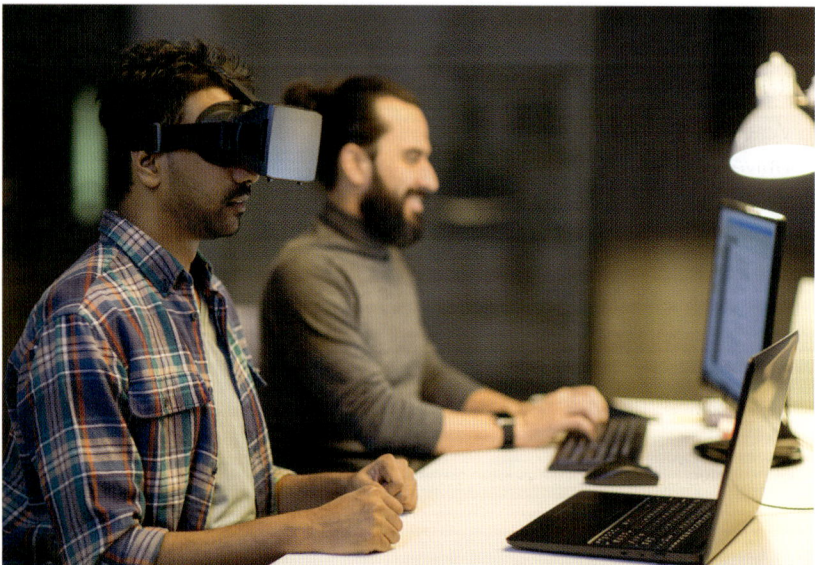

8.4
A video game tester must test every combination of variables in a game.

Source: ©
dolgachov; 123RF.com

PRACTITIONER INTERVIEW

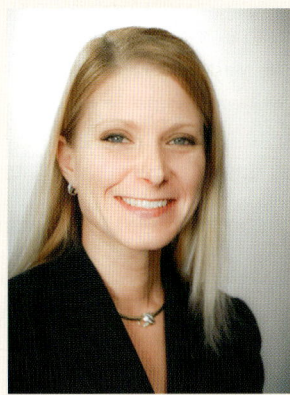

Julie Gaieski

Principal UX Designer, Fidelity—Boston, MA USA
Julie Gaieski is a principal UX designer at Fidelity Investments whose responsibilities include information architecture, visual design and user research for many interactive applications produced within Fidelty. Prior to working for Fidelity, Julie was a front-end developer at a start-up building websites with HTML/CSS and PHP.

What is your educational background and how did you get into this field?

I went to the New England Institute of Art [for] my bachelor's degree in interactive media. After graduation, I got a job as a web design manager at a start-up and got a lot of experience coding HTML, CSS, PHP, and doing some database work. [I also] wrote proposals and [pitched] to new clients. I [wore] a lot of different hats there, but the usability side of things was missing.

When I left to join Fidelity, I met a lot of people who came from Bentley University, [and I became] really interested in a [graduate] program they had that focused around user research. So, I got my master's degree in Human Factors in Information Design [from Bentley]. It focused on user research and usability, but more generally on how people use the products and services that we create.

What kind of interactive media are you producing at Fidelity?

When I joined Fidelity, I thought of it as a financial institution, which it is. But it's almost like a nation of little businesses [with a lot of opportunities for interactive designers]. When I started, I was working on brokerage software [which was for] advisers and brokers who were trading on behalf of clients, so it was very transactional. Then, I moved into the world of enterprise software,

■ Usability

so I was actually supporting employees of Fidelity, designing organizational charts, and informational HR sites, that kind of thing, [which was] much more content-based. Then I moved over to supporting Fidelity International, traveling back and forth from Germany. That work was more marketing based, helping advisors to sell funds to new prospects. Now, I'm helping with Fidelity.com, which is [for] the end customers or investors like you and me, picking out products and making their financial dreams come true.

So, all of your projects represent a lot of different types of users?

Absolutely, but primarily all websites and web-based software, some content sites, some marketing-type sites, but then others that are more like a tool. And then I have done some software that you install on your desktop, but that's pretty rare now.

How do you explain to people what you do?

I try to understand people's needs and goals and then make a design based on that so that it is usable and will actually help [users].

So why is usability in interactive media important?

The customer is the center of everything we do, and without him or her, we have no business! We need to find what makes them tick—not to be just one other commodity vendor, but a partner they'll trust and love! User research helps us with that.

In the pre-planning process, what form does your user research take?

If I'm coming into a new project, I try to understand if there has been research done so far. Do you have personas? Have you done interviews or surveys? What kind of data do you have? How well do you understand what [users'] needs are, and how well does your product fit their needs? Have you heard customer feedback about certain areas that don't work for them, or are you doing really well in some area and you want to build on that? So, it's really understanding the user and how the product is matching the users' needs. If a lot of that is lacking, which typically it is, we'll try to fill in the gaps.

To really understand what's going on in the customer experience, we do a lot of journey mapping. We just try to say, okay, so where does this all begin? Then we go through the end-to-end journey and where the touch points are with Fidelity and ask if those are painful, or where the good parts are and what opportunities we can pull out of that.

What kind of surprises have you gotten along the way when you've done this kind of user research?

One study that totally baffled us was a card sort for our intranet website. We were trying to come up with a structure that was logical to most employees. But there are a lot of different types of employees, and a lot of different types of information. When the results [from the card sort] came back, users either suggested three buckets with twenty items in them, or like 15 buckets with three items in them. And they were all completely different labels and different ways of organizing things. So, we had to make some assumptions, put some things out there and then do some A/B testing between a couple of different structures to see what worked a little bit better.

How are you checking the usability of an interactive product as you are developing it?

We've become a much more agile company. We used to do a lot of heavy usability testing up front, early and often. Typically, if it was a big project, we'd be really rigorous around our testing and making sure things worked pretty perfectly before we went out, because there was such a fear of failure and risk.

Now it's moved in the total opposite direction. It's all about time to market. We try to get things out in front of customers and maybe a small audience first and see how it does and measure and then scale. So, it's been more about getting real data by getting things out there faster versus doing a whole big project, trying to get it perfect, and then putting it out. Then we're challenged with measuring not only traffic, but value. How are our customers reacting to what they're seeing? Is it a satisfying experience, or is it a bad experience? It's been a challenge as a user researcher and a designer to not go through that full process [of usability testing] and just trust that you know what you're doing and that you will measure appropriately and take the time to go back and fix it if it's not right.

What kind of tools do you do use to do that?

We use a program called Clicktail which can measure where somebody is on a page and things that they're clicking on, and align that to demographics. If a customer's logged-in, we know certain things about them, and we can draw correlations between different participants' data and their behavior. But, that's all very quantitative and [does not necessarily reveal] why they are doing it or how the experience was in a qualitative way. We have some thumbs up/thumbs down helpfulness ratings [for users to give us] a sense of [whether the content was] good. If they do vote helpful, there's a little survey [where they can] tell us a little bit more, but it doesn't really get into the meat of the observation that we used to love and trust about usability testing. [Nevertheless,] it is interesting. It's all new for us too, so we're still trying to learn the right ways to test, but that's the direction we're heading.

■ Usability

Do you get much resistance from your development team when you bring back research you've collected and show them something is not working?

Not really, only because we always try to involve our development partners and our business partners early in the process and throughout. So, there's a whole team ownership that goes with that. I think everyone feels like they're part of the process. At least that's the goal. Then, when we hear the feedback, it's much more objective. It's not that I found this thing out and I'm bringing it back to you, it's we can all observe and experience the customer [feedback] together.

Well, that is a good testament for getting the developers involved in the whole process. Are there any other projects you've worked on where you've gotten really unexpected results after it's rolled out?

[It always feels] really great to really nail a couple of these projects, knowing that it was successful because we did our due diligence. [For example, on] the homepage of the company intranet site, we built this this really cool tool bar, [so that the user would not have to] dig around through multiple pages to find all these little widgets. We consolidated everything together and made it really easy to access and easy to use, even on your phone. It was just such a leap from where it was that people just loved it and use this thing all day, every day. It just gives [me] a sense of gratification.

You've been in the industry for quite a while now. How have the changes to the web affected you in in terms of usability?

When I first started out, we didn't have to worry about mobile design. We didn't have to worry about all the different form factors or code or working with the Cloud. We didn't talk about usability much. It was more about making something attractive and interactive and flashy. I first started working on car dealership websites, so it was all about catching [the user's] eye [by displaying] beautiful photos, and then when I moved to Fidelity, it amazed me that that's just one step in this entire journey. It's more about how you interact with a customer. It just opened up my mind to how [important it is to] study human behavior and how companies interact with their customers… much bigger lessons than when I was thinking about my one webpage.

DISCUSSION QUESTIONS

1) Can you think of an example of a product you have encountered that had poor usability designed? What was it? Why?
2) Have you ever played a video game or used a website or app that you felt had poor usability? How and why?

3) What techniques would you use to better understand your users if you were developing a video game? Would these differ if you were developing a website?
4) What are some metaphors (besides the ones mentioned in this chapter) that you have encountered within interactive media? Did they boost your understanding of the application?
5) Do you agree with all of the usability guidelines listed in this chapter? When might you break one of these rules?

REFERENCES

ADDIN Mendeley Bibliography CSL_BIBLIOGRAPHY Abhishek. (2016). How a Better User Experience Can Reduce Uninstalls. *The Being Apptentive Blog*. Online. Available at: <https://www.apptentive.com/blog/2016/09/08/how-a-better-user-experience-can-reduce-uninstalls>.

Aubert, B. A., Christine Roy, M., & Dewit, O. (2001). The Impact of Interface Usability on Trust in Web Retailers. *Internet Research*, *11*(5), 388–398. Online. Available at: <https://doi.org/10.1108/10662240110410165>.

Beck, K., Beedle, M., van Bennekum, A., Cockburn, A., Cunningham, W., Fowler, M., Martine, R. C., Mellor, S., Thomas, D., Grenning, J., et al. (2001). Manifesto for Agile Software Development. *Agile Alliance*. Online. Available at: <https://www.agilealliance.org/agile101/the-agile-manifesto>.

Duran, H. B. (2017). Study: Spending Gap Between Casual and Avid Gamers is Considerable. *A.List Daily*, May 2. Online. Available at: <https://www.alistdaily.com/digital/study-spending-casual-avid-gamers>.

Jayanth, M. (2014). 52% of Gamers are Women – But the Industry Doesn't Know it. *The Guardian*, September 18. Online. Available at: <https://www.theguardian.com/commentisfree/2014/sep/18/52-percent-people-playing-games-women-industry-doesnt-know>.

Kent, S. (2001). *The Ultimate History Of Video Games: From Pong to Pokemon and Beyond—The Story Behind the Craze that Touched Our Lives and Changed the World*. Roseville, CA: Prima Publishers.

Koster, R. (2013). *A Theory of Fun* (2nd ed.). Sepastopol: O'Reiley Media, Inc.

Muiseum (n.d.). Jakob Nielsen. Online. Available at: <https://www.cs.umd.edu/hcil/muiseum/nielsen/nielsen_page.htm>.

Nielsen, J. (2012). Usability 101: Introduction to Usability. *Nielson Norman Group*. Online. Available at: <https://www.nngroup.com/articles/usability-101-introduction-to-usability>.

Nielson Norman Group (n.d.). Jakob Nielsen: Principal. Online. Available at: <https://www.nngroup.com/people/jakob-nielsen>.

Index

24-bit color 71
2D animation 53, 96–99: character 97; on the web 97; programs 97–99
2D animator 53
3COM 37
3D animation 73, 99–102: industry 88; scene composition 101; program 99, 101–102
3D animator 53: artist 50, 53, 93, 99; environment 99; file formats 102; graphics 43, 73, 99–102, 119; model (or object) 93, 99–100; metaball 99; polygon modeling 99; spline modeling 99; surface definition 100–101
3D production process 99–101
3D scanner 100
3D Studio 102
8-bit: color 93, 97; monitors 77, 82; number 71

"A Theory of Fun" 177
A/B testing 146, 180, 183
above the fold 139
acquisition specialist 53
Activision 34
ad network 113
adaptability 43
additive color mixing 81
Adobe After Effects 73, 98
Adobe Audition 73, 105
Adobe Dreamweaver 14, 73
Adobe Edge Animate 98, 111, 151–152
Adobe Illustrator 50–52, 60, 73, 80, 82, 83, 90, 94, 95, 96: Auto Trace 96; Bezier curves 94–95; lines 94; pen tool 94; primitive shapes 94
Adobe ImageReady 86
Adobe InDesign 60, 73
Adobe PhoneGap 151
Adobe Photoshop 72–73, 82, 83, 85, 86, 88, 90–94, 99, 124, 168, 179: channel mixer 87; filters 92; slices 86
Adobe Premiere 73, 111

Adobe Systems, Inc 16, 64, 85, 88, 96, 151, 166, 179
ads 97, 113
Advanced Research Project Agency (ARPA) 36–37, 45
agile development process 174
Aiken, Howard 25
AirBNB 15, 176
alignment (in design) 143–144
Allen, Paul 29–30
alpha version 64
Altair 8800 29–30
Alto computer 31
Amazon 39, 43: Echo 10
ambient: noise 104; sounds 106
America Online 39, 85
American College of Pediatricians 15
analog media 70, 75, 77, 89: film 107; sound 75; to digital conversion 74–77; vs. digital media 70; video 107
Analytical Engine 24
Andreesen, Marc 38–39
Android 43, 151–152, 154: marketplace 154
Andy Tapps Tavern 33
Angry Birds 19, 35, 97, 151
animation 51, 151: cel 98; traditional 97–98
animator 51, 53
Apache web server 165
app: addiction 154; developer 14, 50; development 16, 126, 145; marketplaces 7, 43, 151, 154
Apple Computer 30–32, 43, 48, 86, 111, 151, 153, 154, 168: App Store 154; GarageBand 105; Lisa 31–32; Macintosh (MAC) 32, 38, 48, 72–73, 86, 93, 111, 126, 149, 151, 166
application program interface (API) 86
application, web-based 72, 138
apps, building 153–154
arcade 8–9, 15, 33–34: industry 33

Index

architect 60, 64, 146
archive materials 64
Arduino 155
AroundMe 4, 11–13
Arpanet 35–37, 45–46
"As We May Think" 38
ASCII text system 71
ASP 158, 165
Atari 28, 33–34, 170–171: 2600 9, 33, 170
Audacity 105
audio: digital 107; editing 73, 105; engineer 17, 53; file formats 104–105; immersive 117, 119; levels 104; mixing 105; post-production 116; recording 104–105; spatial 118–119; specialist 50; stereo 118; streaming 78; surround 118
auditory feedback 106, 176
auditory nerve 102
audits 112
Audodesk 3DS Max 101
Augmentation Research Center Lab 45
Augmented Human Intellect Research Center 30
augmented reality (AR) 20, 43–44, 152: definition of 9
authoring: application 14, 98, 149; interactive media 14, 64, 149–169
Authorware 149
AutoCAD 101
Autodesk Maya 101
Avid Media Composer 111
Avid Pro Tools 73, 105
Axure 174

B-Corporation 65–66
Babbage, Charles 23–25
Babyon.JS 151
bandwidth 7, 53, 78, 109, 112, 150, 164
Bardeen, John 27
BASIC 29
Bauhaus School of Design 123
Bell Labs 27
Bentley University 181
Berners-Lee, Tim 38
beta version 64
bit depth 76–77, 91–93
bitmap (or raster) image (or graphic) 90–97, 107, 119
bitmapped screens: invention of 30
bits 70–72, 77
Blender 101–102
blog 40–42, 115–116
bloggers 115–116, 159
blogging: birth of 41

Bolt, Beraneck and Newman (BBN) 36–37
Boolean operations 95
Bootstrap 144, 157, 168
Bosack, Len 37
branding 162
Brattain, Walter 27
"brochure-ware" 40
"Brothers: A Tale of Two Sons" 20
budget 11, 57–58, 66
bug 26, 64, 178, 180
Bush, Vannevar 25, 38
Bushnell, Nolan 33

C# 14, 52, 152
C++ 152
camera, digital 85, 92, 108, 154
Candy Crush 35, 139–140
card sort 67, 172, 182
Carton, Jans 165–168
cartoons 151
casual game 9, 35, 151: development 16
CD (or CD-ROM) 34, 40, 149
Cerf, Vint 48
CERN 38
circuit boards 155
Cisco Systems 37
Clark, Jim 39
Clicktail 183
client 51, 54–55, 57–58, 60, 64, 66–67, 112, 163, 167–168, 178, 181
client-server model 156
clipping (audio) 104
Cloud 74, 184
CMYK color 81, 94
code 149
coders 159
coding 14, 64, 73
color: analogous 128–129; associations 127; branding 131–132; complimentary 128–129; contrast 128; cool 127; legibility 130–131; meaning 127, 131–132; on screen 80–84; palette 108, 127–131, 135; physiological response to 127; preferences 133; trends 133; relationship of 127–129; relationship of 127–129; split complementary 128–129; subtractive 81; triadic 128–129; warm 127; web safe 82; wheel 127–128, 130
comic book industry 87–88
command based encoding of media 79–80
command-line interface 30, 38
competitive analysis 57
compiler 152

Index

composers 53
compression 78–79, 92, 108–109: codec 78–79, 108; definition of 78; inter-frame 108; intra-frame 108; lossless 78, 93–94; lossy 78–79, 93; variable bit rate encoding 108
computer science 16
computer: origins of 23–26; as women 25–26
content management system (CMS) 68, 149, 156, 158–159, 164, 166
content: expert 54; writer (or strategist) 54
contract specialist 53
contrast (in design) 140, 148
conversion: analog to digital media 70, 89; vector to bitmap 95–96; bitmap to vector 95–96
copyright law 53, 109
core web languages 156
Cox, Chris 84–89
cross-platform compatibility 72
CSS 14, 52, 73, 83, 86, 125, 151, 154, 156–158, 166, 181: function of 157
Cycling ' 74, 155

Dallas Cowboys 162
Dark Wave Studio 105
data visualization 148
data-driven design 145–146
database 11–13, 158, 165, 181
defense industry 87
deliverables 59, 67
DELTA Soundworks 116–119
description based encoding of media 79–80
design: conventions 173; narrative 19; phase 58, 60, 67
designer 50, 54, 60, 64, 67, 69, 121: combat 52; game play 52; graphic 51; industrial 146; interaction 51, 145, 147; interface 51; level 50, 52; lighting 52; narrative 50, 52; systems 52; user experience (UX) 51, 145, 172, 181; video game 51–52; visual 51, 181
desktop: applications 7; computer 157
developer 54, 67, 69, 86, 95, 97, 106, 112, 126, 149, 151–159
Difference Engine 23–25
Differential Analyzer 25, 38
differentiation (in design) 136–138
DigiPen Institute of Technology 20–21
digital certificate 154
digital media, pros of 77–78
digital video 107–109: editing 77, 111; obtaining 109; shooting 109–110; working with 108–109
DNS servers 161–162
domain: extension 160, 163; top-level 47

domain name 7, 162–163, 167–168: choosing 162–163; definition of 160; registration 149, 156, 160–162; registry 160; system 45, 47, 160–161; transferring 164; registrant 162
dot com boom 39
dots per inch (dpi) 75
downsampling 92
Dropbox 74
Drupal 42, 68, 164
DSL 164
dumb terminals 28
DVD 34, 109

e-commerce 4, 5, 7, 17, 39, 57, 158, 170, 175–176
e-learning 106, 149
E.T. The Extraterrestrial 170–171, 174
eBay 39
Eckert, Presper 25
email 4, 7, 36–37, 46, 124: account 164; invention of 36–37, 46
emphasis (in design) 139–141
Englebart, Douglas 30–31, 45–46, 48
ENIAC 26–27
Entertainment Software Association 20
Epic games 153
escape rooms 20
Ethernet 37
Etsy 92

Facebook 14, 42–43, 55, 113, 162
Fairchild Semiconductor 27
fake news 14
Far Eastern culture 131–132
Feinler, Elizabeth (Jake) 44–48
Fidelity Investments 181–184
file format 72: 3DS 102; AAC 73; AEP 73; AI 73, 96; AIFF 73, 79, 105, 107; AVI 73, 111; BLEND 102; EPS 73, 96; EXE 73; FCPX 73; FLV 111; GIF 73, 90, 92–92, 97, 99; IFFb 102; INDD 73; JPEG 73, 78–79, 90, 93, 108; MIDI 79, 107; MOV 73, 99, 111; MP3 73, 78–79, 105, 107, 111; MP4 (or MPEG4) 73, 99, 111–112; OBJ 73, 102; PDF 73, 96, 126; PNG 73, 90, 93–94; PRPROJ 73; PSD 72–73, 93; PTX 73; STL 73; SVG 95–96, 168; SWF 98–99; TIFF 78, 93; WAV 73, 79, 105, 107; WMV 111; ZIP 78
file formats: PPJ 73
file size 76, 92, 108–109
file transfer protocol (FTP) 46, 165
file type: application 72; data 72
files: native 72–73
Film Academy Baden-Wurttemberg 117

Index

film 3, 19–20, 53, 65, 70, 74, 77–78, 91, 98–99, 101, 107, 108–111, 117, 125–126, 167: editor 53; super 8 109
filmmakers 53
Final Cut 73, 111
Firefox 72
flash drive 108
Flash: Video 111; website 97–99
flexbox 167–168
floppy discs 40
Florsheim shoes 40
flowchart 51, 60, 90
focus groups 59, 172
Foley techniques 116
font 51, 123
Ford, Henry 172
frame rate 108
Franklin Institute 9
frequency 76, 102, 104, 106, 118
Frick, Tim 65–69
front-end developer 181
functional specification 59
FutureSplash 166

Gaieski, Julie 181–184
game: artist 52; authoring 73; cartridges 34; console 9, 15, 33–34, 152; design document 54–55; engine 98, 152, 168; publisher 54, 58; script 113
Game Boy 34–35
gamers: diversity of 20
gamification 15
gaming, networked 34–35
Gannt chart 58
Gates, Bill 28–30
Gdevelop 151
generation decay 77
gestural interfaces 43
GIFs, animated 97, 99
Gift Rocket 140–141
gigabyte 71
GIMP 94
Gingiber 142
Goat Simultor 19
GoDaddy 47
gold master 64
Google 113, 125, 157, 166: Analytics 68; Fonts 126, 138; Play 153–154; Sheets 11; Wave 4
Googling 163
GPS 13–14, 43, 154
graphical user interface (GUI) 30–33, 38, 48, 152: invention of 45

graphics 90: applications 90, 125, 144
grids 144
guides 144

hard drive 74: portable 109
Harmony 99
Harvard University 25, 29
help screens 113–114
Henry Architects 162
Henry, Alix 162
Hertz 102
hexadecimal code 83
hexadecimal color 89
high-definition TV 108
Hilbert, David 25
Hoefler, Don 28
Holberton, Elizabeth Snyder 26
Home Brew Computing Club 28–29
HTML 14, 52, 64, 73, 86, 106, 111–112, 115, 125–126, 150, 151, 154, 156–158, 166, 168, 181: alt tags 115; anchor links 114; body copy 124–125, 138; Canvas 151, 168; forms 144–145; frame sets 167; function of 157; headings 115, 138; links 114–115, 138; subheads 138; tables 167; title tag 115; VIDEO tag 112
HTML5 99, 106, 112
HTML5 Maker 98
human-computer interaction 28, 175
Hunter Wines 143
Hypercard 149–150
hyperlink 30, 38
hypertext transfer protocol (HTTP) 156

IBM 25, 30, 32
icon 114, 141
iconography 132
illustration program 94
illustrators 52
Image: carousels 97; editing 73, 94
iMovie 111
Indian culture 132
information architect 50–51, 60, 67, 172
information architecture 67, 181
Information Processing Techniques Office (IPTO) 36
Instagram 55
Intel 27–28
interactive digital media: career opportunities 16–17; definition of 1; forms of 6–10; impact of 14–15; in public spaces 155; pervasiveness of 21; within an exhibit 9

189

■ Index

interactive performance: definition of 10
interface design 60, 63, 93, 132
Internet Explorer 39
Internet Hall of Fame 48
internet: birth of 35–37; difference from web 40; growth of 37
InVision 174
iOS 73, 152
IP address 160–163
iPad 7, 43, 151
iPhone 7, 9, 42–43, 49–50, 56, 92, 106, 151, 154
iThrive Games 18–21

Jacquard weaving machine 23, 27
Java 154
JavaScript 14, 52, 97–99, 144, 151–152, 154, 156–158, 166, 168: game 151–152
Jennings, Elizabeth 26
Jobs, Steve 28–31, 48, 151
Joomla 42, 164
journey map 67, 182
Jquery 52

Kahn, Bob 48
keywords (or keyphrase) 11, 115, 154
Kilby, Jack 27
kilobyte 71–72
kiloHertz 76, 102
Kinect 34
kiosk 149: airport 113; application development 155; definition of 6–7; invention of 40; museum 6–7
Koester, Ralph 177

labeling systems 6, 51
Lang, Fritz 125–126
layout principles 133–144
legal specialists 53
legibility 124–125, 143
Lerner, Sandy 37
Lichterman, Ruth 26
Licklider, J.C.R. 35–36
logo 80, 92, 131, 158
Lovelace, Ada 23–24, 27
Lucid, Brian 145–148
Lynda.com 176

Macromedia Director 149–151: Flash (Adobe Flash) 97–98, 151, 166; emergence of 151
mainframe computer 28, 30, 33, 36
"Man-Computer Symbiosis" 36
Mark 1 25

Mary Baker Eddy Library for the Betterment of Humanity 9
Massey University 145–148
Mauchly, John 25–26
Max 155
Maya 73–102
McDonald, Heidi 18–21
McNulty, Kathleen 26
megabyte 71
Meltzer, Marlyn Wescoff 26
"Memento" 3
Memex 38
memory card 107–108
Metcalfe, Bob 37
microchip 27
microphone 104
microprocessor 27–28
Microsoft 11, 16, 29–30, 32, 34, 39, 111, 162: as Micro-soft 29; Excel 11; Theater Lounge 155; Visio 60; Windows 32, 86; Windows 95 34, 39; Windows Server 165; Word 7, 72
Middle Eastern Culture 132
MIDI system 107
Mightybytes 65–69
Missouri Botanical Garden 138
MITS 28–30
Mittal Children's Medical Centre 178
mobile application 64: definition of 7–8
mobile browser 99
mobile device 151, 170
modems 37
Monsanto 132
Monte, Ana 116–119
Monument Valley 136
moodboard 59
Moore, Gordon 27
Moore's Law 27
Mosaic 38
"Mother of all Demos" 48
motion graphics 97
mouse 32–33, 48: invention of 30, 45
MS-DOS 30
multimedia 40, 111, 149: authoring 149–151
museum exhibits 16
Myspace 42
Myst 149

Napster 77–78
navigation 86, 132, 177
negative space 141
Nelson, Ted 38
Netflix 78

Netscape Navigator 39
Network Information Center (NIC) 44–48, 160
networking: invention of 37
New England Institute of Art 181
Nielsen, Jakob 175
Nintendo 34–35
noise floor 104
non-screen based experiences: definition of 10
noise removal 106
normalization 106
Noyce, Ronald 27
Nyquist Theory 76

Objective-C 50, 52
Oculus Rift 9, 43
"On Computable Numbers, with an Application to the Entscheidungsproblem." 24–25
Optimal Sort 172
Optimal Workshop 67
out of gamut 82

packet 36: switching 36
Pantone 133
PBSKids.org 174
PDP-1 33
persistence of vision theory 107–108
personal computer (PC) 30, 33, 36–38, 48, 72, 86, 93, 126: birth of 28–30; game 34, 73, 152
Phaser 151
photo editor 52
photographer 52
PHP 14, 52, 73, 158–159, 165, 181
physical computing 43
physical interactive experiences 9–10, 155
physical interface 43
pigments 80
Pinterest 59
Pixar 88
pixel 79, 88, 90–92, 95, 108, 125
pixel based images (or graphics) 90–95, 151: file formats 93–94
Pokemon Go 43
Pong 8
Popular Electronics 28–29
printers 85
producer 51
programmer 52, 60, 64
programming language 14, 64, 154: client side 157; compiled 152; object-oriented 152; server side 158, 165
Processing 155

project manager 50–51, 67
Project Xanadu 38
proposal 53, 55, 57–59, 66, 69, 112: description of content 56; description of context 56; objective 55; projected outcomes 56–57; target audience 55–56
prototype 4, 59–60, 64: definition of 63–64
punch cards 23–24, 27
Purdue 45
Pure Data 155

QR code scanner 138
quality assurance (QA): department 54, 180; tester 54, 180; testing 64, 180
Quicktime 111

rapid prototyping 146
Raspberry Pi 155
Regions Bank 162
release notes 64
resolution 74–75, 77, 91–92, 95, 124: screen 75, 92, 108
responsive: web design 43; web site 43
reverse sort 172
RGB color 82–83
Roberts, Ed 28–29
rule of thirds 110
Russell, Steve 33

Safari 151
scanners 85, 92
Schell Games 19
screen shot 93
search engine 115, 126, 166: optimization 68, 115–116
Secure Socket Layer (SSL) 164
Sega 34
sensors 155
Seventeen Magazine 115
Shockley, William 27
Shockwave 150
"shoot in twos" 98
Silicon Graphics 39
Silicon Valley 28, 36, 38
SiteKiosk 155
Sketch 174
Skin and Bones exhibit 9
Small Design Firm 10
Small, David 9
smartphone 35, 151, 157: addiction 14; emergence of 14, 42

■ Index

Smithsonian 9
social media 14, 55: birth of 42; channels 55; manager 16; posts 113–114; specialist 55; strategist 55
soft launch 68
software: companies 64; development 16
solid-state memory 108
Sony 34: Sound Forge Studio 105
sound: analog editing 77; and the user experience 106–107; composing with MIDI 107; designer 52; digital editing 77; distortion 104; duration 103–104; effect 53, 106, 119; how it's is made 102–103; in video game 106; manipulation 105–106; on the web 106; recording 104; representation of 103–104; pitch 103–104; sample rate 77; sampled 107; sampling rate 74–76; speech 106; volume 103; within interactive media 119
Soundation 105
soundscapes 53
soundwave 75–76, 104: amplitude 103
Southwest airlines 176
Space Wars 33
Spence, Frances Bilas 26
Spielberg, Steven 170
Spotify 78
Stanford Research Institute (SRI) 30–13, 36, 45–47
Stanford University 28–29, 36–37
Stanford Virtual Heart 17, 116
stock: image website 93; video footage 109
storage media 74
storytelling 148
style guide 51
subroutine 26
Sun Microsystems 175
SureFox 155
Swift 14

tablet: emergence of 14, 35
Target 134
taxonomy 67, 172
Taylor, Bob 36–37
Tech Model Railroad Club 33
technical support 164
technical writer 54
Texas Instruments 27
text editor 151
The Knot 125
"The Mother of All Demos" 30, 45, 48
TinyAnim 98
Tomlinson, Ray 37
tool tips 176

Toon Boom 99
Touchdesigner 155
Transfer Control Protocol/Internet Protocol (TCP/IP) 37
transistor 27
Treejack 67
Triple A 19
tripod 110
Trokia Ranch 10
Turing Machine 25
Turing, Alan 24–25
tweet 42
Twine 151
Twitter 42, 55, 113
typeface 121–123, 126, 128, 135, 138, 148: Arial 123; Helvetica 123; Palatino 123; sans serif 123–124; serif 123–124, 148; Times 123
typography 121–126, 128, 146–148: alignment 125; case 124; condensed 123; contrast 137–138; extended 123; justification 125; kerning 124–126; leading 124–126; properties and definitions 123–125; stroke weight 123; tracking 124–126; uppercase 124; within interactive media 126

Uber 15
UCLA 46
United States Department of Defense 36
Unity (game engine) 14, 19, 73, 117, 152–153
unity (in design) 133–136
Unity Technologies 73, 152–153
University of California at Los Angeles (UCLA) 36
University of Illinois 38
University of Pennsylvania Moore School of Engineering 25
University of Utah 33
Unreal Engine 19, 117, 153
upsampling 92
usability 4–6, 51, 106, 121, 135, 145–147, 170–185: labs 179; test 4, 68, 174, 178–180, 183
user behavior 4, 43, 68
user experience design (UX) 13–14, 16, 51, 146, 148, 166
user flows 67
user personas 59–60, 172
user research 59, 67, 172, 181–183
user scenarios 4–5, 60–63
user testing 54, 64, 68
user-generated content 40

vacuum tubes 26–27
vector 94, 96

Index

vector graphic (or vector-based images) 90, 94–96, 107, 119, 151
vector shape 95–96
vector-based drawing 73, 80, 94
VHS machine 109
VHS tape 109
video camera: mini dv 109
video compositing 73
video conferencing 30
video editing 73: analog 111; digital 110–111; Preview 111; programs 111; rendering 109, 111; splitting 105, 111; time stretching 106; timeline 58, 66; trimming 105
video game 19, 33–35, 51, 55, 58: addiction 15; authoring 151–153; benefits 18–19; company 55; definition of 8; design document 52; development 50, 126, 168; industry 9, 15, 33, 51–52, 171, 180; impact of 15; monetization 19; origins of 33–35; web-based 151
video game tester see (QA tester)
video in interactive digital media 111–112, 119: shoot 109
video shot: cutaway 110; establishing 110; over the shoulder 110; pans 110; point of view 110; reverse angle 110; zooms 110
video: file formats 111; streaming 78; tape 108
virtual reality (VR) 9, 20, 43, 50, 116–119, 152
virtualization 168
visual hierarchy 140, 146–147, 148
visual metaphors 173, 185

Warshaw, Howard Scott 170, 174
waveform 103–104
weaving industry 87
Web 2.0 40–42
web analytics 59
web applications 7, 16
web assembly 168
web browser 38, 72, 95–97, 126, 150–151, 157, 161–162, 168
web copy 114

web developer 14, 50, 95, 126, 159, 163, 165
web development 16, 145, 156–166
web hosting 68, 149, 156, 162–166
web server 149, 156–158, 163, 165, 168
WebSanity 165–168
website 16–17, 40,- 43, 53–56, 59–60, 64–69, 97, 99, 106, 112–115, 124–126, 13, 132–133, 135, 139–143, 151, 156–164: ads 10, 13; definition of 7; Flash 97; responsive 7, 157–158
West Liberty State College 45
Western culture 125, 131–132
Western music 103
whitespace 125, 141–143
Whois lookup 47, 162, 168
Wii 35
Wikipedia 40
Williams Sonoma 125
wireframes 59–63, 67, 90, 174
wireframing 135, 137
WordPress 41, 68, 159, 164
Words with Friends 35
World War II 25
world wide web 38–40, 72, 78, 86: birth of 37–40; emergence of 149, 166; how it works 156
Wozniak, Steve 28–31
writing: efficient 114; instructional 113–114; persuasive 112–113; search engine optimization 115–116

Xbox 34, 56
Xcode 14, 73
Xerox PARC 31, 37

Yahoo 160, 173
Young House Love 115
YouTube 112, 119

Zaans Museum 155
zip disk 74
zip drive 74
Zuckerberg, Mark 162

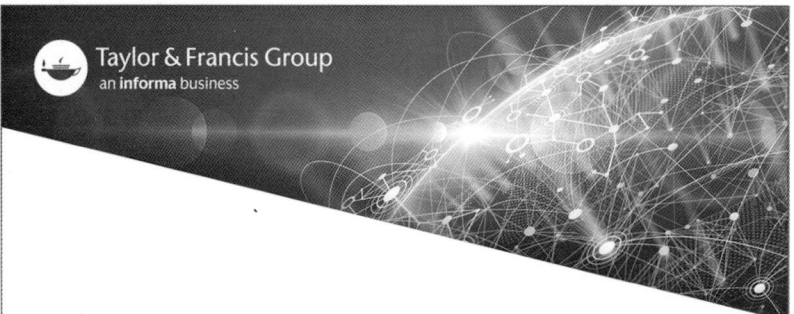